# JAPAN'S ENCOUNTER

# WITH

# CHRISTIANITY

## THE CATHOLIC MISSION IN PRE-MODERN JAPAN

### Neil S. Fujita

PAULIST PRESS
New York † Mahwah, N.J.

The publisher gratefully acknowledges use of the following materials: Excerpts from *The Christian Century in Japan: 1549–1650* by Charles R. Boxer, Copyright © 1951, 1979, Charles Boxer, University of California Press; *Valignano's Mission Principles for Japan* by Joseph Franz Schutte, translated by J.J. Coyne, Copyright © 1980 and 1985, Institute of Jesuit Sources; and *Francis Xavier: His Life, His Time* by Georg Schurhammer, translated by M. Joseph Costelloe, Copyright © 1973 and 1982, Loyola University Press.

*Book design by Theresa M. Sparacio.*

Library of Congress Cataloging-in-Publication Data

Fujita, Neil S.
   Japan's encounter with Christianity : the Catholic mission in pre-modern Japan / by Neil S. Fujita.
     p. cm.
   Includes bibliographical references and index.
   ISBN 0-8091-3206-0
   1. Catholic Church—Japan—History.  2. Missions—Japan.  3. Christianity and other religions—Japanese.  4. Japan—Religion—To 1866.  5. Japan—Church history—To 1868.  I. Title.
BX1668.F86     1991
266'.252—dc20

                          90-21189
                          CIP

Published by Paulist Press
997 Macarthur Boulevard
Mahwah, New Jersey 07430

Printed and bound in the
United States of America

# CONTENTS

iii

Lorenzo Ruiz 1633 - 1637
Dominicano

Sept 28

# ACKNOWLEDGEMENT

This book is dedicated to the Rev. James Hicks for his valuable advice and long-time friendship. Thanks are also due to my brother-in-law, George McKee, for furnishing the maps, to my nephews, Toru and Takeshi Fujita, for collecting many pertinent sources in Japan, and to my wife, Eleanor, for her loving support. Finally, this endeavor would not have been undertaken without the encouragement given by the Rev. Lawrence Boadt, C.S.P., Editor at Paulist Press.

*List of maps*

# ACKNOWLEDGMENT

# CHRONOLOGY

1543 Arrival of the first Portuguese in Kyushu
1549 Arrival of Francis Xavier in Kyushu (the beginning of the Christian mission)
1563 Conversion of Sumitada Omura (first of the Christian lords)
1568 Seizure of Kyoto by Nobunaga Oda
1579 Arrival of Alessandro Valignano (his first visit)
1582 Assassination of Nobunaga Oda
1585 Appointment of Hideyoshi as regent
1587 Edict expelling the missionaries
1592 Invasion of Korea; arrival of the Spanish friars
1596 The San Felipe incident
1597 Martyrdom of the twenty-six Christians (first instance of official persecution of the Christians)
1598 Death of Hideyoshi and the withdrawal from Korea
1600 Arrival of the Dutch traders
1601 Ordination of the first Japanese to the priesthood
1603 Assumption of the title of shogun by Ieyasu Tokugawa
1605
-23 Shogunate of Hidetada Tokugawa
1609 Establishment of the Dutch trading firm at Hirado
1612 The bakufu's decree prohibiting Christianity
1614 Decree expelling the missionaries (beginning of the general persecution)
1616 Death of Ieyasu
1623
-51 Shogunate of Iemitsu Tokugawa

1636 Restriction of all European residents in Dejima and ban of Japanese travel abroad
1637
-38 Shimabara rebellion
1639 Expulsion of the Portuguese traders
1708 Arrest of Sidoti
1792 Visit of the Russian envoy
1797 Visit of the British envoy
1853 Arrival of Commodore Perry
1867 Enthronement of Emperor Meiji and the end of the Tokugawa shogunate
1868 Opening of Kobe and Osaka to foreign trade; establishment of Tokyo (former Edo) as the new capital
1873 Revocation of the law prohibiting Christianity
1889 Promulgation of the Imperial Constitution

# PREFACE

> They have rites and ceremonies so different from those of all other nations that it seems that they deliberately try to be unlike any other people. The things they do in this respect are beyond imagining and it may truly be said that Japan is a world the reverse of Europe (Cooper, 1965, p. vii).

These are the words of Padre Alessandro Valignano, who is expressing his utter bewilderment over the cultural differences between Europe and Japan. This Jesuit priest visited Japan three times between 1579 and 1603 and, as the official Visitor-General, established Jesuit mission policy there. The European missionaries, despite many hardships, engaged in the propagation of Christianity for approximately one century from the first attempts at evangelization by Francis Xavier in 1549 to the tragic end brought about by the systematic suppression by the central government in the mid-seventeenth century.

Just as the padres were at a loss in Japan, the Japanese were also greatly perplexed when faced with strangers from "a world the reverse of" their own. They encountered a totally heterogeneous religion and culture. The nation had never before heard of one absolute and transcendent God, the creator of the universe; it had never before seen a people who ate food with knives and forks.

When these "reverse" religions and cultures met each other historically for the first time, what happened? In that extraordinary situation, what did the western visitors do and what was the Japanese response? What kind of problems did this encounter create? What can we learn from this page of history? These are the fundamental questions which

1

the present book attempts to elucidate. It is particularly important to reflect upon these questions in view of the pluralistic world today. It is now more exigent than ever that peoples of different religions and cultures understand each other so that they can learn to live together peacefully and thereby find their own heritage enriched.

# PROLOGUE: A BRIEF SKETCH OF THE ERA OF THE CHRISTIAN MISSIONS IN JAPAN

The mid-sixteenth century, when European missionaries came to Japan, was one of the most turbulent periods in Japan's history, for the whole country was plunged into a series of civil wars. The emperor and the aristocracy existed without actual authority. The central government (called *bakufu*) was ruled by a warrior family by the name of Ashikaga (the head of the bakufu was called *shogun*). During the second half of the fifteenth century, the controlling power of the bakufu had been weakened due to continuous inner feuding and corruption.

A virtual end to the Ashikaga bakufu was brought about as a result of a protracted war fought between two rival factions within the bakufu from 1467 to 1477. This power contest eventuated in disaster for both sides, as neither won. The result was total political chaos and the horrendous destruction of the capital city of Kyoto, which was the central arena for the battles. The emperor and his courtiers were left impoverished and barely survived by begging alms from individual lords. When, for instance, Emperor Go-Tsuchimikado died in 1500, his body was left unburied for forty days for lack of money for a funeral, and the coronation of his successor, Go-kashiwabara, had to be postponed for twenty-two years for the same reason.

The national plight was even more devastating for the commoners. More than eighty thousand people reportedly died from famine and pestilence between the years 1460 and 1461; the streets of Kyoto were filled with rotten corpses. Even after the war, starvation, conflagrations, contagious diseases, and fighting continued to plague the capital area.

3

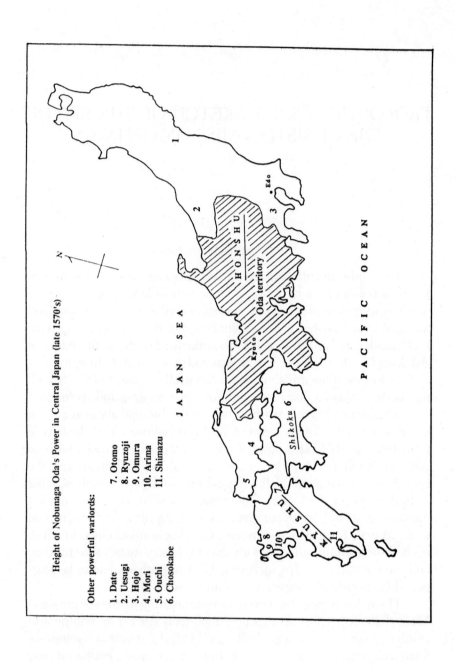

Height of Nobunaga Oda's Power in Central Japan (late 1570's)

Other powerful warlords:

1. Date
2. Uesugi
3. Hojo
4. Mori
5. Ouchi
6. Chosokabe

7. Otomo
8. Ryuzoji
9. Omura
10. Arima
11. Shimazu

Such was still the state of the city when the first Christian missionary, Francis Xavier, visited there in January of 1551. He had had a burning desire from the moment he decided on his Japanese mission to meet the emperor and tell him the Christian message in person. He was bitterly disillusioned indeed; what he saw was a ruined city with the imperial palace looking no different from an ordinary farmhouse. Worse still, he was not able even to have an audience with the emperor.

The decline of feudalism under the Ashikaga shogunate prompted its subordinate warrior clans to begin asserting each their own independence. During the sixteenth century, close to one hundred and fifty of these feudal clans segmented the whole country, which consisted of three main islands: Honshu, Kyushu, and Shikoku. (Hokkaido, the northernmost island of the four major islands of modern Japan, was not settled by the Japanese until the nineteenth century.) Some of these clans were small and weak, simply trying to survive, while others were strong enough to ambitiously attempt to fight their way even to national hegemony. Deputies usurped the domains of their superiors, retainers overthrew their overlords, and branch families supplanted the power of the main families. It was indeed an age of warlords. (The feudal lord was called *daimyo*, and the warrior, *samurai*.)

## DYNAMISM OF THE ERA

The stormy conditions which prevailed in the entire country worked both for and against Christian missions. On the one hand, missionaries did not find the expected peaceful garden in which to sow seeds of faith, but on the other hand, they did encounter an era of great dynamism which could well afford to be open to a new flowering of opportunity. Many of the warlords were most anxious to establish trade with the Portuguese because they were desperately craving financial gain, firearms and other items. The missionaries took advantage of this situation for the propagation of Christianity.

The economic factor was of great significance in deciding the fate of Christian activities, but it was not the only element; there was a strong political constituent as well. This was typically operative in the policies of Nobunaga Oda, who, having emerged as a national figure from the sanguinary struggles among the warlords, eventually opened a path toward the reestablishment of national unity and stability. From a small province surrounding the modern city of Nagoya, east of Kyoto, he used military might and diplomatic skill to subdue his rivals and finally to seize the capital in 1568. A massive use of artillery served as the major means for his military success, and he thus became the virtual dictator of central Japan. (Firearms were introduced by the first Portuguese traders who reached Japan accidently in 1543 because of a rough sea.)

### NOBUNAGA AND HIS FOES

Besides those contending warlords, another tenacious foe Nobunaga had to fight fiercely to subdue was the militant Buddhist groups. Some of the Buddhist sects had become increasingly political, each attempting to assert their independence and maximize their influence on secular affairs. The Ikko (literally meaning one-orientation) sect, above all, grew into a formidable political force comprising well-armed monks and laity with its center in the strongly fortified and well-financed temple compound of Honganji in Osaka.

The Ikko sect was a branch of the Pure Land (paradise) sect, which preached absolute devotion to Amida Buddha, a personification of the manifestation of the infinitely merciful and transcendent Buddha. The simple doctrine of salvation through faith alone by calling on Amida especially attracted the masses who were suffering from social unrest, physical danger, and poverty caused by the exploitation of large landowners and ever-continuing warfare. Their painful experiences of the ugliness and transience of this life drove them in fanatical fervor toward the paradise which the sect promised.

With such a fervent religious faith as a binding force, small landowners and peasants formed leagues (*ikki*) to fight back against the local government officials and feudal lords. Lower class warriors, some out of similar desperation and others seeking opportunity and fortune, joined them. Thus *ikki* developed into a huge military power, spreading its influence to various parts of Japan. Feudal lords often found it very difficult to contain the waves of uprisings. The Ikko-ikki was by no means the only rebellious force; there were many other ikki groups such as those connected with other Buddhist sects (the Nichiren sect, the Tendai sect, and the Shingon sect) as well as those without religious ties.

Nobunaga Oda was never a religious man; he declared publicly his disbelief in gods or Buddha. His struggle of many years with the Buddhist ikki fostered his intense hatred of Buddhism. When, possessed by such a psychological state, he encountered the Portuguese priests, he evidently decided to make use of this new foreign religion to counter-balance the Buddhists' power. He was also a man full of curiosity and open to new ways. European culture and the financial benefits from trading fascinated him. The missionaries enjoyed warm, friendly treatment from this contemporary strong commander of power.

### HIDEYOSHI

Nobunaga's attempt to achieve his goal of winning hegemony over the whole country was cut short when one of his treacherous vassals abruptly ended his life in 1582. The assassination of the lord was immediately avenged by his other general, Hideyoshi. Here was a man who could well epitomize the dynamism of the era. Though born a poor peasant, Hideyoshi rose to power by virtue of his sheer ability and perseverance. Within three years after Nobunaga's death, Hideyoshi gained supreme authority over all the warlords by eliminating the remnants of his former master's family and loyal vassals. This accomplishment prompted the imperial court to honor him by appointing him *kampaku* (regent) and also by granting him the new family name of Toyotomi.

His ambition hardly abated at this point, however; Hideyoshi was obsessed by the megalomaniacal dream of conquering China. In 1592 his troops invaded Korea as the first step in his aggressive plan. They swiftly overran almost all of the Korean peninsula. But the overtaxed army, upon encountering Chinese military reinforcements, had to retreat to the south where they became entrenched. This stalemate was broken only by Hideyoshi's death in 1598; the Japanese (gladly) abandoned the dictator's costly and senseless venture.

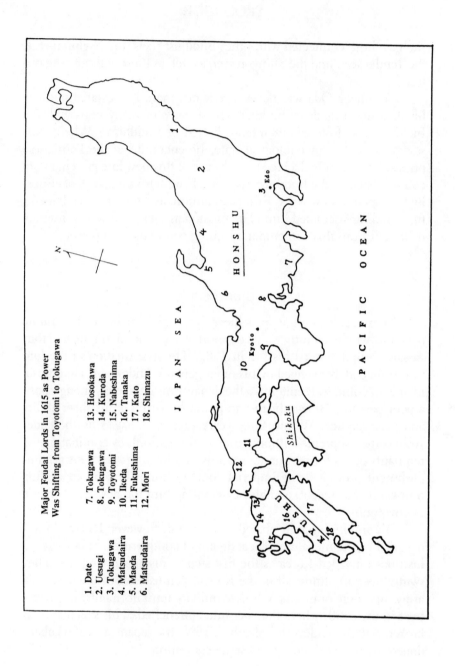

Major Feudal Lords in 1615 as Power
Was Shifting from Toyotomi to Tokugawa

1. Date
2. Uesugi
3. Tokugawa
4. Matsudaira
5. Maeda
6. Matsudaira

7. Tokugawa
8. Tokugawa
9. Toyotomi
10. Ikeda
11. Fukushima
12. Mori

13. Hosokawa
14. Kuroda
15. Nabeshima
16. Tanaka
17. Kato
18. Shimazu

## TOKUGAWA BAKUFU

Hideyoshi's death revived the power struggles among the feudal lords for national sovereignty. Since Hideyoshi's heir was still a very young child, a political vacuum was created. The indomitable contender who filled this vacancy was Ieyasu Tokugawa, whose resident castle was in Edo, the future Tokyo. Just as his predecessor had eliminated the Oda family, he destroyed the remnants of the Toyotomi family and subdued his rivals. Having learned from the downfalls of Oda and Toyotomi, he took extreme care in laying the groundwork for the perpetual stability of the reign of his family. In this, as a matter of fact, he was remarkably successful. His dynasty (the Tokugawa bakufu) lasted for considerably more than 250 years after he assumed the title of shogun in 1603. It ended only when the Imperial Government took over the rule of the nation in 1867.

## CHRISTIAN MISSIONS

Both Hideyoshi and Ieyasu, following the precedent set by Nobunaga, initially at least accepted the Christian missionaries. In 1587, however, Hideyoshi suddenly reversed his heretofore friendly attitude toward the Christians, issued an edict banning Christianity and ordered the padres to leave the country within twenty days. As a result of the ensuing persecution, twenty-six Christians (including six European Franciscans) were executed in 1597. Hideyoshi's order of expulsion, nonetheless, was not strictly enforced. The regent, in fact, in 1593 permitted Spanish Franciscans to stay in the land, which, incidentally, broke the Jesuit monopoly over the mission work in Japan.

Ieyasu likewise initially allowed missionary activities by the Jesuits, the Franciscans, the Dominicans, and the Augustinians. The Catholic mission, in fact, enjoyed its peak around that time. In 1606 it was reported that there were 750,000 believers with an annual increase of five or six thousand. Bishop de Cerqueira called Nagasaki, a predominantly Christian city in Kyushu, "the Rome of the Far East."

In 1612, however, the Tokugawa bakufu changed its policy and issued decrees prohibiting Christianity. And in 1614 the expulsion of the padres was ordered. Some years later all other Catholics were ordered expelled as well; the country closed its doors to the outside world, excepting the Dutch traders in Dejima at the head of Nagasaki Bay. This marked the beginning of systematic persecution which persisted in horrible magnitude until 1873 when the new imperial government relaxed the prohibition after pressure from western countries.

International pressure, in fact, constituted a major reason for the fall of the Tokugawa bakufu and the establishment of the imperial regime itself. By the third decade of the nineteenth century, social unrest reached new heights; this serious crisis was caused by a long-lasting famine and widespread uprisings, which the bakufu had failed to control. Many feudal lords no longer remained loyal to the shogun. And then when the Russians, the French, the English, and the Americans came demanding an opening of the country, the Tokugawa government proved to be totally inept.

In an attempt to save the country from such a chaotic condition, several powerful feudal lords forged an alliance, which forced the abolishment of the shogunate and the establishment of direct rule by the emperor. This effort was successful; in December 1867 Emperor Meiji declared a new government. Historians usually regard this turn of events as marking the beginning of the modern era in Japan's history.

The temporal scope of our discussion in the present book is set within Japan's pre-modern era covering the period beginning with the arrival of the first Europeans and the rise of Nobunaga Oda to the end of the Tokugawa bakufu. We will now proceed in the following chapter to observe the first scene of Japan's encounter with Christianity where the celebrated saint, Francis Xavier, played a vital role.

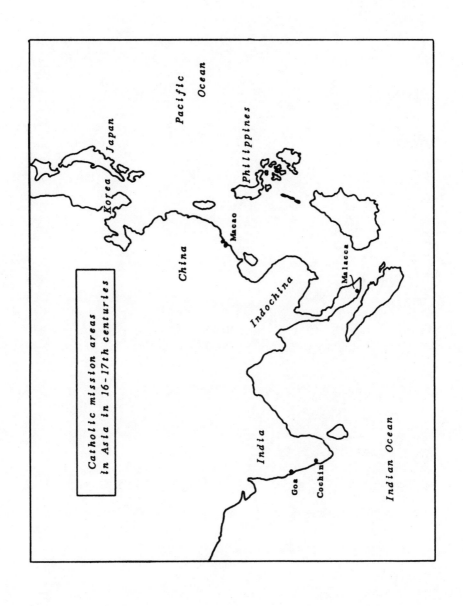

Catholic mission areas
in Asia in 16-17th centuries

Pacific Ocean

Korea  Japan

Philippines

China

Macao

Indochina

Malacca

India

Goa
Cochin

Indian Ocean

# 1

# Francis Xavier and His Work in Japan

## ENCOUNTER WITH YAJIRO

It was when Padre Francis Xavier (1506–1552) was conducting a wedding in the chapel of Our Lady of the Mount in Malacca on December 7, 1547, that he noticed his friend, Captain Jorge Alvares, enter the chapel with a stranger, apparently an Asian. That was how the priest came to make his first Japanese acquaintance. With this man he later traveled to Japan and opened the Christian mission there.

The Japanese man was called, according to Xavier and others, Anjiro, and was about thirty-five years old at the time. He was a samurai (swordsman) of Satsuma, a province of southern Kyushu, where the Portuguese traders had begun their business. After becoming involved in a homicide in his hometown of Kagoshima, he had taken refuge in a Buddhist monastery, where he assumed the name of a monk, Ansei. (According to Padre João Rodriguez in his *History of the Church in Japan*, written in Portuguese in 1620–1621, because of this Buddhist name, he came to be called mistakenly Anjiro, though his real name was Yajiro. This information, as modern Japanese scholars agree, seems to be accurate.) Still fearing his pursuers, Yajiro then fled to the Portuguese ship whose captain he had known earlier. Although he failed to find that specific captain, by accident he met Alvares, who was kind enough to take the fugitive in his ship and to sail from the country.

During their voyage, Yajiro, who was suffering from feelings of guilt, was advised by Alvares to consult with the "holy priest," Padre Francis, to obtain peace of conscience. The considerate captain personally introduced Yajiro to the Christian gospel as well. This was the background which led to the appearance of Alvares and Yajiro at the chapel of Our Lady of the Mount, where they had heard Xavier could be found. This encounter turned out to be indeed a happy one; all three shared a great joy. Xavier was delighted to meet a person from a country about which he had considerable curiosity. As for Yajiro, as he stated in his letter to Ignatius of Loyola on November 29, 1549, he received deep satisfaction and comfort from this opportunity which he believed to be arranged by divine providence.

Yajiro's interest in Christianity proved to be quite serious; he became an excellent student in Christian doctrine at the College of St. Paul in Goa, where Xavier advised him to study. People frequently saw him praying at the church. Yajiro was baptized in 1548 and received the religious name of Paulo de Santa Fe (Paul of the Holy Faith). With him two other Japanese men were also baptized, one called João (his brother or servant?) and Antonio (his servant).

Padre Luis Frois wrote in his *History of the Church in Japan* in 1582–1586 (in Portuguese) that Padre Torres, at Xavier's suggestion, gave Paulo a special lesson on Matthew's gospel every day, and that according to the instructor's report, his student learned the entire gospel by heart. Frois applauded Paulo's intellectual and spiritual excellence by saying that few in the college excelled him. Xavier, too, found him rather unusual among the non-Christians he had met in Asia and therefore decided to use him as an interpreter in Christian missions in Japan. The padre envisioned embarking upon this mission within the next few years.

### PREPARATION FOR THE JAPAN MISSION

Even before he had met Yajiro, Xavier had heard from Portuguese traders that Japan and China were countries where the people were intelligent enough to possibly respond to Christian preaching. The bright vision he had of northeastern Asia was heightened by his disappointment with the progress of the mission in India. The Catholic Church's attempt to evangelize Asia was initiated by João III, the king of Portugal, who requested the pope to send missionaries to the east to spread the gospel. It was hoped that Christianization would militate against the power of the Muslims, the current dire enemies of the Christian west. The Portuguese procurement of pepper and spice possibly would be made easier as well.

Responding to the king, Pope Paul III commissioned Ignatius and his Jesuit companions to select two priests as papal legates to go to India. The choice initially fell upon Rodrigues and Bobadilla, but it was later decided that the former was not to go, and the latter became ill. As a substitute, Xavier, who was then secretary of the Society, was asked to go. He reportedly responded immediately by saying, "Good enough! I am ready." After receiving the papal blessing, he set sail from Lisbon in 1541. He was thirty-five years old at the time.

The religious and moral situation of the Portuguese colony in India was found to be quite deplorable. Xavier's report in 1545 included bitter references to the corruption and greed of the Portuguese officials there. The European colonists became notorious for their cruel exploitation and enslavement of the native population; they were also known for their promiscuity. The response of the local people to Christian preaching was far from satisfactory as well. Conversions were among the poor, whose comprehension of Christian teachings was doubtful; on the other hand, intellectuals of India gave no serious heed to the new religion because ancient Hindu tradition was deeply embedded in their society.

The encounter with Yajiro (later called Paulo) certainly prompted the papal legate to look further east for the next stage of his missionary work. He gathered as much information as possible from Paulo concerning the many facets of Japanese society, such as the political structure, culture, language, customs, religions and so forth.

Serious and bright a person though he was, Paulo unfortunately lacked any extensive and accurate understanding with regard to the Japanese religions: Buddhism, Shintoism, and Confucianism. Even though he could converse reasonably well with the padres in Portuguese, it was still far from facile for him to explain the intricacies of those religions to the westerners who had absolutely no knowledge thereof. As a result, he unintentionally gave a series of bizarre distortions which eventually created the totally false impression that the

Japanese were believers of one creator God called Dainichi and three deities in one God—the Trinity! The padres were also led to assume the Japanese belief in paradise, hell, last judgment, devils, the five commandments (similar to the decalogue), infant water purification (as in infant baptism), last rites, and so on.

These notions were not at all a figment of Paulo's imagination; each was based on certain practices or beliefs of this or that Buddhist sect. Overly anxious to explain to (or even impress) the western priests, he ended up by fabricating, so to speak, a pseudo-Christianity in Japan. One cannot simply blame Paulo, for he tried his best. This comical yet sad misinformation, however, caused serious confusion and conflicts later during Xavier's missionary undertakings in Japan.

With such a "remarkable" discovery about this enchanting land, the papal legate became convinced that Japan must be "the most adequate place for the promulgation of our Holy Teaching," as he wrote to Portugal in his letter of January 20, 1549. This great missionary vision drove him to embark upon a perilous journey over the sea to Japan, accompanied by Padre Cosme de Torres, Br. Juan Fernandez, and a few servants, besides the three Japanese returners, Paulo, Antonio and João. They finally arrived in their Chinese junk in Kagoshima, a city located in southern Kyushu on August 15, 1549.

### XAVIER IN KAGOSHIMA

Kagoshima was Paulo's hometown. Upon his homecoming, he became an instant celebrity. The townspeople had forgotten his earlier deeds and welcomed him as he reappeared after many years of absence with the white bonzes of the Southern Barbarians (the Iberians were called so because, due to the route they followed, they arrived from the south) and their dark-skinned servants from India, the homeland of Buddha. The hometown hero was compelled to meet curious visitors constantly, and he took advantage of the opportunity to tell them about his new religion.

Even the lord of the province (Satsuma), Takahisa Shimazu, invited him along with his foreign companions and questioned them intensively about the world abroad. The gifts they presented to the lord included a decorated copy of the Bible and a painting of the madonna and the Christ child (perhaps an altarpiece) which entranced the lord and his mother. (Apparently they accepted the latter to be a Buddhist picture of Kannon, Bodhisativa of mercy and compassion; the Shimazu family belonged to the Shingon Sect of Buddhism.) The lord was willing to grant permission for a mission to be opened in his territory. His gracious action was motivated not only by genuine hospitality and curiosity toward the foreigners but also by a keen interest in trade with the Portuguese. It was the lord's profound expectation that the padres would help him in a commercial venture.

Thus Xavier's mission activities in Japan were launched. During a period of approximately ten months of labor propagating the Christian teachings in Kagoshima, according to Br. Fernandez's report, a hundred and fifty people were baptized. Among them were Paulo's family, relatives, and friends. There was also an old man, a retainer of the lord of the city of Ichiku, who not only became a Christian (his baptismal name was Miguel) but was later instrumental in converting the whole family of his master (excepting the master himself).

Another good example of local conversions is that of a young man who like Miguel was also from the warrior class, though not with as high a rank. He admired Xavier so much that he decided to follow him. He later became the first Japanese person to visit Europe, where he won wide respect for his exemplary life as a Christian. He was allowed to enter the Society of Jesus in Rome and spent the remainder of his life at the Jesuit College in Coimbra, Portugal.

João Rodrigues, who became a Jesuit in Japan in 1580 and worked as a useful interpreter there for thirty-three years, wrote in his *History of the Church in Japan* that Xavier performed various miracles. Twenty-two of them were later officially recognized by the Holy See when Xavier was canonized in 1622. Among the miracles reported there was one incident where Xavier resurrected a dead girl in Kagoshima. According to Rodrigues, the news spread widely and was recorded in Japanese. (In fact, this story has been orally handed down among the descendants of these Japanese Christians.) Rodrigues also reported Xavier's healings of a leper and an infant with a swollen body. (He claimed that these stories were found in a printed text written by a certain Portuguese who was staying in the area where those incidents occurred.)

Xavier visited several Buddhist monasteries to converse with the monks, who, for their part, were also full of both curiosity and respect for the monk of this new religion from a distant place. Despite serious attempts on both sides, unfortunately, the dialogue evidently did not always develop smoothly, due mainly to the language barrier. Paulo, as mentioned above, was not well versed in Buddhist teachings, and the westerners' Japanese linguistic skills were far from accomplished enough to engage in profound philosophical and theological discussions. (Xavier had no facility in Japanese when he arrived in Japan.)

The differences, of course, lay much deeper than that of language; the very systems of thinking lay counter to one another. This is found cogently illustrated in one discussion regarding the immortality of the soul between Xavier and Ninshitsu, an abbot of the Zen monastery called Fukushoji. Xavier later wrote: "In many talks which I had with him, I found him unsure—unable to decide whether our soul is immortal, or whether it dies with the body; sometimes he told me yes, at other times no, and I fear that the other wisemen are similarly uncertain." For Xavier it was a self-evident truth that the immortal soul resided in a mortal body. The ambiguity shown by the Buddhist totally puzzled him.

The abbot, for his part, was perplexed at the westerner's opinion. For him, the whole universe was constituted by one single, ever-changing composite, including the human soul and the body. There should not be, he thought, an essential incongruence between the soul and the body, and if conflict was felt to exist, one should train both one's mind and one's body to overcome it. Unfortunately, both Xavier and the abbot fell far short of realizing this fundamental difference in their concepts and terminology.

They, nonetheless, seem to have fostered a cordial friendship, as Xavier commented that the old abbot was "so great a friend of mine that it is a marvel to see." Here the encounter between the Christian west and the Buddhist east, albeit with enormous differences, set a positive tone. According to Br. Fernandez, Ninshitsu later "understood the things of the Christians and longed to become a Christian," but his high position prevented him from receiving baptism. "But he afterwards died with great sorrow for this." This information may or may not be quite accurate, but it is certain that some years later when other missionaries visited there, they were welcomed by several elderly monks who still cherished a warm and respectful memory of Xavier. They reportedly wanted to be baptized as well.

Such a courteous reception, however, did not always occur; Xavier had to face hostile opposition from many Buddhists, particularly when he spoke out openly against them. That which appalled him in particular was pederasty, which was a widespread practice among the monks. (Buddhism, as will be discussed later, was in a state of deep spiritual and moral decline in those days.) The priest's condemnation, however, fell on deaf ears. Another target of the priest's strictures was abortions, which were often performed in Japanese society. The missionaries, expressing their disgust and outrage, denounced it repeatedly in their public preaching as well as through personal conversations with local people.

### XAVIER'S CATECHISMS

Xavier, realizing the high rate of literacy among the Japanese population, decided to instruct the Japanese in Christian doctrines through written as well as oral communication. During the winter of 1549, he supervised Paulo, who translated a small catechism which he had used in India. It was a collection of articles of faith and prayer to be recited and consisted of the following twenty-nine items:

1. An opening prayer
2. The Apostles' Creed
3. Acts of faith
4. The Lord's Prayer
5. The Hail Mary
6. The ten commandments
7. A statement that those who observe the ecclesiastical law are to ascend to heaven and those who do not are to be cast into hell
8. A prayer of petition for grace to observe the law this day
9. A prayer to the Holy Mother
10. A prayer to Christ, asking for the forgiveness of sins for this day

11. A prayer to the Holy Mother for forgiveness of sins for this day
12. The commandments of the church
13. Salve Regina
14. A prayer of confession
15. Seven capital sins
16. Seven cardinal virtues
17. Three supernatural virtues
18. Four supreme virtues
19. Seven corporal works of mercy
20. Seven spiritual works of mercy
21. Five senses
22. Three functions of the soul
23. Three enemies of the soul
24. The consecrated host
25. The consecrated wine
26. The act of faith and restitution for unbelief
27. A petition for protection by the Holy Mother and saints
28. A petition for the protection of the Archangel Miguel
29. A prayer before meals

One other catechism was also prepared in Japanese. It included an explanation of creation, the fall of Adam and Eve, the life of Christ, the Trinity, and the last judgment.

These two Japanese catechisms were transcribed, using the Portuguese alphabet, for utilization by the missionaries. Xavier himself read it out loud in front of Fukushoji. (But the Japanese audience unfortunately did not seem to have quite understood him because of his foreign intonation.) Printed Japanese copies were distributed to the converts for memorization. The text often had to be corrected and revised, however, since the translator consistently used Buddhist terms, which caused a considerable amount of misunderstanding (as will be discussed later). In spite of all of these problems, these catechisms were used until 1556 when Vice-provincial Belchior Nuñez replaced them with another version comprised of twenty-five items of similar content. Unfortunately, neither version of the catechisms has survived.

### ICHIKU AND PAULO'S FATE

Xavier was not ready to be content with the success of his mission work in Satsuma. Ever since he decided on the Japan mission while in India, his plan was to meet the highest authority of the nation and tell him about the Christian gospel in person. So he went to the lord of Satsuma to ask for permission and aid to travel to Kyoto, the capital of the country, where hopefully he could receive an audience with the emperor. Lord Shimazu was reluctant to respond positively to this request for several reasons: first, he did not want to lose the padres as his contact with the foreign traders, and second, he was quite aware of the devastation of the city. Despite his caution that the journey would likely be futile and dangerous, Xavier and his companions left Kagoshima and headed for the capital.

On their way to Kyoto, they stopped at various towns. According to Padre Luis Frois, who worked as a missionary for thirty-four years in Japan (1563–1597) and wrote a lengthy volume of a history of the Catholic mission in Japan in 1582–1586 in Portuguese, they were welcomed by the lord of Ichiku, a town northwest of Kagoshima. This region was entrusted by lord Shimazu to his viceroy Niiro who resided in what some Portuguese visitors called "one of the strongest castles in the world" in Ichiku. Niiro welcomed Xavier, and with his family and retainers willingly listened to his preaching. Though he himself did not receive baptism for political reasons, his wife, son and daughter, and fifteen others became Christians. Frois also commented that when he arrived there in the early 1560s, the townspeople asked him about Xavier, and further that he found them so well instructed in the Christian teachings that he had nothing to add.

Frois' report sounds quite gratifying. The situation, however, in reality seems to have been quite different. A rueful illustration is found in Paulo's life. Xavier entrusted him with the young Christian community in Ichiku as he left the town. But several months later, Paulo and his mission companions encountered severe persecution from the Buddhist monks, and Paulo himself was expelled from the town. Out of desperation, he sailed to China where he later died.

Padre Couros mentioned in 1612 that Paulo became a pirate and died a miserable death while carrying out a raid on China. Padre Frois put it: "He (Yajiro) came back from India much changed and well instructed in the things of faith, and in all that time he gave a good example in keeping with his maturity and wisdom. And yet some later said of him that he was like the star which led the Magi from the East, but which, in spite of this, did not approach the crib of Bethlehem with them. For, after he had advised his wife, his children, relatives, and friends to become Christians, which they did, he chose another way a few years later (although it is not known that he ever gave up the faith or ceased to be a Christian)." Georg Schurhammer, the author of four large volumes of a thorough study of the life of Xavier (*Francis Xavier: His Life, His Times*, ET. 1973–1982), surmises: "We suspect that Anjiro, who had perhaps served in the military marine, had been forced through the persecution of the bonzes to join one of these (pirate) fleets" (Vol. 4, p. 130, n. 22)

In view of his serious devotion to Christianity when he was with Xavier, it is indeed surprising that he ended his life in such misery. One cannot help wondering why he did not take refuge in his spiritual director's arms after the expulsion from Ichiku. According to Fernam Mendes Pinto, an adventurous Portuguese merchant and friend of Xavier, Paulo was killed by pirates on his way to China. Rodrigues, trusting this information, gave high praises to the "good man" Paulo and said his death was tantamount to martyrdom. Xavier, he testified, commented from time to time on how virtuous Paulo was. He also gave credit to Paulo for the increase of Christians in that region from less than one hundred in the year when Xavier left to five hundred in 1563, despite the absence of padres during that period.

## ON THE WAY TO KYOTO

Xavier and his companions left Ichiku, headed north by ship, and landed in Hirado, a town located on a small island off the coast of the northwestern edge of Kyushu. This town later became an important Christian center. Lord Takanobu Matsuura, with an eye on trade with the Portuguese, welcomed the padres. According to Rodrigues, two hundred people were baptized there within twenty days of missionary work. Br. Fernandez, talented with linguistic abilities, preached in Japanese. A church was also built with the financial help of the Portu-

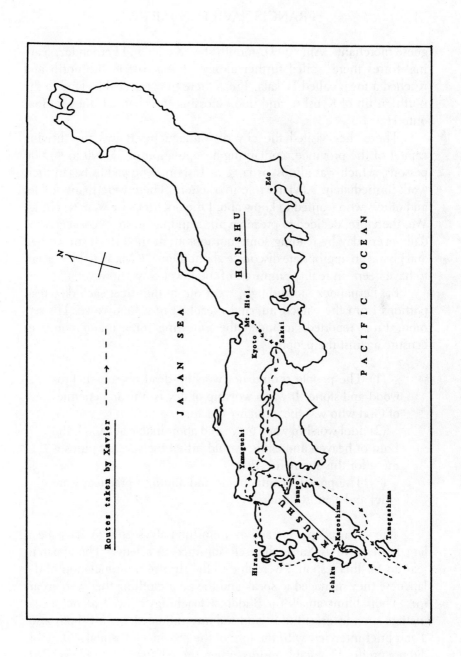

guese merchants. After a two-month stay, Xavier and Fernandez, leaving Torres there, sailed further along the seacoast to the north and reached a town called Hakata. From there they traveled by land to the northern tip of Kyushu, and upon crossing the channel, they set foot onto Honshu.

There they visited the city of Yamaguchi. It was the thriving capital of the province, containing a population of 35,000 to 40,000 persons, which was almost as large as Lisbon. The padres began their work immediately. Xavier wrote in a letter: "There were many nobles and others who wanted to know about the doctrines we were teaching. We, therefore, decided to preach while standing on street corners twice daily every day by reading some portions from the catechism we had and giving an appropriate discourse about them." ("Many nobles" seem to have been, in reality, samurais of the lower class, however.)

Br. Fernandez, accordingly, went out to the street each day, read portions from the catechism, and preached in a loud voice. His sermon, Frois reported, included the following three major points of censure against the people:

(1) The people should not worship dead objects such as wood and stone. It was a worship of devils, the archenemies of God who was the almighty creator.

(2) Idol worship was a grave and abominable act; God, the Lord of heaven and earth, would inflict the severest punishment for this shameful sin.

(3) The prevalent infanticide and abortion practices were cruel and against humanity.

The townspeople's reaction unfortunately seems to have been largely negative as Xavier himself admitted in a letter. The apparent reasons for this response were due to the strange pronunciation of the Japanese they managed to speak and the poor clothing they were wearing. Their blunt attack on Buddhist teachings as well as on sexual matters such as prostitution and sodomy militated against them also. Their brief interview with the lord of the province, Yoshitaka Ohuchi, did not produce favorable results either, though they were not expelled.

The missionaries did not give up, however; they continued their street preaching each day. It was reported that one day when Br. Fernandez was talking about the life of Christ, a man approached him and spat on his face. The insult did not affect him at all; he calmly wiped off his face and kept on with his speech. The incident had the reverse effect than the precipitator intended—one person in the audience was so impressed that he later asked to be baptized; he was the first convert in Yamaguchi. His name was Uchida, whose house the missionaries were renting.

The seeds Xavier sowed in his first visit to Yamaguchi, albeit small in number, remained alive. About fifty years afterward, when a padre visited the town, he happened to meet a seventy year old woman who had been baptized by Xavier. She told him her recollection of "the first priest who came to Japan and then returned to Namban, a tall man of fine appearance who could not speak the Japanese language and thus preached with the aid of an interpreter, and whose face became all red and fiery while preaching."

### AT KYOTO AND MT. HIEI

In December 1550 Xavier, Fernandez, and a Japanese companion began their journey on foot from Yamaguchi and headed toward Kyoto. It was a painful trip; the snow was knee-deep in places and the rivers they crossed were ice-cold and waist-deep. Many local people were often scornful toward the poorly clad strangers who resembled beggars.

There were, nevertheless, kind-hearted people as well. Padre Frois mentioned Br. Fernandez' information indicating that at one harbor where they stopped, a prominent man felt sorry for the helpless foreigners from the land of Buddha (India), so much so that he gave them a letter written to his friend in Sakai, a thriving commercial seaport not far from the capital. The letter intended to request that the addressee find someone who was going to Kyoto to accompany and provide safety for the alien travelers.

The addressee of the letter turned out to be a very wealthy merchant in Sakai. He was kind enough to welcome Xavier and his companions to his beautiful estate. After a short stay there, they were able to go to Kyoto with a nobleman who was introduced to them by their influential host. Xavier was full of joy with the anticipation of his long-planned missionary work in the capital city after such a lengthy and hard journey.

In January of 1551 Xavier and his companions finally reached the capital. But what disillusionment! As we mentioned earlier, the city lay almost completely in ruin after the long series of civil wars and depredation by bandits. The plan Xavier had in his mind before he arrived in Japan was that he should speak with the emperor in person and get permission to spread the Christian gospel and also to open an ambassadorial relationship between the Japanese emperor and the Portuguese governor in India.

However, according to Seisai Emura, a physician in Kyoto who wrote *Mélange of an Old Man* (in Japanese) toward the very end of the sixteenth century, the royal palace that Xavier saw was "no different from a farmhouse." Emura narrated further: "There was no wall surrounding the palace but only a bamboo hedge linked together with bushes. When we were young, we played with clay on the balcony of the palace and fashioned little figures from it." Under such pitiful conditions, the emperor and the court nobility were barely surviving by desperately soliciting donations from wealthy warlords and merchants. The poorly clad foreigner, therefore, was not at all a welcome visitor. Without any gifts to present, his request of an audience with the emperor was abruptly turned down.

Gravely disappointed, Xavier had one other plan—to visit an important "university" in Mt. Hiei near Kyoto. This was a great monastic center of the Tendai sect of Buddhism which was established by a priest by the name of Saicho in the eighth century. Having heard about its reputation, Xavier intended to meet with leading scholars there, engage in philosophical discussions with them, and preach Christian doctrines. Unfortunately, here again he encountered a cold rejection from the monastic authority because he lacked any impressive appearance or any gifts. Sadly, thus ended his short visit to Kyoto. Despite the high hopes with which he had come, he decided to return to Yamaguchi.

BACK IN YAMAGUCHI

The disappointing trip to Kyoto compelled Xavier to concentrate his efforts on Yamaguchi. Upon arrival in the provincial capital, he, dressed in silk appropriate to his role as ambassador of the Portuguese governor of India, went to the lord, Ohuchi, with two letters of recommendation, one from the governor and the other from the bishop of Goa. He also presented thirteen various gifts, including a large and intricate clock, a richly ornamented musket with three barrels, expensive brocades, beautiful fine glassware, a mirror, spectacles and other things, all of which were a novelty to the Japanese. (These things were provided by the Portuguese governor in Malacca, Pedro da Silva. In the chronicles of the Ohuchi family, Xavier's gifts are mentioned.) Ohuchi was so delighted with all of these presents that upon Xavier's request, he immediately issued an order permitting free Christian mission work in his territory. He also provided the missionaries with a plot of land for the purpose of building a church and mission residence. (These were built in November of 1552.)

The lord's official assistance definitely had a positive effect. After several months of apostolic work in Yamaguchi, Padre Torres wrote in September of 1551: "Those who come to these regions must be very learned in order to answer the very deep and difficult questions which they ask from morning till night. They are very insistent in their questions. From the day on which Padre Mestre Francisco came into this city, which is now some five months or more ago, there has never been a day on which there were not priests and laymen here from morning until late at night in order to ask all kinds of questions."

Not only were the Christian teachings totally new to the Japanese but also the information regarding natural science which Xavier shared with them surprised them greatly. Xavier stated afterward, "They do not know that the earth is round, nor do they know the course of the sun; and they ask about these things and others such as comets, lightning, rain, and snow, and similar things. We answered and explained these to them, and they were very happy and content and regarded us as learned men, which was no little help in their giving credence to our words."

The astronomical knowledge Xavier demonstrated to the Japanese was of course very new in Europe as well. Copernicus' revolutionary theory was published only some ten years previous, and Galileo was not yet even born at the time. The great admiration Xavier won from the Japanese for his scientific knowledge was not what he was seeking, however. He was too anxious to teach Christian doctrines to tarry with such discourses on nature.

It is of interest, incidentally, to compare Xavier in this respect with Matteo Ricci, a Jesuit missionary in China toward the end of the sixteenth century. Unlike Xavier, Ricci capitalized on his scientific and mathematical skill in his successful attempt to gain acceptance by Chinese intellectuals. He took pains to explain Christian doctrines by making use of (often by drawing parallels with) Confucian teachings. He, for instance, called God the Lord of heaven, which afforded an easier means to designate the Christian God to the Chinese. This stood in sharp contrast to Xavier's decision to use only the Latin word Deus for God after abandoning a mistaken adaptation of a name for Buddha, Dainichi. The approach Xavier adopted can be characterized as basically one of confrontation with the local culture and religion, whereas Ricci's policy was definitely one of accommodation. (This question will be discussed more extensively further on.)

### DEBATE WITH THE BUDDHISTS

During the second audience with the lord of Yamaguchi, Xavier was asked by several monks who were present about God. The questions and answers, as recorded by Frois, went as follows:

Question: Does your God have form or color?
Xavier:    He has neither form nor color nor any accident, because he is Pure Substance separated from all the elements. He is, instead, the Creator of them all.
Question: What is the origin of God?
Xavier:    God exists by Himself. He is the Prime Principle; he, therefore, is omnipotent, omniscient, beneficent, without beginning and without end.

The first question raised by the Buddhist monks concerned whether or not God had taken any visible form in this world; the question was not really asking about some actual shape or color which God possibly possessed, for the word "color" in the Buddhist sense was indicative of the phenomenal world. The second question was a corollary of the idea expressed in the first. In Buddhist thought, everything was interdependent and thus nothing existed in total self-sufficiency. Both questions clearly betrayed the typical Buddhist rejection of the notion of a transcendent creator God. Xavier's answers, on the other hand, came straight from European scholasticism. He, of course, tried to counter the questions the best he could. Unfortunately, however, the padre and the monks were not communicating with each other; they were not even aware of the difference in the fundamental premises of their thinking. The conversation, therefore, bore no fruit. Padre Torres commented later: "For since they are people who are accustomed to practicing great meditations, they asked questions to which neither St. Thomas nor Scotus could have given answers that would have satisfied them, as they were men without faith."

During the discussion, Xavier came to a puzzling discovery: what his Buddhist partners of the dialogue meant by Dainichi was radically different from what he thought it designated—the Christian God. Ever since Yajiro suggested this Japanese term as the equivalent of God while they were still in South Asia, Xavier had been using it in preaching as well as in personal conversations. As a result, his Japanese audience was led to believe that the western missionary "from India" was talking about the Buddhist Dainichi. The same consequence resulted in a most emphatic way during this discussion in front of lord Ohuchi, for those Buddhist monks belonged to the Shingon sect which taught devotion to Dainichi.

Shingon Buddhism was an esoteric school which flourished most prominently in Japan from the ninth century when a Japanese monk by the name of Kukai brought it to his country from China. The basic teachings of this school originated in the Tantric form of Mahayana Buddhism and spread to China in the seventh and eighth centuries. Kukai learned it from Master Kui-kuo (746–805), the patriarch of esoteric Buddhism in China, and developed it further into his own esoteric philosophical system.

The principal scripture of the Shingon school was Dainichi-kyo (the Great Sun Sutra), according to which the phenomenal world is a manifestation of the ultimate reality known as Dainichi, "The Great Sun Buddha." (This had nothing to do with worship of the sun. The Shingon notion ultimately derived from a cosmic mysticism of ancient India. The "Great Sun" symbolized the mystical cosmic Buddha as the great spiritual illuminator.)

This timeless eternal Buddha (as distinct from the historical Buddha) was beyond all this world's dualism and illusory concepts. Yet at the same time it was within all existence as the Buddha nature. As such, it was believed to be the all-embracing ultimate reality as well as the all-creating source of the universe. The realization of the identity of one's own Buddha nature with the Dainichi (Great Sun) Buddha was the salvific enlightenment of Shingon Buddhism.

The sect used various esoteric (mystical ritualistic) methods for training aspirants to attain the enlightenment. One of them involved a contemplation of pictures or diagrams called *Mandala*. Some drawings represented Dainichi, surrounded by his emanations (various Buddhas and saints) each with a white halo, seated in deep and serene meditation on a white lotus. The ritualistic recitation of Buddha's names, the sacred texts, and mystic formulas—cosmic speech of Dainichi—was also an oft-repeated practice. In fact, the name of the school, Shingon, which means "the true word" (corresponding to the Sanskrit *mantra*), was indicative of this exercise.

Yajiro and the missionaries, as well as the Shingon monks, made a grave mistake by hastily jumping to the conclusion of identifying Dainichi with the Christian God because of some superficial similarities between the two: both of them were considered ultimate and supreme, the creative source and abiding grace of all existence, and the true power of salvation. As such, they were the objects of human devotion. They were also believed to have been manifested in earthly form. Both Shingon Buddhism and Christianity preached the existence of devils as well. Sacred pictures, hymns, and prayer formulae were common to both religions. As for ritualistic practices, both observed purificatory rites of initiation via the sprinkling of water on the novice: the Christian baptism and the Buddhist *kanjo*.

The essential differences between the two were in reality beyond dispute, however. Dainichi was not at all the same as the transcendent

and personal creator God of Christianity. The pantheistic manifestation of the former was absolutely incompatible with the incarnation of
God in Jesus Christ. Kukai, for instance, wrote:

> Existence is my existence, the existence of the Buddhas, and
> the existence of all sentient beings. . . . All of these exis-
> tences are interrelated horizontally and vertically without
> end, like images in mirrors, or like the rays of lamps. This
> existence is in that one, and that one is in this. The Exis-
> tence of the Buddha (Dainichi) is the existence of the sen-
> tient beings and vice versa. They are not identical but are
> nevertheless identical; they are not different but are neverthe-
> less different. (English translation by Y. Hakeda in his *Kukai:
> Major Works*, 1972, p. 93)

When Xavier sensed the basic discrepancy between his faith and
that of the Buddhist teachings, he asked the Buddhists pointed questions attempting to elicit their responses to the Christian doctrines of
the Trinity and incarnation. The inquiry led him to the palpable
conclusion that Dainichi had absolutely nothing to do with his God.
He then immediately instructed Fernandez to tell the people not to
worship Dainichi, for it was not God but instead a product of evil.
From that time onward, he decided to call God "Deus" and not use
any Japanese name.

The missionaries' blunt censure of Buddhism as a deception of
the devil, needless to say, caused the Buddhists to drastically change
their attitude toward the Christians from that of a general friendly
curiosity to one of fury and hostility. The monks refused to meet or
speak with them any longer. Their animosity became so intense, according to Padre Frois, that the missionaries feared physical persecution. The monks carried out a counter-attack on the Christians by
calling Deus "Daiuso," meaning a big lie. Malicious rumors were
spread that the foreigners' preaching would bring disasters, the appearance of ghosts, the coming of turmoil and perpetual darkness.

SUCCESS IN YAMAGUCHI

Despite all this opposition, the missionaries continued their task and reportedly were successful in gaining some five hundred converts in about two months. (This number is reported in a letter by Xavier; Rodriguez put the number at three thousand, which is obviously inflated.) Most of those persons seemingly came from the lowly ranked samurais, merchants, and farmers who felt alienated from the thriving society of Yamaguchi. They became excellent Christians. Br. Pedro de Alcaçova stated in a letter in 1552:

> I stayed in Yamaguchi for a long time and I know there are many Christians who are just like *religioso* (monks or members of a religious order). In view of their compassionate minds and their love for us, they seem to be no different from our Brothers. We cannot praise their excellence too much. To them, the Portuguese were like their real brothers. Whenever they meet non-Christians, they do not forget to talk about Deus. In Japan, it happens more often than in any other country that the father may belong to one religious group, the mother to another, and the son to still another. This is so because there are so many religions in this country. Such a practice cannot be found as far as the Christians are concerned, however. For as soon as they become Christians, they begin inviting others to join them so as to incur the resentment of non-Christians. They converse with one another with affection so special that it even appears unnatural. They speak about Deus without shame wherever they may be. There are some who even reprove non-Christians and destroy their idols in front of them.

Among these strong converts there was a twenty-five year old itinerant bard who later became an able interpreter and preacher. He was born poor and had no formal education, yet was quite intelligent and knowledgeable about, among other things, Japanese religions. In addition to congenitally weak health, he had no sight in one eye and only a little in the other. He was baptized by Xavier and received the name Lourenço. According to Padre Frois, he was allowed to enter the Society of Jesus as the first Japanese brother. Frois wrote: "It pleased our Lord to make him the foundation, as it were, of all the Christianity in the region of Miyako (Kyoto)." Frois also reported that because of Lourenço's preaching, several thousand Japanese persons were converted to Christianity. He never flinched from debates with reputable scholars of Buddhism and Confucianism nor from witnessing to the Christian gospel to many powerful feudal lords. Some of them, in fact, did become devout Christians. Despite poor health, his tenacious efforts continued for forty years until he was totally exhausted at the age of sixty-five.

There were many reports which attested that other Portuguese missionaries in later years met Japanese who had held fast to the faith to which they had been initiated by Xavier. For example, when Padre Cabral visited a small island called Miyajima (not very far from Hiroshima) in 1574, he was greeted by a poor fisherman, whose Christian name was Felipe, and his wife. They had moved from Yamaguchi to this island and were the only Christians there. They wept for joy and showed the priest their rosaries with lead crosses affixed. Felipe told him that he prayed every day for Padre Francis, the other priests and the Pope.

Padre Frois mentioned an incident which occurred in 1586. He was visited at midnight by two ladies over eighty years of age who were the daughters of prominent nobles. They were also baptized by Xavier some thirty-seven years before and maintained their faith despite having had no contact with any Christians and in the midst of much criticism of their beliefs. The priest gave them catechetical instruction for an hour as well as an Agnus Dei and some corals and medals. They departed with tears of joy and sorrow.

Not only Xavier, but Padre Torres also had considerable success in his apostolic work in Yamaguchi. He reportedly baptized two thousand people there. We read in his writing: "When they (the Christians in Yamaguchi) once accepted the faith, there are, from what I have seen and heard, and from what I have experienced with them, no people in the world so tenacious. It seems to me that the majority of those who have become Christians, and of these there are many, are ready to endure any calamity for the love of God."

Those Christians, in fact, had to experience much suffering when some years later the land came under the control of the Mori family who persecuted them. They kept in contact with Padre Torres through letters. It was reported that in 1563 many of them made the fifty-hour-long journey for confession with the padre. During the period of fiercest persecution in the early seventeenth century, many were martyred.

### MISSION IN BUNGO

In September of 1551 Xavier received a letter from the lord of Bungo, the northeastern coastal province of Kyushu, informing him of the arrival of a Portuguese ship in his territory and requesting that he come to speak with him. A letter from the captain of the ship, an old acquaintance of his, came as well. He then decided to go there at once, entrusting Torres, Fernandez, and the others with the apostolic work in Yamaguchi.

The lord of Bungo was Yoshishige Otomo, who, though only twenty-two years of age, was a capable and ambitious ruler of this poor mountainous territory. His young mind was morally uncompromising as well. In 1544, for example, the Chinese crewmen of a Portuguese ship which had arrived in Bungo plotted a mutiny and asked the father of Yoshishige, the then sovereign of the region, to kill the Portuguese from the ship in exchange for the cargo. Yoshishige's father favored the scheme from sheer greed, but the son objected to it violently, declaring that he would defend the foreign merchants himself. Thus the ship was able to stay there safely for three years until it set sail.

This incident was indicative not only of the young lord's moralistic nature but also of his friendliness toward the westerners, a characteristic which remained unchanged until his death. He welcomed Xavier and inundated him with questions about Portugal and India. It was his strong desire to send an ambassador to the representative of the king of Portugal in India. (According to Giovanni Batista Sidoti, the last martyred missionary, Otomo indeed sent an ambassador to Rome; in fact, this emissary died and was buried there.) Being an aspiring warlord, Otomo was hungry for new weapons. This desire prompted him to continue being congenial toward the Portuguese. The use of the imported cannons, in fact, later made him one of the most powerful lords in Kyushu.

Nonetheless, his interest in Christianity was genuine; he was willing not only to permit Christian mission work in his territory but also to provide the missionaries with such necessities as lodging, a piece of ground for a church and other gratuities. He listened intently to their explanations of the Christian doctrines, though he did not receive baptism until a later time for personal and political reasons. It was divulged that when Padre Balthazar Gago came to Japan and met Yoshishige Otomo in 1552, the lord lamented that there were still no Christians in his land. But there were, according to the Jesuit records, six or seven hundred native Christians there in the following year. This lord, at any rate, proved to be one of the best protectors of the Christians. (His life will be discussed further in chapter 4.)

### XAVIER'S DEPARTURE FROM JAPAN

Two and a half years had passed since Xavier landed in Japan. He felt keenly the need to actualize further his vision of the Christian faith in East Asia. While in Japan, he learned that the cultural roots of Japan were to be sought in China. To make the mission in Japan truly effective, he deemed, China should be evangelized first. This conviction led him to decide to leave Japan and return to India so that from there he could plan a China mission and also take care of the situation in India as superior of the India mission. There as well he intended to select and send able missionaries to Japan as reinforcements. Bidding farewell to the sad Christians and Lord Otomo, he set sail from Bungo with several Japanese converts in November of 1551.

Did the departure suggest that he was disappointed with the Japan mission? The available evidence indicates otherwise. In his letter written in Kagoshima addressed to Goa, he said of the Japanese:

> The people with whom we have thus far conversed are the best that we have yet discovered; and it seems to me that, among pagan nations, there will not be another which will surpass the Japanese. They are a race of very fine manners and are generally good and without malice, a people of an

astonishingly great sense of honor, who prize honor more
than any other thing; they are in general a poor people; and
the poverty that exists among noble men (referring to samurai) and those who are not, is not considered to be a re-
proach. . . . A large portion of the people can read and
write, which is a great help for learning the prayers and the
things of God in a short time. They do not have more than
one wife. It is a land where there are few thieves, and the
reason for this is the severe justice which they employ with
regard to those whom they discover to be such, since they do
not spare the life of anyone; they have a profound abhorrence
for this vice of theft. They are a people of great good will,
and very sociable, and eager to know. They have a great
delight in hearing about the things of God, especially when
they understand them.

I would have you know one thing for which you should
give frequent thanks to God our Lord, namely, that this
island of Japan is greatly disposed for the great increase of our
holy faith; and if we knew how to speak the language, I have
no doubt that many would become Christians. (English translation in Schurhammer, *op. cit.*, vol. 4, p. 84)

He criticized and condemned many of the Buddhist monks and wrote:
"It seems to me that the laity will not contradict or persecute us on their
part were it not for the great importunities of the bonzes."

In another letter from Kagoshima, he instructed that the College
of St. Paul in Goa enroll and educate Chinese and Japanese boys in
Portuguese as well as Christian doctrines in order to make them inter-
preters for the missionaries.

Such a generally favorable view of the Japanese and a high hope
for the nation's evangelization as expressed in these letters were verified
by Frois, who wrote to Rome in 1564 that he had often heard Padre
Master Francis speak thusly. Frois himself tendered a full agreement
with Xavier in another letter addressed to his confreres in Goa when he
wrote, "It was not done without the mighty assistance of the Holy Spirit
that Padre Master Francis sought with such zeal after this nation which
lies at the far end of the discovered world separated from the Maker

because of its total ignorance of Him." Betraying his ill feeling toward the Spaniards, he continued: "These people are, regrettable for me to admit, superior to the Spaniards in many respects in their culture, manner and customs. . . ."

### CONCLUDING REMARKS

What was the significance of Xavier's mission to Japan? Through him, for the very first time in its history, Japan encountered a radically different monotheistic religion and the culture related to it. Xavier wrote the first line of a unique chapter of the "Christian century" in Japan's history.

From the point of view of a "success rate" (as we moderns are obsessed with), however, Xavier's life was, unfortunately, not all full of glory. The course of his life, in fact, often had to be altered because of the circumstances he encountered. He, the young and brilliant student that he was at the college in Paris, surrendered his worldly ambition when Ignatius told him the words of Jesus Christ: "What will it profit a man, if he gains the whole world and forfeits his soul?" Next, his dream of going to the Holy Land with fellow Jesuits failed. Then, while he was fulfilling an important duty as the secretary of the Society in Rome, he was suddenly sent to India to fill the vacancy created because of the sickness of his friend (he had, therefore, not been the first choice as the papal legate).

The mission in South Asia, however, was not enough to satisfy him. The encounter with Yajiro inspired a great vision of the evangelization of Japan, which proved to be much more difficult than he had anticipated. The total number of Japanese persons he baptized during his two and one half years there numbered approximately one thousand. Early misinformation later caused him to suddenly and drastically change his teachings from "Worship Dainichi" to "Don't worship Dainichi," which inevitably caused enormous confusion among his listeners and a profound animosity on the part of the Shingon monks. The long envisioned audience with the emperor and other dignitaries did not come to reality in war-torn Kyoto.

The experience in Japan led him to plan a mission in China. It was, unfortunately, impossible for him to enter the country because its government was prohibiting the admission of foreigners into the land. An attempt at secret entry with the aid of some Chinese merchants in exchange for a considerable amount of spice did not materialize, for the Chinese failed to fulfill the promised deal. And while he was still awaiting the Chinese boat on the island of Sancian where he had a view of the Chinese mainland on the horizon, he fell gravely ill and died several days later on December 3, 1552. He was forty-six years old.

The series of unfulfilled plans and visions Xavier had to bear, however, does not have to be deemed as a sign of failure but can be understood instead as a witness to his sincere struggle in opening up new possibilities—clearing the tough obstacles in order to make paths that others could follow. The prophet Isaiah's words, "In the wilderness prepare the way of the Lord, make straight in the desert a highway for our God" (40:3), could well describe the saint's contribution to Christian missions in the east. For this, canonization in 1622 was duly accorded him. Furthermore, he was declared the patron saint of the foreign missions by Pius XI in 1927.

The path through Japan blazed by Xavier, Torres, Fernandez, and their companions was followed and extended by still other missionaries from Portugal and, a little later, from Spain. It is our task in the following chapter to discuss the next stage of the Christian mission in Japan.

# 2

# The Successors of Xavier

PADRE TORRES IN YAMAGUCHI

The person who carried on the work of the fledgling Christian missions in Japan was Padre Cosme de Torres (1510–1570). He not only shared with Xavier from the very beginning the many hardships of apostolic labor, but also succeeded Xavier as superior of the missions, providing leadership after Xavier's departure. Under his guidance which lasted twenty-one years, Christians grew in number quite steadily, despite continued bitter opposition from local Buddhists. Overshadowed by his widely acclaimed companion, Francis Xavier, Torres was indeed an unsung hero.

After Xavier left Japan in 1551, Torres stayed in Yamaguchi until the city succumbed to an aggressive neighbor, the Mori clan. The new ruler was totally hostile to Christianity; thus the padre was compelled to move to a friendly haven in Bungo in 1556. It was indeed a heartbreaking experience for him to see the successful missions in which he was engaged for several years in Yamaguchi completely destroyed along with the once greatly thriving city. Torres, in fact, told Padre Nuñez that he had never lived with such joy and satisfaction in his entire life as he did during his six years in Yamaguchi (cf. Nuñez's letter from Cochin, India, dated January 10, 1558). With the formal approval of Lord Ohuchi, he was able to build a church there and subsequently baptized more than two thousand people. He worked also self-sacrificially to help the townspeople who were suffering from the devastation caused by warfare; he even gave up what little money he had in

39

order to buy food for the starving people regardless of their religious affiliation.

Torres' effort, however, elicited jealousy and animosity on the part of the Buddhists. They first attempted to defeat the padre and his companions through debate. Br. Fernandez wrote a lengthy report in Spanish on the exchange of opinion between the missionaries and the Buddhists, which he sent to Xavier on October 20, 1551. (G. Schurhammer published the original text along with three of Torres' letters, adding his translation and comments in German in *Die Disputationen des P. Cosme de Torres, S. J. mit den Buddhisten in Yamaguchi im Yahre 1551*, Tokyo, 1929.) What they discussed and in what ways they differed and agreed are of a great interest, as we shall see in the following section.

RELIGIOUS DEBATE

*(1) God and human destiny*

The Buddhists maintained that since every being came from nothing (*nada* in Fernandez's rendering), everything was destined to be reduced to the same state. The Christians agreed with the first part of the Buddhist thesis because of the Christian belief in God's creation of the world out of nothing. Here, however, lay a significant misunderstanding of the term "nothing." The Buddhist notion, rendered "nada" by Fernandez, was totally different from the Christian idea of nothing, i.e. physical non-existence. The Buddhist "nothing" (*ku* in Japanese; *shunyata* in Sanscrit) was a philosophical or psychological concept indicating void or nothingness. It implied a radical denial of anything thought to be permanent and immutable.

Xavier had already encountered this topic of dispute during his conversation with Abbot Ninshitsu in Kagoshima. The Buddhists had rejected the notion of the existence of an immortal soul (in contrast to a mortal body) in each person. In their view, it was, in reality, nothing but a figment of one's imagination, and one's attachment to such an illusory entity constituted the very cause of vain selfish desire, conceit, hatred, and anguish. Only when one, in a true sense, realized the delusiveness of "self," therefore, could one free oneself from all of these problems which resulted in human suffering. This spiritual liberation, Buddhism taught, would awaken one to discern the real reality. Consequently, what the Buddhists meant by "nothing" was not at all the same as that which the missionaries took it to mean. They intended to convince the western Christians of the non-substantiality of empirical existence, including the notion of "self." This unfortunately was not comprehensible to the westerners.

The whole of empirical human existence (with no dichotomy between soul and flesh), in the Buddhists' opinion, came from and would go back to the four fundamental elements: earth, water, fire, and wind. These basic components would simply change in their combinations and forms at every new birth and death. In this sense, there was no difference between human beings and animals. Every existence was to share the same destiny. And that was the "principle" (*principio* in Fernandez's rendering) which was applicable to everything in the world. The "principle" was, they insisted, neither good nor bad, neither glorious nor grievous. One would, however, judge it in any of these ways, according to Buddhists, as long as one's mind remained preoccupied by the desire to protect and preserve an illusory and superficial ego.

By sharp contrast, the Christians asserted that such a principle could only come from the almighty creator's will, which was all good and glorious. God created all things by his will and word alone, and he was not in need of any matter to do so. Human feelings of bad, good, remorse, and happiness were indicative of a sense of morality, a precious ability of the soul given by Deus only to human beings.

## (2) Sin and evil

If there were an invisible and immortal soul in humans, existing independently of the body, the Japanese disputants asked, would this not be the same as Deus, for he, as the Christians believed, was similarly invisible and immortal? To counter the question, the missionaries contended that the difference between Deus and human souls could be attested to by the fact that there were evil souls, while Deus was nothing but good. He created all souls good, but some of them became corrupt while others remained upright. Good souls, while in the flesh, could not see Deus, just as a precious stone, however splendid it might be, would fail to shine as long as it lay buried in mud.

The use of moral and rational grounds for proving the existence of God and the human soul was characteristically a traditional Catholic theological approach. According to this way of thinking, the capability of moral judgment was unique to humanity and it marked an essential difference between persons and animals. There should be a radical conflict between good and evil, God being the embodiment of supreme goodness as against Satan, the unmitigated evil. Good souls would ascend to the domain of eternal bliss, whereas wicked ones were to be doomed to damnation forever.

All of these Christian ideas sounded so foreign to the local people that they asked what the source of evil would be. The Christian answer was the evil power which comprised Lucifer and many other fallen angels who had been deprived of original glory and cast away by Deus because of their arrogance. It was they who would tempt people to fall into sin and misery.

Then another question followed: Why did Deus, who supposedly created only good things, have to make such unmitigated evil? Padre Torres' reply was that Deus bestowed Lucifer and other angels with the intelligence and free will to distinguish good from evil. But they misused this God-given ability and chose the wrong. There were good angels, on the other hand, who remained obedient to the maker and thus won eternal glory.

According to the Christian way of thinking, the opposition between good and evil, Deus and Lucifer, was a self-evident reality. It was the responsibility of human beings to be discerning by choosing good and rejecting evil. In the Buddhist view, however, good and evil were perceived as being essentially relative and therefore with no radical and metaphysical conflict between them. The standard by which good and evil were to be judged could change according to the point of view one would take. Buddhism taught that a society should possess and enforce moral norms; it refused to accept the existence of absolutely unchangeable codes of morality such as the divine mandate which Christians believed in.

Such essential differences are evidently manifested in many places in Fernandez's report. For example, when asked by the missionaries what a person should do to become a saint, the Zen Buddhists replied with laughter that saints did not exist and therefore it was unnecessary to seek sainthood. Fernandez also mentioned a statement made by some Japanese to the effect that the unwise would worry because they were concerned about heaven and hell, whereas the wise would be without anxiety, for they knew human desires would become extinct upon death. The dearth of a belief in the absolute and metaphysical ground for good and evil prompted such assertions.

### (3) The merciful Deus and human suffering

As a sequel to the discussion concerning good and evil, the subject of the meaning of human suffering came up. Why does Deus allow Satan to wrong people if he created human beings for obtaining eternal life? This is so, according to the Christians, because people are given intelligence and the freedom of choice. When one elects to do evil, this is one's own responsibility.

But why does the all-merciful Deus require us to follow such a hard way, including the toil and drudgery of daily life, in order to attain glory? The answer is that the law of Deus is, in reality, quite easy to follow if people utilize the weakness of flesh in the right way. Deus would, for example, never order starving people to die nor command them to try to perform impossible miracles. His only commandments are to worship the one who made and saves people and also to love one's neighbors.

Then what of suffering in the afterlife? Do those who were sent to hell have any hope of salvation? Would Deus be merciful enough to rescue those unfortunate souls who died without having had any opportunity to know of Deus? Since the Japanese had always had a strong feeling of venerable affiliation with their ancestors, these questions were quite vital to them. Xavier also had to handle the same subject. He wrote in a letter to the Society of Jesuits in Europe from Cochin, India, on January 29, 1552 as follows:

> One of the things that most of all pains and torments these Japanese is that we teach them that the prison of hell is irrevocably shut, so that there is no egress therefrom. For

they grieve over the fate of their departed children, of their parents and relatives, and they often show their grief by their tears. So they ask us if there is any hope, any way to free them by prayer from that eternal misery, and I am obliged to answer that there is absolutely none. Their grief at this affects and torments them woefully; they almost pine away with sorrow. But there is this good thing about their trouble—it makes one hope that they will all be the more laborious for their own salvation, lest they, like their forefathers, should be condemned to everlasting punishment. They often ask if God cannot take their fathers out of hell, and why their punishment must never have an end. We gave them a satisfactory answer, but they did not cease to grieve over the misfortune of their relatives; and I can hardly restrain my tears sometimes at seeing men so dear to my heart suffer such intense pain about a thing which is already done with and can never be undone. (English translation by H.J. Coleridge, in his *The Life and Letters of St. Francis Xavier*, 1881, vol. 2, p. 347)

As Xavier's letter eloquently witnesses, the subjects of human suffering and eternal damnation troubled the Japanese audience most. It was evidently very hard for them to reconcile in their minds the belief in an almighty and all-loving Deus with the harsh reality of the suffering particularly of the innocent, and the absolute irredeemability of the damned. Many seem to have felt that Christian doctrine on these matters was too rigid and less merciful than the teaching of Buddha's compassion.

The question of God's mercy was brought up rather often in various contexts during the discussions between the missionaries and the people in Yamaguchi. God's mercy was mentioned, not only in regard to human suffering on earth and in hell, but also in response to the following query: Why did Deus, the savior of the whole world, not let his law be preached and manifested in Japan until the present time? The missionaries' reply was that the law of Deus was clearly revealed and expressed through the intelligence of people throughout the whole world, including the Japanese. Every person had the ability to know good and evil through conscience, the inner voice of God. It was, therefore, not always necessary to learn from preachers what Deus taught. If one would use one's intellect, one would inevitably come to recognize the existence of a creator.

How then could unintelligent people discover Deus and his law? To this question the answer was given that no matter how little their intelligence might be, if they would use it efficiently and lead their lives morally, then Deus would give them an understanding within their hearts regarding the worship of God and the avoidance of idolatry. The sin of worshiping wood, stones, devils, and humans was contrary to reason.

From these exchanges between the missionaries and the people of Yamaguchi, a pattern emerged: the western emphasis on reason and God's sovereignty as against the Japanese emotional inclination of presuming on divine compassion. The same pattern is even more pronounced in the following questions and answers: if Deus were merciful, then he would be generous and understanding so as to permit men to have sexual relations with unmarried women, and even to allow pederasty and bestiality. The missionaries replied by saying that even if a woman did not have a husband, she always had brothers or relatives. Just as one would be insulted when someone fornicated with his sister or relative, so one should not take an unmarried woman in order not to insult her relatives. Against pederasty and bestiality they maintained that Deus created a male and a female of each species for the sake of increasing the number of the respective species. Those acts were, therefore, sins against the law of nature which Deus had preordained.

If the increase of species was Deus' wish, the questioners persisted, it would not be a sin then for a married man whose wife was barren to take another woman to produce offspring. The Christian answer was again negative. If Deus would not want to give him children by his wife, he should not do so by another woman.

Why would the merciful one not give children to those parents who wanted them? Because he would teach men that he was the creator and they were not. If he gave children to those who wanted them but yet were ungrateful and forgetful of divine blessings, then they would deny him. To this answer, according to Fernandez, the Japanese agreed.

A lack of any direct Japanese sources prevents us from verifying the reason why they agreed, but we may assume a possible motive at work in their minds: ungratefulness was considered to be a capital vice in the Japanese society. (Even today, for example, an ingrate, *onshirazu* in Japanese, is often equated with an inhumane person, *hitodenashi* in Japanese.) Consequently, a man who forgot the kindness of the one who gave offspring in the first place (i.e. God) should deserve nothing. If this was the reason why they agreed with the missionaries, this is another example of these people from Yamaguchi understanding a Christian teaching in a characteristically Japanese emotional way and deriving from an interpersonal relationship a sense of obligation. They appear to have had no grasp of the western concept of absolute law and order mandated by the sovereign God.

### (4) Heaven and hell

The understanding of heaven and hell was a significant item during the discussions in Yamaguchi. For the Christians, heaven and hell constituted two opposite eternal destinies for everyone. The missionaries tried hard to convince their audience of the seriousness of this matter by emphasizing the reward of heavenly paradise and punishment in hell. The Buddhist opponents, countering the Christian assertion, rejected the existence of these two realms, and insisted that hell was not a place for the evil one to go after death but was a horrible condition which could be experienced here and now in this life. (This did not mean that the Buddhists denied the hereafter; rather they maintained the endless and inevitable continuation of life and death cycles for all sentient beings. This view was called *samsara* in Sanskrit and *rinne* in Japanese.)

Fernandez did not identify what sect those Buddhist disputants belonged to. The views concerning a hereafter varied among various Buddhist sects. The Buddhist images of heaven and hell originated in the cosmology of ancient India, according to which the world was constituted of several layers, the lowest comprising a vast number of hells and the highest, the heavens.

But the central message of Gautama Siddharta, the originator of Buddhism in the sixth century B.C., concerned the spiritual awakening of each individual by ridding himself/herself of what he considered to be illusory concepts (e.g. an immutable eternal supreme being, an immortal soul, an abode of eternal bliss, earthly wealth and power, etc.). Life, as he saw it, was filled with suffering and anxiety, which were caused by the inability of people to realize truly the transient nature of life and to discard the desire to cling vainly to the illusive values. The pain of hell thus could be experienced in this world. Early Buddhism, therefore, contained essentially no teachings of paradise and hell as two separate eternal territories, as Christians believed.

In the Mahayana school of Buddhism which spread later northward from India to China, Korea, and Japan, the images of paradise and hell were often used to instruct the masses, because of an emphasis on the salvation of every sentient being, monk or lay folk, learned or unlearned. The Pure Land sect (which we referred to in the previous chapter), in particular, preached fervently about the rebirth of good people in the blissful land of Buddha. (Some modern scholars have suggested that such an other-worldly orientation of the Pure Land sect originated through the strong influence of Nestorian Christianity in China.)

One of the greatest masters of Pure Land Buddhism in Japan was a monk by the name of Shinran (c. 1173–1262), who preached total surrender to the merciful hand of Amida Buddha. This abandonment of selfhood (the "self," according to Buddhism, was never in existence in true reality in any case) would lead to one's spiritual rebirth. In Shinran's thought, the immense compasssion of Amida overwhelmed the dark curse of hell. What was crucial here was one's inner enlightenment through devotion to Amida and not the immortal soul's destination (whether up to heaven or down to hell) after its physical death.

Other sects, notably Zen Buddhism, denied totally any notion of paradise and hell. Lourenço, an excellent Japanese preacher in the Christian missions, wrote in his letter to the Jesuits in Bungo on June 2, 1560 that when Padre Vilela and he conversed with several Zen Buddhist scholars in Kyoto, they "revealed an almost total ignorance with regard to the hereafter."

We may conclude, consequently, that paradise and hell were talked about by Buddhist teachers essentially as a means to instruct the general populace. The masses thus widely believed in the blissful land of Buddha and the horrible nether world. The missionaries' fiery preaching about the hereafter as an actual future event, therefore, often made successful inroads into the religious mentality, particularly among the less privileged. The misery and suffering caused by the tumultuous conditions of that era also prompted them to long for a better world to come. The majority of the converts, in fact, came from the lower strata of the society. The Annual Letter of the Jesuits for 1579 reported that heretofore the converts had been almost entirely confined to the poor.

Br. Fernandez's report eloquently demonstrates the intensity and seriousness of the discussion between the missionaries and the Buddhists in Yamaguchi. The subjects dealt with were quite extensive and difficult, yet concerned issues vital to all, such as human suffering and one's ultimate destiny. No purely theoretical and academic discourse seems to have been offered during the debate.

Despite serious attempts at discussion on both sides, unfortunately, a meaningful mutual understanding did not apparently materialize. Each side was convinced of its own position and thus attempted naturally to arrive at some explanation of the other's contentions according to its own scheme of thinking. Both of them fell far short of obtaining an accurate grasp of the other's views. Fernandez wrote, for instance, that what the Buddhists were saying about Shaka (Gautama Siddharta) did not make sense at all, and consequently he concluded that it was all nothing but a deception by "men without faith." Despite barren results, this dialogue was significant, since it was one of the first instances in history of a serious debate between Christians and Buddhists.

### TORRES IN BUNGO

After more than six years of successful ministry in Yamaguchi, Padre Torres had to take refuge in friendly Bungo. Yoshishige Otomo, the lord of that region, welcomed him by providing him a good house and estate from his own personal property. The padre used a portion of the land for a cemetery and another plot for a hospital. A cemetery was necessary for the Christians to bury their dead because Buddhist temples usually refused to accept them. The medical facility was also desperately needed; the record shows that there were a number of sick people such as lepers in the land. The lord was so pleased with the padre's effort that he offered a subsidy for the facility's operation.

Padre Frois reported many incidents which clearly demonstrated Torres' self-sacrificial ministerial work in Bungo. According to Frois, Torres was a large-framed man and was rather heavy despite a very poor diet. (The missionaries kept a vegetarian diet rigidly in order to keep with the custom of strict Buddhist monks.) He was always walking around barefoot with a hat except when he visited noble people. Even during the severe cold of winter, he did not try to warm himself with a fire.

He performed his priestly duty conscientiously; he, for instance, offered mass while leaning on the altar when he was gravely ill. He never once failed to show a warm concern for the people. As Frois put it, "the first greeting he presents to visitors is tears (of love) from his eyes." Frois also stated that Torres' "modesty and religious maturity suited the nature of the Japanese" so much that he won profound love and respect from them. Some of the Japanese Christians adored him so much that they even kept locks of his hair or pieces of his old clothes as precious treasures.

Christian education was also Torres' primary concern; he worked hard to make his congregation familiarize themselves with biblical stories and catechisms. His attempts seem to have borne fruit. At Christmas in 1560, for example, he encouraged them to stage some pageants. In response, they chose to perform "the fall of Adam and hope of redemption," "Solomon's judgment," "the angels' proclamation to the shepherds of the birth of the savior," and "the last judgment." The pageants were reportedly so well performed that the audience was thoroughly inspired. At Easter time of the following year as well, the pageant of Christ's resurrection was presented quite successfully. These facts suggest that the congregation became acquainted with the Bible rather thoroughly.

The second area of Torres' educational program specifically concerned the instruction of children. It was reported that forty to fifty youngsters attended catechism classes every day. They were taught to recite prayers in Latin. In addition to Christian education, lessons of reading and writing in the Japanese language were also given to them by a Japanese brother.

An extreme shortage of missionaries necessitated extensive participation of the Japanese Christians in spreading and maintaining the
missions' activities. As will be discussed later, the small units of Christians (called confraria) began to be formulated. They were quite effective in providing spiritual as well as material assistance. Caring for sick
and helpless people and providing a Christian burial of the dead were
also among their important tasks. There is thus no doubt that under
the leadership of Padre Torres the Christian missions made a solid
advance in the areas of education, medical missions, and the structural
formulation of a Christian community, as well as the propagation of
the Christian message.

CONVERSION OF SUMITADA OMURA

Lord Matsuura of Hirado never opened his mind to Christianity,
although he allowed missionary activities in his territory because of his
desire to keep foreign trade in his port. Having been wary of what the
missionaries termed the "veiled animosity" of Matsuura, Padre Torres
decided to negotiate secretly with Lord Sumitada Omura, a southern
neighbor of Matsuura. In order to get permission for missionary work
in the Omura territory, he had to offer a proposal for opening trade
with the Portuguese at Yokoseura, a small fishing port in Omura's
land. The plan proved to be a great success; Omura not only accepted
his request but also showed a personal interest in Christianity.

Torres first dispatched Br. Luis de Almeida to Yokoseura along
with a Japanese helper whose religious name was Damian. Lord
Omura warmly welcomed them and donated to the missions half of the
port town so that the Christians could live without any disturbances.
The lord's generosity was soon rewarded; a Portuguese ship surely did
arrive in Yokoseura. Shortly after that, Padre Torres himself moved
into the town. All this happened in 1562.

Unlike many of the daimyos whose friendliness toward the Portuguese was motivated solely by the prospect of financial gain, Omura
took Christianity seriously. After studying the catechism diligently, he
received baptism from Padre Torres. The religious name given to him
was Dom Bartholomeu. Thus he became the very first Christian
daimyo in Japan's history. He was a sincere believer in Catholicism.

According to Frois, he often told his retainers confidently to ask him any questions concerning the Christian faith. In order to prevent them from requesting to be baptized for purely political reasons (e.g. intending simply to please the lord), he asked the padre not to baptize anyone who had not listened to sermons at least several times a month for the duration of two months.

Inspired by the missionaries' story about Constantine the Great, the first Christian Roman emperor (c. 288–337), Omura publicly displayed his faith by hanging a gold cross on his chest and actively promoted Christianity in his land. It was reported, for example, that when he was on his way to a battlefield, he stopped by a shrine of the military patron deity as was the usual practice. Instead of praying for victory while kneeling in front of the statue, however, he struck it down with his sword and said, "Oh, you have deceived me so many times!" He then ordered the whole shrine to be burnt to ashes. Later at the lord's command an impressive-looking cross was erected at that site. Besides this shrine, many other Buddhist statues were demolished in his territory.

Sumitada Omura was by birth a younger son of the Arima family who ruled a territory adjacent to the Omura domain. He was adopted by the Omuras who did not have an heir to be the ruler there. This arrangement thus made these two clans close allies. Lord Omura attempted to influence his older brother, Yoshisada Arima, to become a Christian. Padre Torres sent Br. Almeida to Arima, who received him quite cordially. And thus Christian missions commenced in the Arima region as well. In due course a thriving seaport called Kuchinotsu became a Christian center; an old abandoned Buddhist temple was converted into a church, and several hundred of the townspeople joined the church. The lord's active assistance helped to make all of this possible.

In addition to this encouraging development in the Arima territory, the neighboring town of Shimabara emerged also as a good prospect for missions. The ruler of the town allowed Christian activities there, though there was stiff opposition from the local Buddhists.

Kuchinotsu and Shimabara gained in importance to Christians not only because of their fresh and promising future for Christian missions, but also because of the loss of Yokoseura. Lord Omura's vigorous anti-Buddhist campaign caused a serious strain among his retainers, many of whom remained loyal to their ancestral religious affiliation. A revolt against the lord finally broke out. The rebels caught him off guard, and Omura barely managed to escape from their attack. The castles in the capital as well as in other towns in the domain were captured. Yokoseura was burnt to ashes.

Nonetheless, Omura soon fought back with the help of his natural father and brother; he never regained the power he once had, however. The incident made Christian activities there more difficult not only because of the open opposition to Christianity among the citizens but also because of Omura's father, who, though he had rescued him, had remained a committed Buddhist and now began to exert pressure on Omura to curtail Christian activities in his domain. The Christians, nonetheless, endured and their contributions, particularly in the areas of education of the young and medical care for the local people, were in fact widely appreciated. A person who deserved much credit for these valuable efforts was Br. Almeida.

### BR. LUIS DE ALMEIDA

Br. Almeida (1525–1583) played a unique role under Padre Torres' direction in the missionary activities in Japan. He was different from other European missionaries in the following ways: first, he was by birth Jewish; second, he was a convert from Protestantism; third, he came to Japan originally as a merchant; finally, after becoming a Jesuit brother, he contributed greatly to the medical missions in particular.

Shortly after arriving in Japan in 1552, he decided to donate everything he owned to the Jesuit missions in Japan and was accepted as a brother by the society. He thus became the first layman from Portugal to become a Jesuit in Japan. Frois spared no words in praise of this man; he stated that there was no Jesuit who possessed greater talent than Almeida in understanding the Japanese. Frois also commented on his "unusual skill and facility" in negotiating with Japanese officials. Being originally a merchant, he was clever and patient in sounding out better possibilities and striking good deals for the sake of the expansion of the missions.

Torres, knowing these distinctive qualities of Almeida, often sent him to create new mission fields. The success in the Omura project was undisputed proof of his talent. He was also quite effective in developing Christian communities in several small islands off the northeast coast of Kyushu. The ruler of these isles, Koteda, became a devout Christian and actively participated in converting his subjects. The number of Christians increased rapidly—some fourteen hundred in less than two months! Sometimes the whole of one village became Christian at once. The mass conversions based on a village unit took place because of the villagers' strong loyalty to their tightly knit community. As will be mentioned later, such remarkable cohesion within individual communities often helped sustain the faith of community members even during horrendous persecutions.

Several beautiful churches were built in the Koteda islands. Though he was a brother, Almeida was performing the pastoral tasks of preaching, baptizing, and taking care of the young congregations. (He eventually became a priest.) The scarcity of missionaries compelled him to visit other parts of Kyushu such as Hakata, Kagoshima, and Ichiku, where he found, to his great joy, that the seeds sown previously by Xavier and others were still very much alive.

The area of the missions to which Almeida contributed most was medical assistance for the poor. This particular concern, in fact, was one of the major motivations which led him to decide to dedicate his life to the missions. His donation enabled the missions to build a clinic in Funai, the capital of the Bungo prefecture in 1556. The clinic focused on the treatment of patients who were either poor or suffering from contagious diseases such as leprosy. It also accepted many infants of poverty-stricken parents. (Infanticide was often practiced in those days.) By virtue of this medical facility, consequently, many babies were rescued and baptized. It was reported that the clinic accommodated more than a hundred patients in addition to daily visitors.

Almeida, though not a professional surgeon, was excellent in surgery. He also taught surgical techniques to the Japanese. There were also in the clinic a few Japanese physicians trained in Chinese medicine whose effectiveness impressed him so much that he ordered drugs from China. (This marked the first occasion in Japan's history of technological cooperation between the west and the east.) With Almeida's help, clinics were constructed in several other places as well. The medical work thus became an integral part of the Christian missions in Japan. Br. Almeida deserved full credit for this charitable endeavor.

## PADRE BALTAZAR GAGO

Despite Herculean efforts made by these missionaries, more missionary support from Europe was desperately needed; this is mentioned repeatedly in the letters sent from the Jesuits in Japan. To meet this need, Padre Baltazar Gago (1515–1583) arrived in Kagoshima with Br. Duarte da Silva and Br. Pedro de Alcaçova in 1552. Padre Gago immediately began working with Br. Fernandez in Bungo, and Br. de Silva joined Padre Torres in Yamaguchi, while Br. de Alcaçova returned to India shortly after his arrival, for the purpose of correspondence.

Padre Gago, in spite of Lord Otomo's protection, constantly had to face Buddhist opposition in Bungo. Many Buddhist monks repeatedly insisted that there was no need for converting from Buddhism to Christianity since the teaching of Deus was identical in essence with that of Buddha. To this typically Japanese eclectic view, Gago felt it urgently necessary to clarify the differences between the two religions.

A primary problem which concerned the padre was that of language. In his letter of September 23, 1555, addressed to the Jesuit brothers in India, Gago wrote: "[We] came to realize that the use of false words to explain the truth has caused misunderstandings, though we have adopted words which the Japanese, according to their sects, have been using, in order to preach the truth. . . . [We, therefore, have] decided to teach them our words in place of the words which are considered to be harmful." According to Gago, there were more than fifty Japanese words which needed to be replaced with European (i.e. Latin or Portuguese or Spanish) vocabulary. Gago further stated that the differences between Christianity and Buddhism had been made clearer after having employed the new terminology.

Xavier had already had to deal with this problem when he realized that Dainichi had nothing to do with Deus. Since then, in order to avoid misunderstanding, the Latin word, Deus, had usually been used not only by the missionaries but also by the Japanese. Nonetheless, several Japanese words were continually employed for Deus, as various documents from that period indicate. A Latin and Portuguese-Japanese dictionary published in 1595 listed *tendo* (the way of heaven), *tenshu* (the Lord of heaven), *tenson* (the reverend of heaven), and *tentei* (the king of heaven) as the translations of Deus. The 1603/4 version of the Japanese-Portuguese dictionary, too, confirmed that *ten* (heaven), *tenshu*, *tendo*, and *tenson* were being used to designate Deus.

One other example of the misleading translation which Gago mentioned was the word "cross." It was rendered *jumoji* which designates in Japanese the letter or sign of the number ten; that number was written like a cross (✝). The Japanese audience was apparently confused about how this number related to the Christian symbol of the cross.

The Portuguese words which were used to replace other "harmful" Japanese words in Gago's list include, for example, *anima* (soul), *paraiso* (paradise), *inferno* (hell), *graça* (grace), *confissão* (confession), *cruz* (cross), etc. The Japanese Christians pronounced these Portuguese terms with a heavy Japanese accent (or in a Japanese way). Consequently, these words were pronounced *haraiso*, *inheruno*, *garasa*, *konhisan*, and *kurosu*. Be that as it may, these exotic words became established as the Christian vocabulary in the pre-modern Japanese language. Yoshishige Otomo, the lord of Bungo, for example, reportedly said at his deathbed, "Padre, I ask you to take care of my anima."

Padre Gago's contribution to the missions cannot be underestimated particularly with respect to his attention to the terminological as well as conceptual differences between Christianity and Buddhism. His health, however, did not sustain his admirable endeavor very long. In 1561 serious sickness compelled him to return to India, where he died in 1583.

In addition to the extremely strenuous journey by the sea, the different climate, unfamiliar food, and mental strain often disturbed foreigners' health. The letters of the mission superiors, such as Xavier, Torres, and others, repeatedly urged the mission headquarters in India, Portugal, and Rome to send workers who were blessed not only with spiritual and intellectual capacity but also with excellent health. Br. da Silva who came to Japan with Gago also suffered from poor health and finally passed away in Kyushu in 1564.

The same unfortunate condition curtailed Provincial Belchior Nuñez's stay in Japan. He landed in Funai with Gaspar Vilela and some others in 1556, but he fell ill and had to return to India after just several months' work in Japan. The progress made by the missions impressed Nuñez, but on the other hand the difficulty of the missionary task was perceived quite clearly as well. Realizing the significance of Gago's effort to clarify the verbal and ideological differences between Christianity and Buddhism, he urged Gago to write a book on this matter. Gago, in fact, published a treatise in 1557.

With the Provincial's encouragement as well, he edited a catechism entitled *Twenty-five Articles*, as it consisted of twenty-five chapters. It was based on Xavier's earlier edition, but many misleading and controversial words and expressions were changed and corrected. Lourenço, the former bard and now eloquent preacher who was knowledgeable about Japanese religions, contributed greatly to the improvement in this new version. According to Frois, it was so well done that it convinced Lord Koteda's father to become a Christian. Unfortunately this catechism is not extant.

### PADRE GASPAR VILELA

According to Frois, Vilela (1525–1575) "possessed excellent ability and personality fit to carry out the mission. He had by birth strong health by which he could bear many hardships and an appearance suitable to the Japanese." Coached by the veteran missionary Torres, he worked successfully in Bungo for two years. Frois stated that he was well liked by the local Japanese. The experience in Bungo was indeed inspiring to him as well. The genuine faith and love the innocent villagers felt, he said, was like that of the earliest Christians in the New Testament.

During the third year after coming to Japan, Vilela, at Torres' direction, worked in Hirado. As mentioned before, Matsuura, the lord of that region, was most anxious to entice Portuguese ships to come to his port, while harboring what the Jesuits called a "veiled animosity" toward Christianity. He even wrote a letter of invitation to Nuñez. Vilela labored hard there despite the ambivalent attitude on the part of the ruler. But he had a strong supporter in Lord Koteda, who was a brother and viceroy of Matsuura. He not only vigorously promoted Christianization of his territory but also aided the padre's attempts in Hirado. In the Koteda domain, Buddhist temples were converted into churches, and many Buddha statues were burned. Such aggressive evangelistic activities led by Vilela and Koteda, however, invited emotional reaction from local residents. Finally, riots broke out and developed into open revolt. Unable to control the situation, the indecisive Lord Matsuura asked Vilela to leave Hirado, though he allowed the Christians to continue practicing their religion there. As in the case of Omura, here again the policy of confrontation with the local religion and tradition failed when carried out too drastically.

### KYOTO MISSION

The debilitation of the missions in Hirado prompted Torres to plan a renewed attempt at evangelization of the capital area. Vilela, Lourenço, Damian, and a few others were chosen for this endeavor. They arrived in Sakai in October 1559. There they tried first to approach the monastic establishment at Mt. Hiei where Xavier's abortive attempt was made some years earlier. This time, however, an elder monk received them cordially. Lourenço was asked twice to speak about Christianity to several of the monks there. Their response was courteous but negative. The elder monk, though rejecting totally what the Japanese preacher had to say, kindly arranged for the Christian visitors to obtain passports to travel to the capital city.

Kyoto, albeit still in a desolate condition, was nonetheless the capital of the whole nation, and it was the party's ultimate target. They found a shack in which to lodge and prepared to evangelize. Vilela assumed the appearance of a Buddhist priest by shaving his head and wearing a monk's robe, but he carried a crucifix in his hand. They thus commenced preaching, standing on the street. The townspeople's reaction was extremely tepid, however.

Vilela, therefore, decided to adopt Xavier's method of approaching the top echelon of the society with the hope of reaching the lower classes with their support. (This approach was employed consistently by the Jesuit missions in Japan and China.) Luckily an influential Buddhist priest was generous enough to introduce Vilela to the shogun, Yoshiteru Ashikaga.

The shogun was willing to meet the padre. To prepare for this important audience, according to Frois, Vilela was extra cautious not to neglect any aspect of protocol and decided this time to wear a Jesuit habit, hoping to appeal to the exotic taste of the Japanese. He presented to the host a sand-clock, the only valuable item the poor missionary possessed. The interview turned out to be a success; the shogun showed warm interest in the foreign visitor. He, in fact, offered the padre wine from his own cup, a display of special favor.

Having secured the shogun's good will, not only did the harassment stop, at least for the time being, but street corner preaching suddenly began to attract the attention of the people. They had to handle numerous questions and engage in debate day and night. Here again the persuasive orator Lourenço seems to have played a vital role. And although this blind preacher with congenitally feeble health became totally exhausted to the point of even vomiting blood, he nonetheless never gave up working.

It is interesting to note what Lourenço wrote in a letter to the padres in Bungo on June 2, 1560 from Kyoto. In it he stated that some of the monks of the Shingon sect claimed the identity of Deus with Dainichi, some from the Pure Land sect insisted on the sameness of Deus with Amida, and certain Zen Buddhists contended that there was a similarity between the Christian understanding of salvation and their teaching of enlightenment. Even some people of the Shinto religion told him that Christianity was simply an ancient branch of their religion. But all of them, Lourenço concluded, were in reality representing ideas which were "one flight lower on the stairs" leading to the truth (the truth being Christianity). Lourenço was one of the first in history to present the view that all eastern religions constitute a pre-stage of Christianity.

This "inclusivist" perspective is not at all archaic nonsense either; a number of scholars since his day, even to the present, have expressed opinions similar to that of this sixteenth century lay preacher. Lourenço was, though having no formal education, a self-made scholar of comparative religions, so to speak. Lourenço's view, however, seemed to be inconsonant with the padres' "exclusivist" position which refused to see any continuity between Christianity and eastern religions. (Various opinions apropos of the relationship between Christianity and other world religions will be discussed further in the epilogue.)

Despite the missionaries' hard labor, however, converts were scarce in the Kyoto mission. Those who did accept Christianity often had to meet the fate of ostracism from families, relatives, and neighbors. Among the small numbers of converts, there was a physician by the name of Yohoken (given the religious name of Paulo). After receiving baptism, he decided to work with Padre Torres in Kyushu, where he was later allowed to enter the Society of Jesus. He was instrumental in publishing a grammar of the Japanese language for use by the Europeans (published in 1594), a Latin and Portuguese-Japanese dictionary which contained as many as 908 pages (1595), a catechism (1593), the stories of the saints (1591), and other European literature such as *Imitatio Christi* by Thomas à Kempis (1596) and the *Aesop's Fables* (1593).

Meanwhile the political situation in Kyoto remained very unstable. The shogun's power was practically non-existent, and his vassals attempted to control the capital and its vicinity. The whole area became again an arena of intense fighting. At Torres' direction, Vilela and his companions moved to Sakai. This city, "Venice in Japan" as Frois called it, was a thriving commercial seaport powerful enough to maintain its own independence. As the wealthy merchants viewed Christianity as a religion for the poor, they were not willing to listen to the mission team's preaching. A modest Christian community was built there, nonetheless. Because of the city's neutrality, the Sakai congregation often functioned as a haven thereafter, whenever the Christians in the capital region ran into hardships from their opponents.

### GREAT SUCCESS IN THE CAPITAL VICINITY

A dramatic new development took place in the Christian missions in Kyoto: the surprise conversions of two highly ranked officers of the shogun's government. They were Yamashiro no kami Yuki and Geki Kiyohara, both of whom were highly respected for their wide-ranging knowledge and profound wisdom. Having been entrusted to control the security of the capital city, they had to deal with the Buddhist monks who were constantly attempting to exert pressure on the government as well as on the residents. A ban of the missionaries was one of their demands. In order to handle the question in a fair manner, Yuki felt it necessary to obtain an accurate understanding of Christianity and requested Padre Vilela to come for an interview with him.

The Christian community, out of fear and suspicion of the possibility of a malicious plot against the padre, sent Lourenço instead of Vilela to Yuki. The undaunted Lourenço was more than happy to risk his life for this mission, and he not only clearly explained the teachings, intentions, and activities of the Christians, but, lo and behold, he also succeeded in convincing both Yuki and Kiyohara to become believers! His extraordinary effort thus opened a path to the highest dignitaries of the shogunate.

The encouraged padre immediately joined Lourenço. They converted more people of high rank, including Lord Takayama and his family. As will be observed later, both the father and son Takayama proved to be exemplary Christians. The father received the baptismal name Dario and the son Justo. Through their influence, several more men of power also became Christians. In 1564, there were reportedly seven churches in active operation in the areas of Kyoto, Nara, and Sakai.

Modern historians detect a political as well as genuine religious reason for this remarkable success. That is, the conversion of those politically important individuals was most likely motivated by an antagonism toward the militant Buddhists. It may very well have been so, because these monk-soldiers were regarded as a significant public nuisance by the political leaders. In fact, Nobunaga Oda, who grasped the hegemony of central Japan, massacred them later.

### FROIS AND ALMEIDA IN KYOTO

While the missions made considerable progress in the capital area, new reinforcements arrived from abroad. In the summer of 1563, Padre Luis Frois (1532–1592) landed on Kyushu with Padre Giovanni Batista de Monte and Miguel Vas. Padre Frois was a talented writer; he had worked as a scribe at the royal library in Portugal before entering the Society of Jesus in 1548. While engaged for thirty-four years in the missions in Japan, he wrote many volumes including a lengthy history of the Catholic missions in Japan; he also edited with Br. Fernandez a

Japanese grammar and a Japanese-Portuguese dictionary for use by the Europeans.

Padre de Monte was born in Italy in 1528, became a Jesuit priest in 1555, and volunteered to go to Japan as a missionary. He worked mainly in northern Kyushu and died in Hirado in 1587. Vas came to Japan as an Indian-born lay worker. A year after arriving in Japan, he was permitted to join the Society. He was sent to Macao to be ordained in 1579. While he was in Japan, he served as the treasurer for the missions. The arrival of these three men had been long and desperately awaited. According to Frois, there were only two padres (Torres and Vilela) and five or six European brothers in Japan at that time.

During the first two years of work in Kyushu, Padre Frois, with the help of Br. Fernandez, became considerably accustomed to the Japanese life and the local language. Following this orientation, he was ready to embark upon the more challenging task in the capital of the country. He went there with Br. Almeida in 1565 in order to advance further the Christian missions opened earlier by Padre Vilela and Lourenço.

Frois and Almeida were fascinated greatly with the refined beauty of the traditional culture in Kyoto. In their writings both of them spared no words in praising the delicate and immaculate nature of the houses and gardens of that area. The exotic enchantment of the Buddhist statues and temples, albeit pagan, amazed them. That which excited them most, though, was the great prospect for the propagation of Christianity in this traditional city. In a letter to his friend in Goa (dated April 27, 1565 and written in Kyoto), Frois confirmed the correctness of Xavier's positive evaluation of the Japanese people and the future of the missions in this country.

However, just when the Christian missions gained excellent prospects, Kyoto was again plunged into turmoil. The shogun was assassinated by his vassal in the summer of 1565. The Buddhists who were adversaries of the Christians were quick to seize the opportunity. They procured from the emperor an edict banning Christianity. (The imperial court was consistently anti-Christian, regarding Christianity as an evil foreign religion which would undermine its authority.) The Christian missions thus suddenly collapsed; the padres retreated to Sakai but continued their work in Kyoto and in the neighboring vicinity.

## DOMINANCE OF NOBUNAGA ODA

The assassination of Shogun Yoshiteru Ashikaga occasioned the emergence of an ambitious warlord, Nobunaga Oda. He eventually took control of central Japan. After having eliminated his rivals, he marched to Kyoto with Yoshiaki Ashikaga, the younger brother of the murdered shogun. The various factions who had been fighting one another in that region were soon subdued. Nobunaga's ostensible support of Yoshiaki, however, was in reality nothing but an excuse to justify his own dominance over the capital. Dissatisfied with the status of being a mere puppet of Nobunaga, Yoshiaki later attempted a plot against him, only then to be deposed. Nobunaga's plan to become the ruler of the whole nation rapidly progressed.

As far as the Christian missions were concerned, Nobunaga's rise to power proved to be a quite fortunate turn of events, because this warlord became a friend of the padres. The amicable relationship was facilitated by one of the loyal retainers of Nobunaga by the name of Koremasa Wada. He was the older brother and overlord of a devout Christian lord, Dario Takayama, and was also deeply sympathetic toward Christianity. At Dario's urging, he pleaded with Nobunaga for Padre Frois' return to Kyoto. Permission was granted; the padre and Lourenço went to the capital city and were able to meet the then most powerful man in Japan. The interview took place in the spring of 1569 at the site of the construction of a castle which Nobunaga was personally overseeing.

## INTERVIEW WITH NOBUNAGA

According to Frois' report, this meeting lasted about two hours with everyone standing under the hot sun at the busy construction site. Nobunaga asked Frois many questions in rapid sequence. (He was noted for his impatient temper.) The questions began with inquiries about the padre's age, his background, the frequency of correspondence with Europe and India, the approximate distance of travel from Europe to Japan, and so on. Then the following conversation ensued:

Nobunaga: "Do you intend to return to India if your teaching does not spread in this country?"

Frois: "We would stay here for the rest of our lives for the sake of the promulgation of Christianity, even if we aren't able to gain a single convert."

Nobunaga: "Why do you not have a house for your community?"

Lourenço: "When the grain sprouted, the brambles were so thick that they smothered the seedlings to death. No sooner had the Buddhist monks realized that the noble people were beginning to convert than they pushed the padres out. They resorted to every possible means to try to eradicate the Christian missions. Therefore, there are many people who are ready to become Christians, but they retreat because of these disturbances. There was a house for the padres, but they were evicted five years ago with no good reason."

Nobunaga: "What made you come here from a place so far away?"

Frois: "There was no other reason than that we wanted to follow the will of Deus, the creator of the world and the savior of mankind, by teaching the people of Japan the way of salvation. We are doing this without seeking any worldly gain. Also for the same reason, we were willing to take upon ourselves the various hardships and incredibly horrible dangers of such a long journey."

All the while this conversation was going on, according to Frois, a lot of people assembled and were listening to them. Then Nobunaga said to the padre loudly and in a furious manner, pointing his finger at the Buddhist monks who were present, "You are not like those liars who are standing there. They deceive the masses. They are crooks and cheaters. They are horribly conceited and arrogant. I thought of eradicating all of them so many times, but I just leave them alone because I don't want to cause too many repercussions among the people and also out of pity for them, though they hate me."

There are several significant points in this conversation, which should be noted. First, Nobunaga wanted to know exactly what Frois' real intention of coming to Japan was since the trip required almost insurmountable risks and difficulty. He who recently took hold of the hegemony of the nation naturally suspected that the foreigners might have had some aggressive political motives, even perhaps the colonization of Japan in the same way the Spaniards were doing in the Philippine Islands. The answer he received from Frois was a definite no; the padre was not in the least interested in any secular matters, political or financial.

Second, Nobunaga as a fearless adventurer was pleased with the missionary's vigor and perseverance for his cause—qualities in tune with this strong man's personality and likings. He was not essentially against religion per se, including Buddhism, but that which he had no patience with was religious people's interference in political affairs. The padre's asseveration of his total disinterest in any material gains gave the general a sense of assurance. Nobunaga evidently felt that the Christians were far better than the Buddhists, most of whom were, he believed, obsessed with greedy desires for power, wealth, and carnal pleasures.

Therefore, third, the complaint made by Frois as well as by Lourenço regarding the Buddhists' persecution reinforced Nobunaga's personal enmity toward the Buddhists. (He had been fighting with the militant Buddhists. Two years later, in fact, he had his soldiers burn the cathedral in Mt. Hiei and slaughter mercilessly every single soul found there.) Thus, in effect, this first interview progressed positively for both sides.

### NOBUNAGA'S FAVOR TOWARD FROIS

The amicable development of this conversation with Nobunaga encouraged Padre Frois to challenge some important Buddhists to a debate in front of Nobunaga. Should he lose, the padre said to the warlord, he would be willing to be expelled from the city, but should he win, the monks would have to accept the teaching of Deus. Until the Christian contentions could be clarified through such an open debate, Frois insisted, the missionaries would always be maliciously harassed as aliens. Nobunaga consented to this proposal with a smile and praised Frois' courage and intelligence.

Acknowledging Nobunaga's approval, Frois made one more request—to be granted a residence permit in Kyoto. He adroitly added that this favor would be deemed as the greatest grace the general could give him and that it would help in spreading the sublime reputation of Nobunaga overseas as far as India and the Christian countries in Europe. These complimentary words flattered the strong man's ego immensely; he received Frois' request and promised a more private meeting the next time. At Nobunaga's order, Wada entertained the visitors by showing them around the interior of the newly built castle.

Nobunaga's favorable treatment of Padre Frois also led to an audience with the shogun, which was successful as well. But the padre was officially still banned by the edict issued from the imperial court five years before. The Christians in Kyoto were, therefore, anxious to receive official permission from Nobunaga. Without his authorization, in fact, no one was secure. In this unstable situation, many people, Christian and non-Christian alike, consequently sent expensive gifts to the general in order to obtain licenses. The Christians also presented him with exotic items from Portugal, such as clothes, hats, leather material from Cordova, fur coats, clocks, and valuable crystal glassware. In addition, Wada and others donated ten bars of silver to Nobunaga on behalf of the padre.

Nobunaga declined to receive these gifts, saying that he would not accept valuable things from a foreigner in exchange for a permit; nevertheless, he ordered Wada to prepare the necessary document for the padre. To the great joy of the Christian community, the document guaranteed the padre's residence anyplace he might choose to live (including the capital city), his exemption from all civic requirements, and protection from any undue harm.

At Nobunaga's recommendation, moreover, the shogun also granted Frois an official letter to the same effect. Frois was, needless to say, very grateful to them all. Expressing special thanks to Wada, who helped engineer this fortunate event, Frois stated that it was none other than God who chose the man, though a non-Christian, to provide him with such a great amount of love and kindness. When asked by the padre about becoming a Christian, Wada replied with a gentle smile that he was already a Christian in his heart.

### FROIS' VICTORY OVER NICHIJO

Padre Frois' challenge to debate with the Buddhists came to fruition by chance when he and Lourenço were visiting Nobunaga at his residence. Present was a Buddhist priest by the name of Nichijo. He was of dubious origin, claiming to belong to the Hokke sect, was an adventurer who had engaged in various shady businesses, but was eloquent and shrewd enough to climb the ladder of success. Nobunaga evidently found him useful, particularly in negotiating with the imperial court. This staunchly anti-Christian Buddhist pleaded often to have his master expel the padres but to no avail.

Nobunaga apparently thought it would be interesting to let Nichijo and Frois debate at this opportunity. Frois later recorded the discussion, according to which the majority of the exchange took place between Nichijo and Lourenço. Only when the latter was physically fatigued due to frail health after two hours of intensive argumentation did Frois take over. Throughout the conversation, Nichijo failed to demonstrate any sign of brilliance or persuasiveness. By contrast, Lourenço totally dominated his opponent. Though Frois' record might naturally be biased in favor of his companion (no report of the content of the debate is available from any Japanese source), the Japanese brother eloquently explained his belief in Deus, the Lord and maker of the universe, who was eternal, invisible, and all-powerful, as the beauty and magnificence of the created world unequivocally bore witness. As such, he argued, Deus deserved to be worshiped and served by every being.

Frois continued the Christian apologetics by underscoring the existence of "anima racional" (rational soul) as distinct from the physical body. Such a soul, he contended, constituted the hallmark of a human being as it was not only rational but also immortal. The tone of the padre's speech betrayed his conviction that he could afford to be even a bit condescending toward his opponent—a sign of an assured sense of victory.

Nichijo, unable to control the feeling of shameful defeat, "pursed his lips, ground his teeth, trembled his hands and feet, raged as if he were in flame, flashed his face, reddened his eyes, jumped up forgetting courtesy toward the king (Nobunaga), and like a shot arrow, grabbed the padre by the collar while cursing him." Then he ran to take hold of Nobunaga's sword and drew it, saying, "If you are right, I will kill your disciple Lourenço, so that you can show me the soul which you claim exists!" But Nobunaga and his attendants swiftly seized and disarmed him.

This confrontation (which was not even a debate) ended in complete victory for the Christians. Nichijo totally lost his master's trust. The story of this incident immediately spread over all the city. The vengeful Nichijo continued in intrigue not only against Frois but also against Wada whom he considered to be the most influential supporter of Christianity. But he later incurred the general's wrath and was expelled for good.

## CONCLUDING REMARKS

Frois' effort in Kyoto was a great success in the sense that it gained political security for Christian missions in the capital city by procuring the good will of Nobunaga, the de facto ruler of central Japan. To this end, not only he himself but also his remarkable helper, Lourenço, played a vital role. But the one who was of decisive significance in this drama was Lord Wada. He, though a non-Christian, rendered willing and consistent assistance to the padre, even risking his own honor and life. Without his help, the missions would not have enjoyed the favor of Nobunaga. The warlord seemingly took genuine interest in the Portuguese, but as a shrewd politician he wanted to use the Christians as a counter-balance to the Buddhists.

It was Xavier's ardent desire to convert the highest authority of the nation so the rest of the population would follow suit. Tumultuous circumstances prevented him from success in this attempt. Padre Torres, the successor of Xavier as superior, concentrated his efforts on Yamaguchi and northern Kyushu. Under his direction, the missions made considerable progress, as the conversions of Omura, Koteda, and some other influential people exemplified. Padre Vilela managed to build a bridgehead in the capital, and it was Padre Frois who attained, at least partially, what Xavier originally intended—an inroad into the ruling class. Thus the Christian mission was now ready to open a new phase of its activity in Japan; this is the subject of the chapter which follows.

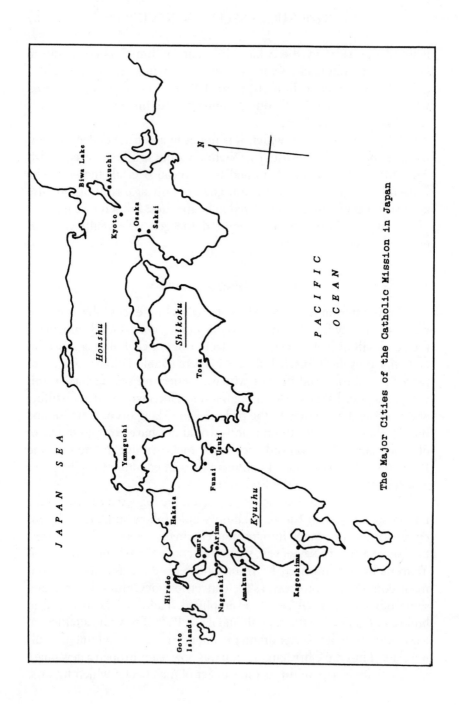

The Major Cities of the Catholic Mission in Japan

# 3

# Growth of the Christian Missions

## PADRE CABRAL'S ARRIVAL

The year 1570 marked the beginning of a new phase of the Christian missions in Japan. During the late spring of that year Padre Francisco Cabral (c. 1533–1609) arrived in Kyushu in order to succeed Padre Torres as superior. Torres, the "good old padre" as Frois amicably called him, died in October of the same year from old age and a long and tormenting illness.

Soon after his arrival, Cabral summoned all the Jesuits to an island called Shiki off the coast of northwest Kyushu. Assembled there were Cosme de Torres and Gaspar Vilela from Nagasaki, Balthasar de Costa from Hirado, Alessandro Vallareggio from the Goto Islands, Melchior de Figueiredo from Kuchinotsu, and Giovanni Batista de Monte from Bungo. Also present were Br. Luis de Almeida, Br. Jacome Gonçalves, Padre Balthasar Lopez, and Padre Guecchi-Soldi Organtino who accompanied Cabral on his voyage to Japan. The conference lasted about thirty days.

The goals which this newly arrived mission superior had in mind for this meeting were first of all to become personally acquainted with his fellow workers and secondly to discuss various problems concerning the missions. The exact items that were on the agenda are not known, but Cabral's primary concern was to give the missions fresh inspiration by tightening up discipline.

For example, Cabral forbade all the mission members to wear silk clothes and virtually terminated commercial trading at mission stations. The former was a custom adopted in order to appear proper as would be expected of clergy by Japanese society. The simple black cotton habits the missionaries originally wore made them look like beggars in the eyes of the Japanese who had no knowledge of the Jesuit vow of poverty. Commercial involvement of the mission, Cabral pointed out, commenced when the former merchant Almeida contributed to the missions a sizable amount of money when he entered the Society. Both silk clothing and commercial trading, in the new superior's opinion, brought to the missions a relaxation of discipline and thus a degeneration from the apostolic ideal.

The majority of the confreres, strongly disagreeing with Cabral, contended that these practices were not signs of indulgence in luxury but were rather legitimate actions taken out of necessity. Padre Xavier, for instance, had made a great success of his second visit to Yamaguchi, clad in attire impressive to the local population and armed with official letters from the viceroy and the bishop in Goa, India.

Also, Br. Almeida's contribution undoubtedly vitalized the missions' work as a result of not only the money he donated but also the business skill and medical knowledge he possessed. The missions were, in fact, desperately in need of funds; two-thirds of the expenditure of the missions were covered by profit from the trade in which they participated. The funds sent from Portugal were in reality far less than the king had promised.

The opposition view went unheeded, however; the new superior enforced resolutely the rules which he had decided to set forth. (He in fact boasted of his success in putting the new ordinance into effect in a letter sent to the Jesuit General from Nagasaki on September 5, 1571.) Cabral proposed a plan to open a residence school where several priests and many brothers could live together under the strict direction of a superior. The purpose of the school would be to train and retrain them in the spirit of poverty and obedience characteristic of the Jesuit Society.

This very rigid disciplinarian policy of Padre Cabral appeared to have stemmed partly from his background and personality. He was a Portuguese knight (fidalgo), who fought in battlefields. A military assignment, as a matter of fact, had brought him to India, where he had become closely acquainted with the Jesuits and, subsequently, entered the Society there. While devoting himself to missionary work as a priest there, he even resorted to military power to eradicate foes and force the local people to convert to Christianity. The same regimentational mentality appears to have caused him to adhere strictly to the standard Jesuit approach of working to convert the higher echelon of society within the mission fields in the hope that the lower classes would follow suit.

Aided by his wealthy and influential Portuguese friends, Cabral successfully befriended several feudal lords in Kyushu; in fact, the wife of Lord Omura, the wife of Lord Amakusa, and then Lord Yoshisada Arima and Lord Yoshishige Otomo received baptism.

In the Omura territory, in particular, Christianity advanced considerably; victory over an enemy in the fall of 1574 prompted Lord Omura (Dom Bartolomeu) to launch a systematic attempt to Christianize his domain. The lord demanded that his subjects receive the Christian faith, demolish Buddhist temples, and build churches; several mass baptisms took place as a result. In the Arima territory also, many from the nobility as well as the common folks volunteered to join the church mainly because of their lord's conversion. The influence of Padre Coelho, Cabral's successor, was instrumental in contributing to this success.

### CABRAL IN CENTRAL JAPAN

Padre Cabral's real goal, however, was the conversion of the highest authority of the land. In early 1572, Cabral went to the capital region, accompanied by Frois and Lourenço, and enjoyed audiences with various dignitaries including the shogun. The party then proceeded to meet Nobunaga at Gifu about forty miles east of Kyoto. As Cabral wrote in his letter of September 23, 1572, they received an exceptional welcome by all of those of high rank.

Frois recorded in considerable detail what took place during their interview with Nobunaga. The powerful feudal lord asked them to tell him about Deus. Responding to the request, Lourenço again performed so admirably that the warlord praised the preacher by saying that there could be no better teaching than what he had just heard. He then said to his aides, "I swear by Hakusan-gongen that my opinion and the teachings of the padres and others here are in complete agreement."

Hakusan-gongen was a deity enshrined in Mt. Hakusan and popularly worshiped in those days. Nobunaga's statement affords a typical example of the eclectic mentality of the Japanese that readily syncretized various religions by obfuscating significant differences. (As will be observed more than once in the remainder of this book, the lax or tolerant attitude toward religious beliefs among the Japanese worked both for and against the Christian missions. This national character would welcome foreign influences as long as they blended in and did not upset the people's tolerant and congenial lifestyle, but if otherwise, the Japanese would tend to become violently exclusive. Such a mentality stood in sharp contrast to the intolerant nature of Christianity.)

After the conversation with Nobunaga, a banquet was served, at which Nobunaga asked Cabral whether or not he would eat fish or the meat of animals. (The Buddhist monks were not supposed to eat either.) The padre answered affirmatively and added a statement to the effect that the padres would not do things in which they did not believe. The lord took the answer in a good spirit, because he had known for a fact that there were many Buddhist monks who were secretly eating the forbidden food. Cabral's statement was not quite accurate, however, because the missionaries had thus far deliberately stayed away from eating meat as was expected of observant religious persons in Japanese society. But this mission superior reversed that.

As mentioned above, Cabral also initiated a change in the Jesuit dress code. When he and his companions appeared in front of Nobunaga, consequently, they were wearing the Jesuit habit. The Japanese general, when he saw their plain cotton garments, offered them silk clothes, which Cabral cordially declined. The interview went well all in all. The then most powerful man in Japan, who liked the Europeans and their culture, had kindly received Cabral.

Pleased with the successful outcome of the trip to central Japan, Cabral visited there once more two years later (1574). This time again he met Nobunaga. A detailed account of the second journey is not available, but it appears to have been satisfactory as nothing negative was reported.

## CABRAL'S VIEWS OF THE JAPANESE

Though cordially received by the Japanese dignitaries, Padre Cabral harbored a very poor opinion of the Japanese in general. His uncompromisingly rigoristic policy, which was referred to earlier, stood in a sharp contrast to the attitude shown by Torres, Vilela, Frois and others which was quite accommodative toward the Japanese ways. Vilela, for example, shaved his head and wore a monkish gown following the Buddhist custom. He and Frois were genuinely fascinated with the refined beauty of the traditional Japanese culture in Kyoto despite its imbued pagan nature.

Cabral evidently cherished a strong sense of what one might call "Euro-centrism." A modern scholar, George Ellison, describes it as follows: "Cabral made a few bad mistakes in judgment, and his main fault was a failure to fit himself into the modes of the mission country. The Roman behaved as though he were in Rome, and the narrow view distorted his sense of purpose" (see his *Deus Destroyed*, Harvard University Press, 1973, p. 55). In fact, Visitor-General Alessandro Valignano, who made three visitations to Japan during the period of 1579 through 1603, mentioned Cabral's frequent pejorative comments as, for example: "But, of course, that's a Japanese for you!" (see *ibid.*, p. 56 and p. 407, n. 6).

In a letter to Rome, Cabral bitterly complained that he had "never seen a people that is so haughty, avaricious, unreliable, and insincere as the Japanese." For them it was "a matter of honor and a sign of prudence to keep their thoughts hidden and prevent anyone from reading them." "From their childhood, they are taught to do so, and are trained to be incommunicative and hypocritical." The Buddhist monks seemed to him to have been the worst of all. They possessed, he wrote, "a proud, grasping, ambitious, and insincere disposition." "They put up with community life and subservience while they have no alternative means of support; as soon as they secure this, they assume superior airs." (These and the following quotations from Cabral's letter are cited in *Valignano's Mission Principles for Japan*, Part I, by J.F. Schütte, English translation by J.J. Coyne, 1980.)

Cabral wrote this letter in 1596 in Goa after he had resigned from his office as mission superior in Japan because of a fundamental disagreement he had with Visitor-General Valignano who adopted a decidedly adaptational policy. The letter, therefore, was infused with a harsh polemical intention. One of the issues concerned the admission of the Japanese to the Jesuit Society. Cabral lamented over the fact that "seventy or eighty have already been admitted," and said that because of this, "it is inevitable that the Society and, indeed, Christianity in Japan will collapse; and it will almost be impossible to find any remedy later." In an attempt to drive this contention home, he described the Japanese character very negatively, as quoted above.

Doom would be the inevitable end of the missions, in Cabral's view, if the Society was to follow Valignano's program of nurturing the Japanese to become priests, teachers, and theologians, because they "lack the necessary aptitude, and then because the climate of the country and the influence of the stars play their part; it is as though there (in Japan) men's hearts were a prey to continual unrest and a love of novelty." By citing some examples, he accused them for their arrogant attitude of assuming superior airs over the padres. There were only two ways, according to Cabral, to keep the Japanese obedient to the order of the Society: the first was by means of the power of grace of the divine spirit, and the second was through the strict regulation by which they might be kept permanently in the status of *dojuku*.

### DOJUKU

*Dojuku* is a Japanese word meaning literally "living together." It was used by Buddhists to designate a novice who lived in the monks' quarters in a Buddhist temple to serve the monks. The Christians adopted the word in order to indicate a lay acolyte who dedicated himself to evangelization by teaching the catechism and preaching. Though officially not clergy, yet he was regarded as such because of his full-time work for the missions, his celibacy, and his appearance (tonsure and a long black cassock). He lived with the padres, brothers, and fellow dojukus and engaged in any necessary chores at their residence though not as a servant. (There were servants working in the residence.)

The dojukus were allotted to each padre, who strictly supervised their religious progress. Their subjugation also involved various rules concerning their life: they were not usually allowed to dine at the padres' table, and their menu was inferior in quality to that of the padres and brothers. Nor were they permitted to sleep in the same room with the padres and brothers. They were to show the greatest respect to the padres, in particular. When speaking with them, for instance, no headcover was to be kept on. If a conversation took place on the street, the dojukus had to assume a humble posture by removing their sandals and placing their hands on their knees. This practice apparently startled bystanders even though they were used to various forms of feudalistic protocol, and invited, at times, bitter criticism from them.

The dojukus were quite useful for missionary activities. The padres, in particular, were definitely in need of their help. Valignano admitted that the padres could not get anything done without their assistance. Padre Cabral too had to resort to the helpful contribution the dojukus could provide, and evidently he believed that this was the status at which the native Christian workers should be kept.

This decision appeared prompted by his proud sense of racial, cultural, and religious superiority as a European priest and former knight. It was also reinforced by his uncompromising and narrow application of the order of the Catholic Church and the Jesuit Society, which matched the spirit of the military training of his previous career. (Valignano, however, criticized him for his "ignorance" of the constitution of the Society and its application.) Furthermore, one could suspect that a latent sense of insecurity as a foreigner in an unfamiliar land was operative as well.

Visitor-General Valignano read the situation differently, however. He recognized the dire need of help from the local Christians and without reservation appreciated their contribution. He even envisioned them being trained eventually to become fully equipped clergy, philosophers, and theologians. In his judgment, the Japanese were capable of fulfilling his expectations without a doubt.

Valignano's adroit realization that Japanese society was functioning on a system whereby gradual advancement in status was deemed appropriate quickened him to plan the authorization of a class of dojuku as a legitimate order in the Jesuit Society. Thereby dojukus were encouraged not only to stay with the missions permanently but also to become brothers even without the knowledge of Latin and, after appropriate training, eventually to receive ordination. Valignano, in fact, sent a formal letter to Rome requesting the acceptance of his plan, and Padre Aquaviva, the Jesuit General, approved of the Visitor's device for providing important incentives to the native workers. This decision was prompted by considering "the Japanese custom" seriously, and it was judged as "adequate to the situation (*ad tempus*)."

Valignano's innovative policy proved to be successful. Previously there were many dojukus who were demoralized, some of whom, as a result, had left the missions. But this trend changed after the Visitor's arrival; dojukus greatly increased in number from 100 in 1580 (one year after Valignano's arrival in Japan) to 284 in 1603 (when he left Japan for the last time). This increase, however, hardly implied an unrestricted recruitment of dojukus. Valignano, in fact, ordered Gaspar Coelho, Cabral's successor, to tighten the standards for recruitment during his second visit to Japan (1590–1592).

### VISITOR-GENERAL VALIGNANO

Visitor Alessandro Valignano (1539–1606) was indeed the principal architect of the Jesuit mission in Japan. Born in a noble family in Italy, the brilliant young man with a terminal degree in law won the recognition of the Society of Jesus as Visitor of the order's missions in India at the young age of thirty-four. This appointment, in fact, provoked stiff opposition from some members of the Society not only because of his youth but also because of his dearth of experience as a superior; by that time, after all, he had been a Jesuit for only seven short years.

The most serious antipathy directed toward Valignano came specifically from some of the Portuguese members of the order (e.g. Luis Gonçalves de Camara) who held the Ignatian style disciplinarian approach in high regard. The independent-minded Valignano with his many new ideas appeared to them to be entertaining dangerous deviation. His Italian origins did not please them either. Their criticisms of him were mounted with great acerbity. "I stood defenseless in their midst," he confessed later.

Valignano, however, fought back with the kind support of Mercurian, the general who wanted to establish a direct relationship between Rome and India by eliminating the strong influence of Gonçalves and others. (All missionaries, correspondence, and material supplies from Europe were dispatched to India by way of Portugal, where they were censored strictly at that time.) Valignano attempted vigorously to fulfill the general's desire.

A dynamic and innovative approach was thus exactly what preoccupied the mind of this young and energetic Visitor before his departure from Lisbon in March 1574 to Asia. During his initial stay in India, Malacca, and Macao for five years (1574–1579), he zealously advanced the program of language training for the European missionaries. High on his agenda as well was the establishment of a more efficient organization of the Jesuit activities in the vast area of Southeast Asia and smoother communication with Rome. (It took about a year and a half for correspondence to be exchanged between Goa and Rome even under the most favorable conditions.)

However, Valignano, albeit dynamic in his thinking, shared with all other Europeans of those days a very low estimate of the peoples of South Asia and Africa. He wrote that they lived like "brute beasts" and were "incapable of grasping our holy religion or practicing it." "In fine, they are a race born to serve, with no natural aptitude for governing" (cf. Schütte, op. cit., p. 131). As Xavier had experienced earlier, Valignano also felt a considerable amount of disappointment with the Indian missions. In Portuguese India, according to him, there was no orderly government, no justice, no obedience, nor sufficient resources in the way of finance and personnel.

Such miserable conditions in India led him (as Xavier before him) to turn his attention eagerly to what they called the "white races" in China and Japan. On the basis of what had been reported, Valignano came to embrace high hopes particularly for the mission in Japan even before he had left the shores of Europe. This was the land, he believed, where the Christian gospel would find a fertile soil in which to flourish, for "they (the Japanese) are a gifted, reliable people, not given to many vices. They are poorly off and not intemperate in eating. After receiving baptism they are quite capable of appreciating spiritual things"; he wrote thus in his letter to the General from Valencia on

November 16, 1573 (cf. Schütte, *ibid.*, p. 61). With such a bright prospect in his mind, he planned a mission strategy for actively recruiting local Christian workers there.

## VALIGNANO'S NEW POLICY

Valignano visited Japan three times (1579–1582; 1590–1592; 1598–1603). Upon his initial arrival in Japan, the situation he found was far from what he had heard or expected. It was indeed an incredible cultural shock for him to find himself helpless in the midst of a totally foreign environment—a world where everything was just the opposite of European ways. In his own admission, he was like "a dumb statue" during the first year.

The difference between what he discovered in Japan and what he had been told before his arrival was "as pronounced as the difference between black and white," admitted the Visitor in his letter to the General on December 5, 1579. He was struck by a painful recognition that only good things had been reported to Goa and Europe; his enthusiastic optimism was replaced by profound disillusionment. The "white race" in Japan, who were supposedly eager to listen to Christian teachings, turned out to be uncommunicable and inscrutable strangers. What they showed outwardly seemed to him quite contrary to what they actually had on their minds. "They are the most dissembling and insincere people to be found anywhere," he wrote as well in the same letter.

This somber realization prompted him to set strict regulations concerning missionaries' reports. The Annual Letters had been sent from the different mission residences, which prevented the superior from examining their accuracy. Valignano decided that the Letters should be placed under his own control; annual reports were to be collected from individual mission stations by the district superior, who were in turn to send them to the Superior General. This new procedure guaranteed the reports' reliability, though it reduced local spontaneity.

Valignano's disappointment with the Japanese, nonetheless, hardly caused him to abandon his missionary zeal there. (Some modern scholars seem to be wrong in assuming that the disillusionment turned his interest from Japan to China. As mentioned earlier, he came to Japan two more times and was planning the fourth visit despite the terrible persecutions of Christians there. This strongly suggests that he did not give up on his mission to Japan.) Instead he doubled his efforts by initiating some more significant reforms in the approach to the missions.

## ESTABLISHMENT OF INSTITUTES

High on the agenda in Valignano's mission strategy in Japan was the recruitment of workers from local Christian communities. This was a plan which he was contemplating before leaving Europe and of which he became even more convinced after arriving in Japan. In his reckoning, there were only fifty-five Jesuits, including twenty-three priests, for 100,000 Christians in Japan in 1579.

In addition to the severe difficulties which arose from differences in language, custom, etc., the heavy schedules were simply overwhelming to the missionaries. Their life was, as Valignano put it, "a continual wayfaring." Reinforcement from Europe came too slow to fill the dire need. It was thus definitely exigent to procure personnel from the native population. Despite the negative impressions which he initially acquired of the Japanese character, he evidently never doubted their intellectual ability. Consequently he was eager to establish residence schools to train young prospects.

The first school was opened in Arima in April 1580. The school building was an old Buddhist monastery which was donated by Lord Arima as a token of appreciation for Valignano's efforts in providing him with Portuguese weapons with which he was able to repel a powerful enemy attack. The Visitor had the monastery remodeled in order to provide better classrooms, living accommodations, and other necessary quarters. Valignano himself wrote the regulations and curriculum for the school's educational activities. Twenty-two youngsters were enrolled as first year students. All of them came voluntarily from legitimate families of the warrior class and with the consent of their parents.

The pupils were trained under the close supervision of a padre and a brother. The daily schedule ran as follows:

4:30 (summer); 5:30 (winter) A.M.—wake up time
                                    prayer and mass

6:00–9:00 A.M.—Latin lesson

9:00–11:00 A.M.—meal and recreation
11:00 A.M.–2:00 P.M.—Japanese lesson
2:00–3:00 P.M.—music lesson
3:00–4:30 P.M.—Latin lesson
5:00–7:00 P.M.—supper and recreation
7:00–8:00 P.M.—Latin and Japanese lessons
8:00 P.M.—litany and bedtime

As this curriculum indicates, the school intended to nurture the young-sters to be prospective members of the Jesuit community in Japan. It was hence called a seminario. The graduates of the seminario were expected to advance to colegio for further clerical education in such areas as theology and philosophy.

Overriding an objection by Padre Cabral, the Visitor vigorously pushed his plan forward. Thus by the end of May 1581 the second seminario was organized in Azuchi (a town where Nobunaga Oda had built a magnificent castle, about fifty miles east of Kyoto). Padre Or-gantino and Lord Ukon Takayama were instrumental in this develop-ment in that region.

By virtue of the wholehearted protection by the lord of the terri-tory, Yoshishige Otomo, Bungo became an important center of the Christian mission in Japan. The lord provided Padre Cabral with a plot of land in Funai (the capital of the region) in order to set up a school to train and retrain the mission workers in the winter of 1576–1577. But the plan did not materialize until the arrival of Valignano.

The colegio of Funai began its function with seven or eight stu-dents toward the end of 1580. In addition to instruction in Latin and Japanese, theology was also taught in the native language. The students were coached in preaching as well. The school also furnished a place for the European Jesuits to learn the Japanese language. For prepara-tion to enroll in the colegio, a novitiate was also opened in Usuki, a town about twenty miles southeast of Funai in the same year. It was reported that six Portuguese and six Japanese were living there as nov-ices then.

Valignano's effort in setting up these institutes proved to be a great success; many excellent Christian workers were produced. By creating the educational centers in these areas, the Visitor also officially estab-lished the three main mission districts: Bungo, Shimo (meaning hinterland, covering the northwest region of Kyushu), and Kami (meaning upperland, indicating central Japan). Each of these districts was overseen by the respective district superior.

These three regions became the arenae of meaningful encounter between the Christian west and the Buddhist-Confucian-Shinto Japan. Not only in the religious aspect, but in many other areas in culture, both traditions met and produced fruitful results. Examples lay in profusion. As will be noted below, many books were printed in both the European and the Japanese languages. The European scientific information and skills in such areas as medicine, astronomy, mathematics, geography, and many other branches of science were introduced. A number of dojukus were trained in western painting, sculpture, and music. Some of them were in fact soon able to produce excellent artifacts of paintings, musical instruments, sculptures, and clocks, which were, according to Frois and other padres, as good as European specimens. All in all, the Christian mission brought to Japan an abundant cultural enlightenment as well as a religious contribution.

CHRISTIAN PUBLICATION

The educational program Valignano envisioned included an ambitious plan of publishing various books. Before coming to Japan, he had been contemplating printing a Latin dictionary and grammar as well as other European literature in Japanese translations. The high number of Japanese ideograms, however, prevented him from putting the project into practice, but a clever alternative was devised—the translated books were printed as transcribed using the Portuguese alphabet. Valignano requested that his colleagues in Europe send him a huge number of books of various kinds ranging from religious and philosophical treatises to stories with moral overtones such as Aesop's fables.

On the second visit to Japan in 1590, Valignano brought with him a printing press. A printing house was set up first in Kazusa, and later moved to Amakusa, then to Nagasaki (these three towns were all located in the Shimo district). Woodcut print was in use in Japan at that time, but the Jesuits started using metallic movable type. (The metallic type had also been imported from Korea, but the traditional wooden type was pleasing to the Japanese taste.)

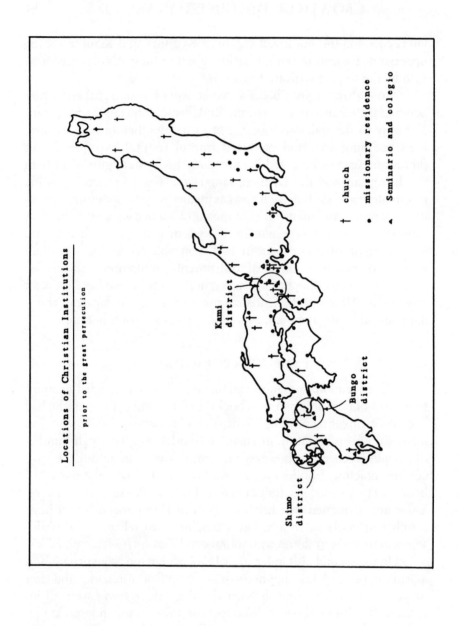

Locations of Christian Institutions

prior to the great persecution

† church

• missionary residence

▲ Seminario and colegio

Kami district

Bungo district

Shimo district

From 1590 until the outbreak of the great persecution in 1612, not only were many European books published in the Portuguese script but several Japanese classics (e.g. *Tales of the Heike*) were published also for the sake of the European students of the Japanese language. (For a complete list of the Christian publications in pre-modern Japan, see *Kirishitan Bunko: A Manual of Books and Documents on the Early Christian Mission in Japan* by J. Laures, Tokyo, 1957.) All of these attempts contributed to the possibility of significant cultural exchange between the West and Japan.

### (1) Valignano's catechism

Cultural exchange was not really what the Visitor had in his mind, however; his intention lay rather in the evangelization of the Japanese. For this purpose, he wrote the *Japanese Catechism of Christian Faith* while staying at the colegio in Funai during the winter of 1580–1581. The original version of this book, written most likely in Portuguese, unfortunately has been lost, but Japanese and Latin translations are extant. The author presented the original version to General Acuaviva, who had it rendered into Latin and published in 1586 in Lisbon under the title of *Cathechismus Iaponensis Christianae Fidei*.

The book consisted of two volumes covering the following topics. Volume 1: (1) polemical discussion on the Japanese religions, (2) Deus, (3) cosmology, (4) Buddhism, (5) Buddhistic ethics, (6) the principal doctrine of Christianity, (7) the Trinity. Volume 2: (1) the decalogue, (2) the sacrament, (3) the resurrection of the dead and the last judgment, (4) heaven and hell.

Large portions of the Japanese version of this book have been discovered in this century. In 1902, Naojiro Murakami, a pioneer in the study of the Christian missions in pre-modern Japan, found several letters of Pr. Frois, Pr. Organtino, and Br. Vincente under the surface of an old damaged *byobu* (Japanese folding screen) at the national libraries in Evora and Lisbon, Portugal. These letters were used as reinforcement for this sixteenth century piece of furniture. Then in 1960, according to Professor Kiichi Matsuda, a contemporary authority in the same field, many more manuscripts were recovered from the byobu at the library in Evora. He successfully separated each sheet of paper with the help of the librarians and came up with some one hundred pages.

A great bulk of the recovered material contained the Japanese version of Valignano's catechism. Its text agreed to a great extent with the Latin version. The treatment of some of the subjects (e.g. the Trinity) in the Latin text is missing in the Japanese counterpart, however. The discrepancies between the two versions can be explained by several facts: (1) that many pages of the text of the Evora byobu have been lost, (2) that both of them are after all translations, and (3) that the Latin version was a result of editing attempts by someone in Rome, which Valignano himself admitted. As for the byobu manuscript, furthermore, Prof. Matsuda determined that it was actually dictation notes taken from a lecture and not a direct and literal translation from the original. It was most likely copied sometime during the period of 1581–1582.

This catechism, though called thus, does not follow the usual question and answer form, but is narrated as an instruction manual for the seminarians. It begins with an introduction which emphasizes the theme of the uniqueness of human beings as against animals distinguished by an intellectual capacity which Deus bestowed upon them. Humans, therefore, must be able to recognize the truth and discern good from evil. After these introductory remarks, the main body of the lecture opens with statements concerning the necessary existence of the creator. Valignano here negates the Buddhists' opposition to this Christian teaching by underscoring the intelligibility of the Christian position as one which is self-evident to the rational human mind.

The author proceeds to explain Deus in terms of the following three aspects: (1) as spiritual nature, (2) as ruler of the world with an unfathomable wisdom and goodness, and (3) as oneness. By referring to the Aristotelian concept of form which makes matter exist, the instructor inculcates the necessary existence of God as the ultimate source of all matter. The subject discussed next concerns the moral quality of the teachings of Deus, whose unparalleled value has been evinced by numerous sages and prophets of old. Compared with it, Buddhism can offer little in regard to ethical persuasion. The Buddhist monks' moral decadence (e.g. sexual misconduct) is mentioned pointedly and bitterly.

The instructor then moves on to the topic of the creation of angels and Adam and Eve and their fall which brought about evil and original sin. This is followed by an instruction in christology: Christ's incarnation and redemption. In explaining the dual nature of Jesus Christ, Valignano uses the metaphor of grafting where a plant remains one while possessing two different natures.

The doctrinal treatment must have continued still further, but unfortunately a considerable amount of the ensuing pages have been lost. The extant remaining sheets contain ethical instructions to an applicant to the Jesuit brotherhood whereby he should receive divine grace for the forgiveness of sins, should not fall into wickedness, and should not neglect his confessions. It is stated that confession is the "sword to kill sins."

Valignano specifically points out some "bad habits" of the Japanese, such as that of duplicity. This particular vice annoyed the padres so much that they condemned the Japanese for it from time to time, as we have mentioned previously. (Actually this reading on the part of the Jesuits seems to have stemmed from a serious lack of communication between the European padres and the Japanese due to the language barrier and different behavioral patterns. This question will be addressed again later.) Valignano strongly urges the applicant to overcome cultural differences and to become a faithful child of the compania (the Jesuit community).

The content clearly demonstrates that this catechism was prepared specifically for the sake of the novices entering the Jesuit brotherhood. Originally it was most likely used by the Visitor at the seminario in Azuchi. The discovery of the handwritten copies of the catechism from the Evora byobu is of great significance, because, first of all, they constitute the oldest extant catechism in Japanese. Second, they provide priceless bits of information concerning the Jesuit mission theology and their views about Japanese society and its culture and religions. Third, their value as educational texts is of importance as well, since they were aimed at training the youngsters eventually for the priesthood.

### (2) Dochirina Kirishitan

Prior to the publication of Valignano's catechism, several concise editions of a catechism had been written in order to instruct the Japanese in the fundamental doctrines of Christianity. Xavier, Torres, and Gago are known to have prepared a few such tracts. After the publication of Valignano's version, a few more catechisms were prepared. The best known is called *Dochirina Kirishitan* (Christian Doctrine), which has survived in three manuscripts. Two of them were printed in the Latin script in 1592 at Amakusa, and the third copy was in Japanese script published in Nagasaki in 1600.

At the Jesuit conference held in Nagasaki in February 1592, it was decided that this *Dochirina Kirishitan* and no other would be used as the official catechism in Japan. Unlike Valignano's text found in the Evora byobu, this catechism is in a question and answer form. But in most of the *Dochirina*, the catechumen asks the questions and the catechist supplies the answers, a reverse of the usual procedure. The author of this catechism is not known, but he (or they) relied on the *Roman Catechism* published in Rome in 1566. (The Council of Trent intended this catechism to be the Catholic Church's official manual of doctrinal instruction for the faithful.)

*Dochirina Kirishitan* opens with a brief introduction, which underscores faith, hope, and love as being fundamental to the Christian life. The main body of the catechism is divided into the following eleven sections. (1) The main aim of the first section is to instruct the student about that which makes a person truly Christian. The answer includes the belief in Deus as the one God and the creator, the immortality of the human soul and its final judgment, and the divine grace through Christ's redemption. A Christian is one who is true, even to death, to this belief by manifesting the image of Christ in himself/ herself.

(2) The second section concerns the significance of the cross: it symbolizes the liberation from the bondage of devils. Instructions for making the sign of the cross are explained. The following subjects are taught in each of the ensuing sections: (3) the Lord's Prayer, (4) Ave Maria, (5) Salve Regina, (6) the Apostles' Creed and the Trinity, (7) the ten commandments.

(8) This section deals with the ecclesiastical laws. The following five items are especially emphasized: (a) the celebration of mass on Sunday and on other festival days; (b) confession at least once a year; (c) the reception of the eucharist on Easter; (d) the importance of fasting

during the season of Lent and abstaining from eating meat on Friday and Saturday. (During the Lenten season, one meal a day and the drinking of wine and water are allowed. Those who are younger than twenty-one and older than sixty, those who are sick and pregnant, and those who engage in hard labor are exempt from fasting); (e) tithing.

(9) This section covers seven mortal sins and the necessity of contrition and the seven virtues. (10) The seven sacraments. (11) Other necessary directions including the importance of neighborly love, virtues, the gifts of the spirit, the beatitudes, prayers of confession, and prayers before and after the meal.

Compared with Valignano's *Japanese Catechism*, *Dochirina Kirishitan* is more comprehensive covering many aspects of the Catholic faith and life. It does not contain any polemical statement against the Japanese religions and philosophies, revealing a sharp contrast to the *Japanese Catechism* which includes a great amount of censure and denunciation particularly against the Buddhists' teaching and practice. *Dochirina Kirishitan* was edited for the sake of all levels of Christians, while the *Japanese Catechism* seems to be aimed specifically at more-or-less intellectual Christians including seminarians. Theologically, both catechisms faithfully follow the directions presented in the *Roman Catechism*.

## VALIGNANO'S MISSION POLICY

As the content clearly indicates, Valignano's catechism was not a series of straight propositional statements of Catholic doctrine; it was rather designed to explicate the teachings of the church by constantly comparing them with the Buddhistic ideas prevalent in Japan in those days. Though firmly rejecting Buddhism as the devil's tenet, Valignano made serious attempts to understand it and urged his European colleagues to do the same. He paid special attention to the Zen sect, because he recognized its profound spirituality and rigorous discipline. The Pure Land sect appeared to him quite similar to Protestantism in Europe, for both underscored salvation through faith alone, which his post-reformation Catholic faith could hardly accept.

There is no doubt that Valignano received help from some Japanese person in order to acquire information about Buddhism when he wrote the catechism. This Japanese source was, according to Frois, provided by a talented Japanese Christian by the name of Yohoken Paulo. This man was originally a physician, and excelled in literary skill in Japanese as well. After becoming a Christian under the influence of Torres, he worked with the padre for eighteen years.

Yohoken was allowed to enter the Jesuit order in 1580 when Valignano arrived in Kyushu. Although Yohoken was already eighty years of age at that time, the Visitor was so impressed by his virtuous personality and useful gifts that he made him his personal aide. "Because of his cooperation," Frois testified, the catechism was completed. "It was intended to preach to the pagans by making use of the knowledge concerning the Japanese sects and archives with which he (Yohoken) was extensively acquainted and was able to supply to us." He was also instrumental in publishing a Japanese grammar and a lexicon for the Europeans' use and in making available the translations of many European books. Frois stated furthermore: "Everywhere in Japan, people loved greatly the beauty and excellence of his literary works."

It is indeed a noteworthy fact that the first official catechism was produced as the result of close cooperation between a European missionary and a Japanese Christian. It was not a document written and imposed one-sidedly on the local people by a western authority alone. This affords an eloquent example of the dynamic and adaptive nature of Valignano's mission policy.

### (1) The policy of adaptation

Valignano's adaptive mission policy was explicitly stated in a document entitled *Counsel for Religious Aspirants,* a copy of which was also recovered from the byobu at Evora. According to Professor Matsuda's judgment, it represents notes taken at Valignano's lecture at the noviatiate in Usuki in 1580. (In the opinion of Professor Arimichi Ebisawa who co-published the byobu documents with Matsuda, this lecture was delivered instead by Padre Organtino at the seminario in Azuchi. But even if that was the case, the treatise must have reflected Valignano's view quite closely, since Organtino was in complete agreement with the Visitor's general approach.)

We read in the text such statements as: "The Portuguese custom is greatly different from that of the Japanese, and it is quite proper (for the Portuguese) to learn the Japanese way in Japan. It is, therefore, important for the Europeans to set aside their original habits and ways and learn the Japanese habits and ways when they come to Japan. . . . Consequently, it is unnecessary (for the Japanese) to imitate the ways of the Namban. It is wrong for Japan and thus should be warned against."

Valignano then admonished the Japanese aspirants to identify themselves truly as integral members of the Christian compania and not to harbor any feeling of isolation or national parochialism. (Such a propensity apparently existed among the Japanese novices, which was the cause of major concern for the padres including Cabral, Valignano, Organtino, among others. We will discuss this question more in detail later.) The Visitor took pains to emphasize that the compania belonged to the Japanese Christians and its leadership would eventually be given to them.

This statement was of historic importance, because, first of all, it guaranteed the acceptance of the Japanese into the priesthood of the Jesuit order. Second, it declared the equality of all members. Third, it promised that the leadership of the Catholic Church in Japan would be consigned eventually to the Japanese Christians. This policy was the hallmark of Valignano's courageous innovation. (As mentioned earlier, Padre Cabral categorically rejected the whole idea.) Valignano's expectation, in fact, seems to have been very well fulfilled by the Japanese pupils; as the Annual Report of 1583 attested, they "made tremendous progress in learning as well as in virtue." It also reported, for example, that they mastered Latin within three or four months!

The mission policy declared in this lecture is indeed remarkably foresighted in view of the fact that it was not until even some years after World War II that the Christian churches (both Catholic and Protestant) would begin to review critically the prevalent tendency of the missions to confuse the cultural indoctrination of the local population (usually followed by economic and political domination) with evangelization. In the sixteenth century, Valignano was already envisioning the establishment of Christian churches run by the Japanese for the Japanese in a Japanese style—literally a Japanese Catholic Church.

Valignano's policy took a measure of profound wisdom and courage, since in those days the Christian missions (including that of the Jesuits) were often quite aggressive and insensitive toward native peoples throughout the world. In the Portuguese and Spanish colonies, the converts were told to adopt European names, wear European clothes, and totally observe European religious practices. Any attempt at altering the European ways, not to mention the European logic in teaching Christianity, was deemed as an offense to God.

In the mission lands such as Latin America, the Philippine Islands, various parts of Africa, and other places, military conquest and proselytization worked hand in hand. Some padres, in fact, actually suggested that this method be applied to Japan and China. Valignano angrily rejected the proposal, saying that it would be not only inappropriate but also impossible. His peaceful and adaptive policy was consistently carried out in Japan. (However, Valignano was once obliged to help the Christian Lord Arima by providing him with weapons.)

*(2) Application of the adaptive policy*

In order to enforce this adaptive policy among the European missionaries, the Visitor also wrote a treatise entitled *Warning and Advice concerning the Japanese Customs* in 1581. This booklet contains detailed instructions in regard to protocol apropos to Japanese society. Some salient examples are as follows. The missionaries should always maintain a polite yet friendly attitude. They should not be gawking around with curiosity, nor should they use big gestures or laugh too loudly. They should not visit non-Christians too often. They should not meet noble people without the proper previous introduction. They should carefully adjust their degree of courtesy depending upon the social rank of persons they meet. They should choose an adequate gift when visiting persons of rank.

The missionaries should follow the Japanese way of building and using their residences. For example, the house, particularly the kitchen and the toilet, should always be kept immaculate. A tea house should be built apart from the residence in order to match the contemporary Japanese craze for the tea ceremony. They should follow the Japanese diet (contrary to Cabral's direction), but should wear the Jesuit cotton cassocks (agreeing with Cabral's decision). The structure of the sanctuary, however, is an important exception in that it should be built in a long rectangular shape following the European church style and unlike the usually square Buddhist temples.

It is really astonishing that Valignano, even if he had the help of others, was able to write such precise instructions as to the desirable social conduct only one year after he came to such a totally unfamiliar country. These directions which Valignano established were evidently carried out rather faithfully by the missionaries. Francesco Pasio, who succeeded Valignano as Visitor, described with fascination how the residence was constructed in the native fashion. But the furniture of the house was European, which suggests that the living style of the missionaries was not quite Japanese.

## DEPARTURE OF CABRAL

Valignano's mission policy, as has been noted previously, brought about a complete reversal of Cabral's ideas. Cabral was convinced of the absolute supremacy of Christianity and the European culture, which, he believed, should be imposed upon non-Christian lands without regard for local situations and traditions. He, according to Valignano, even laughed at the suggestion that the missionaries should study the Japanese language, which he considered impossible to learn, and thus he provided them with no opportunities to learn. He was terribly disgusted at Valignano's request to Rome that priest and brothers who were endowed with not only physical strength but also intellectual excellence be sent to Japan.

It was a profound repulsion on Cabral's part when Valignano decided to promote harmonious equality between the European and Japanese members of the missions by admitting the latter into the priesthood (and eventually even bishopric). We read in the Visitor's report to the General from Nagasaki on August 16, 1580: "Francesco Cabral held that the Japanese could not stand so much charity; if they were to be properly governed, they needed stern treatment which of course must be blended with charity at the proper time. All the other fathers decided on the opposite policy: the Japanese should not and could not be governed sternly; rather they should be treated with great gentleness and affection in the same way as we dealt with the Portuguese; when necessary, however, sternness would have to be mingled with this mild treatment" (see Schütte, *Valignano's Mission Principle*, I, p. 372).

It was thus quite palpable that the difference of views concerning the overall mission principle was too fundamental for there to be any reconciliation between Valignano and Cabral. Having realized this, the latter submitted a request both to the General and to Valignano that he be released from his office; he left Japan for Macao in 1581. The Visitor appointed as his replacement Padre Gaspar Coelho (c. 1531–1590), a more agreeable person, who served as the Vice-Provincial in Japan from 1581 to 1590.

### GREAT SUCCESS OF ORGANTINO

Padre Gnecchi-Organtino (1532–1609) was perhaps the most consistently vocal opponent of Cabral. He made a great success of his missionary efforts in central Japan, which considerably influenced Valignano when he set up his mission principles. A mention of his work may be in order at this juncture.

Organtino's conflict with Cabral had already begun before either came to Japan. In 1568 he was appointed by the Provincial in India to be the official Visitor of the district of Malacca and Macao. When he arrived at Macao, he found that Cabral, who had supposedly already set sail for Japan, had been held there by an unfavorable wind. Organtino considered himself as the superior, whereas Cabral, who had been the Visitor there, claimed his status was still effective. It turned out, therefore, that there were two superiors at the same time in the same place. Quarrels concerning the power of jurisdiction took place between the two. It was unfortunate that because of the impossibility of quick communication and consultation with the authorities in Goa, such a conflict could not be solved immediately.

Despite this personal disagreement, both padres journeyed together to Japan and landed in Kyushu on June 18, 1570. Immediately after the mission conference in July and August of that year, Cabral, now the mission superior of Japan, sent Organtino to the Kyoto region. There Organtino later succeeded Frois as district superior.

Organtino's accomplishment in central Japan is indeed astonishing. When Frois left Kyoto in 1577 (about fifteen years after Xavier's visit as the first Christian missionary), there were about 1,500 Christians there. But, according to him, as soon as Organtino took over the leadership, the number of those baptized jumped by thousands within a few months. This tally seems to be confirmed by Valignano's report in 1580 which mentioned 15,000 Christians in that district.

One may naturally wonder what caused such a spectacular success. Organtino's response to this question credited his success to his mission strategy of adaptation, as he stated in his letter (February 11, 1595): "We should attempt to adapt ourselves in everything as much as possible." This intention led him to an intensive study of the local language. Investigations into Buddhism were also a target of his ardor; he, along with Frois, received personal tutoring from Buddhist monks for a year. His whole life was attuned totally to the Japanese way. Against Cabral's direction, for instance, he continued wearing Japanese silk clothes. After about twenty years of work in Japan, he wrote to the General on March 10, 1589: "I am more Japanese than an Italian, for the Lord of his grace has transformed me into one of that nation."

Privy to the Japanese fondness for novelties, he made a special effort to present grand ceremonies at the chief Christian festivals. Chanting and singing accompanied by European music instruments certainly enticed the visitors into a world of religious fantasy. In order to heighten the effect further, Organtino procured from Europe vestments of brocade and velvet, altar covers, paintings, and other items which were quite exotic to the local population. He requested the Jesuit General to send him men of skill in architecture, sculpture, painting, music, and the manufacturing of musical instruments. (This, unfortunately, did not materialize.)

With an identical aim in mind, Organtino told Nobunaga Oda of his plan of building an impressive looking church. The strong man, who was anxious to demonstrate his grandeur, endorsed the idea immediately and granted some funds and land for the project. The padre, with the devout assistance from local Christians, succeeded in building the three-story-high Church of the Assumption of the Blessed Virgin Mary in Kyoto (which was popularly called Namban-ji, the temple of the Southern Barbarians). It was completed in the spring of 1578 and became a great tourist attraction. (This church was unfortunately destroyed by fire in 1582 when a rebel army attacked Nobunaga at the Buddhist temple, Honno-ji, which was located only a city block away from the church. Only a church bell has survived until today; the date of casting, 1577, is still visible.)

Organtino proved to be a tremendous public relations man; to a huge crowd drawn by such exotic religious buildings and activities therein, he preached the sovereignty and compassion of Deus. He also made every effort to promote mutual love and help among his Christian followers, which served as an admirable model in the society. He certainly knew how to handle the psychology of the masses. Such a psychological approach was used also with the prominent Christian feudal lords in his district where he created a competition among them; those reputation-conscious rulers became anxious to try to make their territories Christian. Naturally, as a result, more converts were gained and more churches were constructed.

It is wrong, however, to regard Organtino as merely a manipulator. He did all these things not simply to obtain converts but also to express his genuine love for the Japanese. Here again the difference between Cabral and Organtino was clear; there was not even the slightest hint of Cabral-like Euro-centrism in Organtino. In his letter to the General (dated September 29, 1577) he repeatedly stated his high estimate of the Japanese character:

> Your Paternity must not think that they (the Japanese) are an uncivilized race; apart from our Christian faith we are vastly their inferiors. Since I have begun to understand their language, I have formed the judgment that in general there is no other people as discerning as they. . . . If (this nation) submits to the faith, my opinion is that no church in the world will surpass (that of Japan). . . .

> I pray Your Reverence to get rid of the notion that this is an uncivilized people; for, apart from the faith we hold, no matter how wise we fancy ourselves to be, when compared with them it is we who are most uncivilized. I confess in all truth I am learning from them every day, and I believe that there is no nation in the world so singularly gifted and tal-

ented as the Japanese (October 15, 1577). (English translation by Schütte in his *op. cit.*, pp. 107f)

Nonetheless, Organtino did not blindly praise the Japanese; he was in fact appalled at some aspects of the Japanese mores such as the cruel forms of punishment used (i.e. execution) and the prevalent sexual immorality. He did not appreciate the Japanese indulgence in drinking parties nor their music which sounded to him totally cacophonous. But his genuine love and respect for the people motivated him to become as one of them and to tell them the Christian message of love. That was precisely the reason why the people returned a profound affection and admiration to him as well. Fondly called "Orugan Bateren" (Padre Organ) by the local people, he was perhaps the most loved missionary in pre-modern Japan.

### VALIGNANO'S VISIT TO CENTRAL JAPAN

Valignano was, needless to say, quite impressed by Organtino's great success in central Japan. What he saw during his visit to that region indeed confirmed the achievement. He traveled from Bungo and arrived at Kyoto in March 1581. His busy itinerary took him immediately to the many Christian communities scattered in that district. Everywhere he visited, he was welcomed enthusiastically by a thriving flock of believers.

A number of churches had been built and were quite active, and the seminario was well into operation in Azuchi by virtue of the vigorous efforts of Organtino and Lord Ukon Takayama. Everything he experienced during the journey satisfied the Visitor greatly. He was convinced more than ever of the appropriateness of the policy of adaptation for the mission in Japan.

The Visitor's assessment of Organtino was of course very high. His letter to the General, dated December 12, 1584, included the following comments: "He is a good religious, virtuous and prudent, with a unique flair for intercourse with the Japanese; he is discerning and clever in employing the proper means of dealing with them. Hence he is very well liked by his household and by externs, and possesses exceptional authority among the Japanese."

Valignano even considered appointing Organtino for the post of Vice-provincial of Japan but decided against it for the following reasons: (1) "Though he does everything possible for the advancement and welfare of the Japanese, he does so with such utter devotion that I (Valignano) fear he would be less useful in promoting religious recollection and the proper formation of ours both in the novitiate and in the colleges." (2) He is too "lavish with money and ventures in putting up buildings." (3) He does not get along with Cabral, though he is "more adroit in finding the proper course to adopt."

In effect, the Visitor's fear was that Organtino would do more for the Japanese than for the missions! He also worried about the possible criticism that he was showing personal favoritism toward Organtino because they shared the same nationality (Italian). For these reasons, at any rate, he chose Gaspar Coelho instead of Organtino, for he was "a very balanced person, a friend of the Japanese, and a man of high courage" (cf. Schütte, *ibid.*, pp. 95f).

The highlight of Valignano's visit to the capital district came when he had an audience with Nobunaga Oda. The powerful general continued to show a warm friendship toward the Europeans; he was delighted to meet this tall (well over six feet) Italian priest. They exchanged a long and cordial conversation. The gifts Valignano presented included, among other things, a large gilded candlestand, crystal, and a velvet covered chair with a gold frame. The chair was reportedly used as Nobunaga's seat for an audience of more than 100,000 spectators at a grand review of the troops in 1581. Nobunaga in his turn gave Valignano his favorite byobu with a splendid scene of Azuchi painted on it by a well-known artist.

This masterpiece was Nobunaga's particular treasure; he loved it so much that he had even turned down a request from the emperor's court to donate it to the palace. Valignano placed it in the mission residence in Azuchi, which attracted hundreds of spectators daily. He later took it with him for an exhibition in Kyoto, Bungo, and finally shipped it to Rome. (Unfortunately it has been lost, but some European drawings based on it do exist.)

All this public display of personal favor toward the missionaries by Nobunaga, in addition to his hatred of the Buddhists, certainly furthered the Christian cause in central Japan. But the Christians seem to have been clearly aware that the strong man would never become a Christian. He was simply not a spiritual man, but was instead a thoroughly worldly materialist.

Nobunaga's self-aggrandizement was in fact so prodigious that he had a temple erected for himself making him a living object of adoration. He claimed himself to be, according to Frois, the lord of all lords. (Such a megalomanic act was not merely an ego trip but stemmed from his political intent to rally the whole country around his regime. He was certainly not the only one to use this tactic. His successors, such as Hideyoshi Toyotomi, Ieyasu Tokugawa and his descendants, did the same.) It is highly doubtful, therefore, that Nobunaga, had he lived longer, would have continued favoring Christianity which denied any form of "human worship."

In contrast to their father, Nobunaga's three sons appear to have been genuinely interested in Christianity. Both Frois and Organtino reported that they frequently had long talks with them about various matters including the Christian faith. In particular, the oldest son, Nobutada, was quite studious resembling a catechumen. Ultimately, however, the sons did not decide to join the church formally out of a fear of displeasing their father. The strict moral codes of the church also made them hesitate.

On the part of the Christians, nonetheless, it was a realistic expectation that these future rulers of the land were going to have at least a profound sympathy toward their religion. Consequently, after a half year of fecund activities in central Japan as Valignano left Kyoto for Kyushu, he was filled with the joy of a great vision of the eventual conversion of the whole country.

### MISSION CONFERENCE AT NAGASAKI

Shortly before leaving Japan in February 1582, Valignano called a conference at Nagasaki. Present there were padres such as Gaspar Coelho, Luis Frois, Lourenço Mexia, and others who were working in the Shimo district at that time. Though the exact topic discussed at this consultation is not known, it seems to have been basically identical with that dealt with at the previous meetings in Usuki and Azuchi. *The Resolutions (Resoluciones que el P. Visitador da acerca de las preguntas de la consulta*) which the Visitor edited on January 6, 1583 contained the major conclusions reached through those meetings.

## (1) Necessity of native clergy

First it was stated that the mission in Japan represented "the most significant endeavor of the age" for the Catholic Church and that therefore the pope, the Jesuit general, and the king of Portugal should be informed thereof accurately. For such a great and important work, however, there was a severe shortage of mission personnel. Not only for this reason, but also because of the vast cultural and religious differences between Europe and Japan, it was suggested that vigorous attempts be made to nurture native clergy.

A policy that only the Jesuits continue the missionary work in Japan was proposed for similarly compelling reasonings. It was thought inadvisable to have missionaries of other orders, since this might create confusion. Valignano emphatically appealed to the authorities in Europe to recognize these facts.

## (2) Necessity of bishopric

In *The Resolutions* there was also a reference to the necessity of appointing a bishop for the church in Japan in the near future. There were 150,000 Christians and 200 congregations, which required a bishop to administer. But the conference's conclusion was that the padres who were experienced with local conditions should be in charge and not a bishop sent from Europe who was unfamiliar with Japan. The Visitor's desire was to establish an independent Japanese province where a Japanese superior, be he Provincial or Vice-provincial, would be entrusted with a wide range of authority.

(At that time, Japan constituted a diocese under the archbishopric of Goa. But Sixtus V decided to send Pedro Martins, a Jesuit, as the bishop of Japan in 1588. His arrival in Japan was delayed until 1596, however. After about a one year stay in Japan, he died on a journey off Malacca in 1597. Luis Cerqueira, likewise a Jesuit, succeeded in the office in the following year and worked in that capacity until his death in 1614. Thereafter the then provincial Valentim Carvalho was voted to take over the leadership, though not as the bishop. He was later expelled from Japan when persecution became intense. The Jesuit monopoly of the Japan mission advanced by Valignano and the many other fellow Jesuits inevitably became fiercely controversial when missionaries of other orders later came to Japan.)

### (3) Training of native workers

The training of native workers for the missions was always one of the central concerns of Valignano; *The Resolutions* emphatically reiterated it. The document required a strict two year period of probation for the novitiate, after which time, with the recommendation of the Japanese consultors, they were then qualified to study Latin, theology, Japanese writings, Buddhist doctrines and the refutation thereof.

*The Resolutions* laid strong emphasis on the importance of harmony between the native and foreign personnel in the missions. The four points of behavioral instruction which Valignano had previously demanded were reasserted: mildness, impartiality, a consistency between one's internal esteem and one's external behavior, and an adaptation to the Japanese way of life. Dining manners, for example, were to follow the Japanese example; all the members were to eat rice, soup, vegetables and fruits. They were also to abstain from meat and fish as the Buddhist monks did. Only newcomers from Europe and the sick were allowed to eat European food.

(The Japanese frowned upon the fact that the missionaries kept pigs and goats in their residential compound, slaughtered cows, and hung up their hides to dry and sell. The smell of lard which the Europeans used liberally in cooking was unbearable to the local people. Their kitchen and dining rooms were not as tidy as those in the Buddhist monasteries. Valignano decided to change all of this and instructed the importance of this change by quoting St. Paul's words in 1 Corinthians 8:13: "If food is a cause of my brother's falling, I will never eat meat, lest I cause my brother to fall.")

As far as the clothing of the Jesuits was concerned, Valignano diverged from his adaptational policy. He insisted that the traditional Jesuit habit be worn uniformly by all members of the order. A distinction was to be made between that of the members of the Society and of the dojukus who wore Japanese dress. Footwear could be either European or Japanese, but, following the Japanese way, it should not be worn inside the house (except for socks).

## (4) Financial matters

Finally, *The Resolutions* addressed the problem of financial security which always plagued the missionary activities. As mentioned earlier, the Jesuits initially participated in the silk trade and gained considerable benefits from it. But this was prohibited by the General because of Cabral's request. As a remedy for the severe loss of revenue, the suggestion was made that some arable land be procured for raising agricultural products. Citing the rule of the order, Valignano was at first adverse to it, but the exigent situation forced him to ask special permission from Rome to carry out this plan in such an emergency. An urgent appeal for financial support from Europe was also made.

### EMBASSY TO EUROPE

To consummate his first visit to Japan, Valignano inaugurated a grand plan to send an embassy to the pope and the king of Portugal on behalf of the Christian lords of Kyushu. The aim of the venture was twofold. First, Valignano hoped to arouse interest in the Jesuit missions in Japan among the Europeans by making what would be received as an exotic presentation of the Japanese envoys so that more missionaries could be recruited and more funds raised. Second, it would be far more effective to let the Japanese ambassadors themselves, upon their return, tell their fellow countrymen how great the civilization of Christian Europe was.

The plan was indeed a noble one, but the Visitor apparently set it up quite hastily. He selected the following four pupils of the seminario in Kyushu: Mancio Ito, fourteen years of age, to represent Lord Yoshishige Otomo, Miguel Chijiwa, fourteen years old, on behalf of both Lord Sumitada Omura and Lord Harunobu Ariuma, Julian Nakaura, fourteen years old, and Martinho Hara, twelve years old. The latter two were to be vice-envoys. All four were said to be relatives of these three lords.

However, according to Padre Pedro Ramon who was working in

Kyushu at that time, these four children were "none other than very poor and miserable wretches." The padre wrote furthermore to General Aquaviva on October 25, 1587 that he was personally acquainted with Mancio Ito, who was only remotely related to Lord Otomo and was an orphan in the custody of the missions. This lord, in fact, asked the padre why these boys were going to be sent to Europe. Ramon expressed in the letter his deep regret as to the choice of these envoys; it would even jeopardize, he stated, the credibility of the Jesuit Society.

It does not seem that Padre Ramon wrote this letter simply out of a personal animosity toward the Visitor, nor did he attempt to undermine the expedition with some malicious intention. There is no evidence to indicate any of these possible causes. He was, in fact, accurate about the unfortunate state of Mancio, who was indeed only remotely related to Otomo as well. According to a careful study done by Professor Matsuda, the whole plan originated solely with Valignano, and it is even dubious to what extent the three lords were consulted. Omura and Arima reportedly consented to the project and were willing to write several cordial letters to the ecclesiastical and civil authorities in Europe, but Otomo appears to have been informed only at the last moment before the youngsters' departure from Japan.

There are six extant letters which carry the signatures of these three lords. They are addressed to the pope, the king of Portugal, the Jesuit General, Cardinal Enrique, and Cardinal Farnese. (Five of these letters are housed in the Jesuit archives in Rome and one in the University of Kyoto.) Matsuda has convincingly shown, however, that Otomo's signatures were forged by someone; the lord of Bungo did not write the letters. He was possibly even unaware of their having been composed until sometime later.

Weighing the whole situation, Matsuda surmises that the scarcity of time prevented the Visitor from discussing the plan with Otomo, but because of his close friendship with the lord, he felt safe that he could receive approval from him after the action was taken. It might very well have been that Valignano had not anticipated that this venture would become the event of such magnitude that it turned out to be. Whatever the case might have been, it was very hastily arranged by the Visitor.

There is no trace of Valignano's attempt to defend himself against Ramon's criticism; perhaps he never knew about it. However, later when some Franciscan friars accused him of "deceiving the pope and the whole world" by scheming this whole venture, he wrote a strong defense (*Apologia en la quel se responde a diversas calumnias*, 1598). There is no doubt that he harbored no such insidious intentions whatsoever; it was a totally sincere attempt on his part to invigorate the difficult mission in Japan.

The only thing for which he was perhaps to blame was that he did not clarify the fact of Mancio's deprived background and also that he failed to consult Otomo in advance. In other words, he was too anxious to get the envoys to Europe to spend enough time to set up the plan carefully. (In fact, Mancio Ito was not his first choice; there was a better qualified young man by the name of Jeronimo Ito who was studying at that time in the seminario in Azuchi. He was a son of Otomo's niece. There was, however, not enough time to summon him to Kyushu.) As far as these young ambassadors were concerned, evidence points to the fact that they presented themselves honestly and accurately before the Europeans.

### THE ENVOYS IN EUROPE

The activities of the envoys in Europe were narrated in a book written by Padre Duarte de Sande and published in Macao in 1590 (*Dialogus de Missióne Legatorum Iaponensium*). The book consisted of thirty-four conversations in which each of the four envoys told of his experiences in Europe to Leo, the brother of Lord Arima, and Linus, the brother of Omura. Though the title cover gave De Sande as the author, the real author was none other than Valignano himself.

In his letter from Macao on September 25, 1589, Valignano clearly stated that by utilizing mainly the envoys' diaries and personal reports, he composed the first draft in Spanish and then asked De Sande to rewrite it in the form of a dialogue in Latin. The whole book reveals that its obvious intention was to impress Japanese readers with the greatness of Christian Europe as eyewitnessed by the four youths. The Latin version was, of course, planned to be rendered further into Japanese.

According to this book, the following events happened during the envoys' journey. The party left Nagasaki on February 20, 1582. When

they reached Goa, India, Valignano unexpectedly received a communi-
qué from the General which ordered him to stay there as provincial of
India. He was consequently obliged to entrust the chaperone responsi-
bilities to two Jesuits: Jacobus Mesquita and Nuño Rodriguez.

In spite of the hardship of sea journey, the party was able to arrive
finally at Lisbon, Portugal on August 11, 1584. (Julian Nakaura, in
particular, suffered from severe seasickness, which unfortunately prevented him from participating in the various reception parties and
ceremonies.) The first official audience with European dignitaries was
with King Felipe II who was the ruler of both Spain and Portugal. De
Sande took pains to underscore how grand and magnificent the royal
reception was. When Mancio approached the king to kiss his hand, the
Royal Highness embraced him instead of following the usual protocol.
He showed the same exceptionally generous greetings to the other
youths as well.

Such an extraordinarily warm reception was extended to them
wherever they visited. Pope Gregory XIII did the same. On February
22, 1585, albeit frail at the age of eighty-four, he was willing to meet
them at the hall which was ordinarily used for audiences only with
kings. The whole city was, De Sande wrote, in a tremendously festive
mood; hundreds of people came out to see the youths from the other
side of the earth. There was a huge procession (the sight of which was
later painted on a wall at the Vatican). Again, when the envoys tried to
kiss him on his foot, the pope extended his arms to embrace each one
of them; he chose to do this, according to De Sande, despite objections
from the cardinals and others. When Gregory XIII, however, passed
away shortly afterward, his successor, Sixtus V, treated them just as
warmly. Honorable citizenship of the city of Rome was bestowed upon
them.

The successful journey proceeded from Rome to several other
cities in northern Italy, where the party enjoyed the same courteous
treatment from the nobility of that region. The local people were
naturally very curious about the unusual visitors. Numerous stories
were written of their impressions, many of which depicted the youths'
physical features (such as the smallness of their eyes and noses) and
their surprisingly polished manners. Each behavior of these "princes"
(as they were called in those stories) drew the people's interest; they, for

example, did not drink wine and skillfully used chopsticks when they ate.

Despite their young age, they seemingly performed their duty extremely well. They made a number of speeches in Latin and had to answer a myriad of inquisitive questions before many dignitaries. They demonstrated their musical skill as well. Mancio and Miguel, for example, played the organ at the cathedral in Evora in front of a huge audience. All of these activities apparently impressed their European hosts tremendously.

All in all, the expedition proved to be a great success. The enthusiasm among the Europeans was far more than Valignano had hoped for. The glory of renaissance Europe certainly overwhelmed the Japanese youth, who were ready and excited to tell of their experiences to their fellow countryfolks. Unfortunately, however, in the meanwhile the political situation in Japan had turned quite ominous toward the Christian missions there.

The party traveled from Italy back to Spain and Portugal. They then departed from Lisbon and later arrived in Goa on April 22, 1587. While still in South Asia, the news reached them that Nobunaga Oda, a friend of the missions, had died during a battle with the troops of his rebellious general. Worse still, two of the important Christian lords, Yoshishige Otomo and Sumitada Omura, had also both died in the same year, 1587.

In the midst of a deep anxiety caused by this sad news, the inconvenience of a sea journey delayed the envoys' schedule, and it was 1590 when they finally returned to their homeland. By that time, another general of Nobunaga, Hideyoshi Toyotomi, had established his hegemony over the whole country. The new ruler, unfortunately, turned out to be a persecutor of Christianity. And thus commenced a new chapter of the Catholic missions in Japan—a period of suffering and sacrifice.

### CONCLUDING REMARKS

The period from 1570 to 1590 constituted a period of expansion and consolidation of the Christian missions in Japan. Padre Visitor Valignano had a principal role in this development. He set the basic policy of the missions: the mission land was officially organized into three main districts (Kami, Shimo, and Bungo); the educational programs were vigorously advanced by launching forth seminarios and colegios in these three areas; a more systematic and accurate way of communicating with the headquarters in India and Europe was established.

Above all, the policy of adaptation was clearly defined and enforced. The Visitor discerned a fundamental fallacy in Padre Cabral's approach which had attempted to impose Christianity on the Japanese from the vantage point of Euro-centrism. He, therefore, required all of the European missionaries to learn the local language, customs, culture, and religions. This, however, did not mean a complete Japanization of the Christian missions; it retained what was regarded to be essential to the spirit of Catholicism. In the way of living, manners, and diet, the missionaries were to follow the local customs as much as possible, yet on the other hand the traditional Jesuit attire was to be preserved for the sake of maintaining the virtue of poverty characteristic of the order.

The policy of adaptation was not devised by Valignano after arriving in Japan. It was rather an idea nurtured in his mind long before he left Europe. He became ever more convinced of its validity when he saw the great success Padre Organtino had in his missionary work in central Japan through the same approach. Organtino, most loved by the Japanese, stood in sharp contrast to Cabral who, though with a good record of converts during his tenure as superior, alienated many of his native Christian workers because of the often harsh and arrogant way he treated them.

Valignano's policy of adaptation was applied not only in Japan but also in China at the hand of his former student, Matteo Ricci. A summary reference to his work in China illustrates Valignano's policy. Valignano was the master of Ricci when the latter was a novice in Rome in 1571, and then later in 1582 they were reunited in Macao when Valignano summoned Ricci to Goa in order to send him as a missionary to China.

The Visitor had established a Chinese parish in Macao; he was resolutely determined to commence Christian evangelism in China despite the fact that "some few who had experience with the Chinese people said that any attempt to win them over was a sheer waste of time, like trying to whiten an Ethiopian," as Matteo Ricci wrote in his diary (see *China in the Sixteenth Century: The Journals of Matthew Ricci, 1583–1610*, tr. L.J. Gallagher, 1953, p. 131). In 1583 Ricci was granted permission by the Chinese government to reside in the country; thenceforth he spent the rest of his life there until he died in 1610 in Beijing.

Inspired by Valignano's policy of adaptation, Ricci made every effort to integrate himself into Chinese society; for example, he wore Chinese attire, ate Chinese food, and studied the Chinese language intensely. His missionary method was in accord with the Jesuit practice in mission lands, namely: "Convert the high echelon, then the lower classes will follow."

By making use of his mathematical and scientific skill and knowledge, Ricci succeeded in befriending Chinese intellectuals. Realizing the fact that Confucianism constituted the basis of Chinese tradition, he devoted himself to a vigorous investigation of it, eventually translating several classic writings of Confucianism such as, among others, *The Analects, The Great Learning,* and *The Doctrine of the Mean.*

Armed with such a wide range of knowledge of both Chinese as well as western culture, Ricci attempted to explain Christian teachings in such a way that the western theological notions could be made more relevant to his Chinese audience. *The True Meaning of the Lord of Heaven,* which he wrote in Chinese in 1584, was a treatise of the Christian faith, cleverly employing various Confucian concepts and terminology. Its contents and structure, nonetheless, revealed its reliance on the legitimately Catholic books such as *The Spiritual Exercises* by Ignatius Loyola, the founding father of the Jesuit Society. Ricci's book was a success, as it drew favorable attention from Chinese literati.

This book, however, suffered much criticism from the Christian world for its use of Chinese words for key Christian concepts. Perhaps the most controversial example was his choice of a Chinese term for the Christian God. In Japan as well, the search for an equivalent word for God was a difficult task which missionaries, including Xavier, had to face, as we have observed before. They eventually settled the question by using the Latin word Deus.

Ricci preferred to employ "the Lord (or master) of heaven." Later, however, following his death, his broad toleration of the Chinese traditional terms and practices (e.g. filial piety) met with condemnation by the Holy See in 1704 and 1715. The Chinese emperor, K'ang-hsi (1661–1722), who had considered it profitable to have European intellectuals in his service, supported Ricci's policy, and thus felt repulsed by the church's condemnation. This conflict militated against Christian evangelism in China for the next two hundred or more years.

It is, consequently, beyond dispute that Valignano's mission policy left a decisive mark in Christian mission growth not only in Japan but also in China during the pre-modern era. As far as Japan was concerned, he was the principal architect of the structure of the missions. Under his direction, evangelization met with considerable success. His policy of adaptation was imaginative and creative; it indeed had a major impact on the Christian missions there.

Despite serious efforts by Valignano and many other Christian workers, however, the political situation in Japan suddenly turned unfavorable toward the Christians. The Catholic missions entered an era of horrible persecution. This troubled period will be the major subject of our next chapter.

# 4

# Christian Missions
# Under Hideyoshi's Reign

## TOYOTOMI HIDEYOSHI

The life of Toyotomi Hideyoshi (1536–1598) presents us with a cogent illustration of his time. It was a period of drastic social transition. By the end of the first half of the sixteenth century, the political power of the central government (the Ashikaga bakufu) had become virtually extinct—the anarchy resulted in a condition where fortunes were up for grabs for anyone who was ambitious. Hideyoshi epitomized the stormy dynamism of this age. And the Christian missions had to deal with this power-hungry despot.

Born a poor peasant, Hideyoshi rapidly climbed up the ladder of success by serving Nobunaga Oda loyally. His undaunted efforts and ingenious mind impressed his sovereign so much that he had become one of the top generals by the time of Nobunaga's sudden death in 1582. When the surprising news of the violent death of his overlord reached him, he was engaged in a campaign in the western province of Honshu. Before the enemy learned of the news, he quickly and adroitly arranged a truce and rushed back to central Japan with a huge number of troops. Hideyoshi's swift and decisive move not only contributed to his success in avenging his late overlord but also paved the way for him to establish for himself a national hegemony.

The next step of his ambitious plan was the elimination of his opponents and rivals through the use of military power and diplomatic maneuvering. By 1590 no one in the whole country dared challenge his authority. The imperial court was obliged to grant him the post of regent (*kampaku dajo-daijin*), the highest rank one could possibly obtain. Later he assumed the title *taiko* (retired regent). Such a rapid and remarkable rise in a person's life from the bottom to the very top of society could take place only during unstable conditions such as the whole nation was experiencing at that time.

Hideyoshi succeeded in unifying the war-torn country under his control. Attempting to consolidate his rule over every corner of the nation, he took several decisive measures which affected everyone. He first enjoined a systematic confiscation of weapons from the peasantry and soldier-monks in order to suppress their hitherto quite rampant uprising. This action was intended also to firmly establish a feudal system where the warriors would dominate other social groups including the monks, farmers, artisans, and merchants.

The second major measure Hideyoshi imposed was a wholesale survey of all arable lands, a practice which was carried out annually from 1582 until 1598, the year of his death. The lands were measured systematically, evaluated for taxation purposes, and assigned ownership. This policy, in addition to providing fiscal benefits, forced the land owners and tenant farmers to be subservient to warrior authority. The regent's eagle eyes were of course directed to the feudal lords and their retainers as well. In an attempt to prevent any possible rebellion from occurring, a careful rearrangement of their fiefs and the methodical demolition of many of their castles and fortresses were conducted.

To encourage economic recovery necessitated by many years of civil wars, Hideyoshi, like Nobunaga, favored a policy of free trade by opening the closed markets and guilds. Tax incentives and other fiscal measures were also put into effect in order to cause economic growth. The warrior government felt it exigent to closely oversee the rapidly developing urban tradesmen's activity so that it could reap as much profit as possible. Special commissioners were appointed to inspect the thriving commercial towns such as Sakai.

A strict control of currency was also of vital concern on the part of Hideyoshi's government. The long-lasting tumultuous social condition had invited the wide use of inferior coins, which had further aggravated the unstable economy. As a counter-measure, a large number of new coins were minted with governmental guarantee. In order to bolster the industry and the economy, Hideyoshi encouraged the extensive mining of gold and silver. Silver, in fact, became a major commodity for trade with the Europeans.

All of these measures certainly precipitated the stabilization of the society and a revitalization of its economy. As far as the Christian mission was concerned, however, all these new developments were not favorable; the mission was totally subjected to this despotic ruler's whims.

### THE EDICT OF EXPULSION OF THE PADRES

Hideyoshi, like Nobunaga, recognized the importance of trade with the Europeans. Both of them were fascinated with western culture. Hideyoshi, for example, loved to wear a Portuguese mantle and sleep in the bed which the Portuguese merchants had given to him. The paintings, musical instruments and clocks from Europe were also his proud possessions.

Neither Hideyoshi nor Nobunaga was religious, but Hideyoshi did not share the intense hatred which Nobunaga displayed against the Buddhists. He instead allowed the restoration of the Buddhist monasteries which Nobunaga had ordered destroyed. As long as the monks remained submissive to his authority, they could even enjoy his protection. As for the Christians, Nobunaga consistently favored them over the Buddhists. The padres' undaunted religious commitment, supplemented by their intelligence, genuinely impressed him. By contrast, his successor showed no trace of such feelings of admiration.

Hideyoshi, nonetheless, occasionally exhibited friendship toward some missionaries such as Organtino. When the padre requested permission to build a church in Osaka, a city where Hideyoshi had recently constructed a magnificent castle, he not only willingly consented to it but even selected a site near the castle. According to Frois, furthermore, he told several Europeans (including Frois himself) and Japanese Christians at the castle in May 1586 that he would "build churches in all parts, commanding all to become Christians and to embrace our Holy Law." But the seriousness of this pledge is highly doubtful; it must have been nothing more than one of those totally spontaneous and hyperbolic statements he was known to make from time to time. In fact, two months after this incident, he did exactly the opposite; he suddenly issued an order expelling the missionaries from the country.

### (1) Occasion of the edict

How did the regent come to make such a surprising edict? The occasion was as follows. The clan of Shimazu, located in the southern tip of the island of Kyushu, constituted a strong power during the era of civil strife. In 1587 they invaded the territory of their northern neighbor, Otomo. By that time Yoshishige Otomo had retired and was spending much of his time solely in devotion to Deus. He was in fact planning to create an exclusively Christian land in a corner of the Otomo domain. His son, Yoshimune, was then the active suzereign, but the young Otomo was not as capable a ruler as his father, and the Otomo family lost much of the power and influence it had once commanded.

In the face of an attack by this formidable enemy, Otomo did not have the strength to fight back; the capital city of Funai was overrun. The father Otomo, returning from retirement and desperate, was obliged to ask Hideyoshi for help. Hideyoshi, who himself had been planning to subdue the Shimazu, was willing to accept Otomo's petition. His massive troops of 250,000 men were soon dispatched, and he himself marched to Kyushu in early 1587. This show of force was too overwhelming for the Shimazu; they could do nothing but surrender.

The triumphant regent settled post-war matters by rewarding those who had rendered meritorious service and by punishing those who had opposed him. On his way back to Osaka, he stopped on July 16, 1587 at Hakata, a harbor town in northern Kyushu, where he met Padre Coelho who came there from Nagasaki in an armed Portuguese ship. The purpose of the Jesuit Vice-provincial's visit was twofold: first to congratulate the regent on his victory, and second to entreat him for a plot of land for a church in Hakata. Hideyoshi met the padre in good spirits and granted his request. The audience ended cordially.

On that night Hideyoshi drank heavily the wine Coelho presented to him. His drinking companion happened to be his physician and personal counselor named Seyakuin Zenso, a staunch anti-Christian

Buddhist. He told the regent that his attempts to recruit young women for Hideyoshi's pleasure were unsuccessful because of Christian influence. The refusal of these Christian women had to be recognized for what it was, he insisted, a sign of disloyalty to Hideyoshi himself. Seyakuin went on vilifying the Christians by listing many incidents of the demolition of Buddhist temples, and concluded that the Christians were none other than a subversive element in society which should be eliminated.

Seyakuin's venomous slander had a horrendous effect on the drunken Hideyoshi, who flew into a fury and decided to suppress Christianity. Despite the late hour of the night, he dispatched a messenger to Ukon Takayama, a leading Christian lord, demanding that he renounce his faith immediately or surrender his entire fief. Ukon faced the despot's order without flinching. Rejecting his advisors' plea that he just feign submission, he answered the messenger firmly that he would give up his fief. At this, the enraged regent took immediate action, and Ukon, taking nothing with him, went into exile in the territory of other Christian lords.

The second move of Hideyoshi on that night was as outrageous as the first. He sent messengers this time to Padre Coelho demanding his immediate reply to the following four questions:

1. Why do you missionaries so anxiously, even forcefully, try to make converts?
2. Why do you destroy Shinto shrines and Buddhist temples and persecute monks instead of being conciliatory to them?
3. Why do you do such unreasonable things as eat useful animals like horses and cows that serve people?
4. Why do the Portuguese buy many Japanese and take them to their country as slaves?

The regent's inquiry took the sleepy Coelho totally off guard, but the padre somehow managed to brace himself to respond to these accusing questions as well as he could:

1. We came here in order to save souls. We attempt our best to gain converts, but we have not forced anyone, and that is not our way.

2. The Japanese are free from us; we have no power over them. We, therefore, cannot force anyone to believe even if we want to do so. What drives the Japanese converts is the truth of the teachings they receive. Only for this reason do they become Christians. They realize that they cannot gain salvation through the teachings of Buddhism and Shintoism, and thus they themselves destroy their temples and build churches of Deus on the temple sites.

3. The Portuguese have never eaten horse meat. If the regent wishes them not to eat beef, it is easy for them to desist.

4. The Japanese slaves were sold by the Japanese. The padres greatly disapprove of it and have made serious attempts to forbid it, though to no avail. We believe that the regent can put an end to it with his powerful authority.

The Vice-provincial's desperate defense failed to appease Hideyoshi's wrath. On the following morning he became more violent in his verbal attack on the padres. According to Frois' letter of February 20, 1588, the regent repeatedly told his entourage that the padres had come to destroy the country by the use of shrewd and deceitful words. Many warriors and lords, he went on to say, had already been taken in by their specious talk. He, however, had uncovered their snare, and had he not, they would otherwise have rallied the converts to rise up in revolt against him. They were, therefore, even more pernicious and dangerous than the militant monks of the Ikko sect. He thus decided to order them to return to their country of origin within twenty days.

### (2) The edict

There are two extant copies of Hideyoshi's edict of expulsion of the padres. One consists of five statements, while the other has eleven. The latter may be summarized as follows. The first article declares that the Christian faith is a matter of individual decision, but the second article restricts the daimyos (lords) and samurais (warriors) from forcefully converting any farmers who are registered in Buddhist temples. The third article states further that should the daimyos and samurais impose their arbitrary demands on the farmers in favor of Christianity, they will be punished.

The fourth article demands that the daimyos and samurais whose fiefs are more than two hundred chos or three thousand kans request formal permission from the central authority, should they wish to become Christians. Others, apart from those already mentioned, the fifth article enjoins, may be free to choose their religion according to the decision of the head of the household.

The sixth, seventh, and eighth articles accuse the Christians of being more pernicious than the rebellious Ikko sect. The ninth article allows the freedom of choice of belief to those of the lower classes (i.e. farmers, artisans, and merchants). The tenth article prohibits the buying and selling of Japanese citizens inside and outside of the country. The eleventh article also forbids the commercial exchange of cows and horses for the purpose of slaughter and food.

This version of the edict was obviously addressed to the people of Japan, while the other version (which contains five articles) was directed to the Europeans who were in Japan. It agrees with the Portuguese translation provided by Frois. It runs as follows:

1. Japan is a country of gods (*shinkoku*). The promulgation of an evil teaching from a Christian country (i.e. Portugal) should never be allowed.
2. It is unprecedented in Japan's history that the padres convert the people to their religion and make them destroy Shinto shrines and Buddhist temples. When fiefs, residences, and stipends are given, it depends upon the recipient's observance of the law of the realm (*tenka*) and his attendance of the mind on all matters. Stirring up the rabble is unforgivable.
3. It is judged that the padres by their cunning teachings have gained supporters as they pleased, and thus violated the Buddhist law of Japan. This is intolerable. The padres should not be allowed to stay in the land of Japan. They must prepare to return to their own country within twenty days. Should anyone harm them during this period of time, he shall be subject to prosecution.
4. As for the black ship which comes for trade, this is a different matter. Trade may be carried on for many years to come.
5. Henceforward, those who do not violate the Buddhist law, not to

mention the merchants, may travel to and from the Christian country.

The above is to be carried out accordingly.

### IMPACT OF THE EDICT

The edict seriously impacted the Christians, both Europeans and Japanese, many of whom were forced to go underground. The Christian educational facilities were either closed or moved to remote areas. The padres finally assembled on February 11, 1589 at Takaku, Kyushu, to discuss how to cope with this critical situation. A suggestion was made that they ask for military support from the Philippines against Hideyoshi's regime. All of the padres, including Vice-provincial Coelho, agreed, but a lone dissenter was Organtino. This plan was, in fact, carried out; firearms and ammunition were acquired and stockpiled in Nagasaki. This move indicated how desperate the padres were at that time. Valignano, however, rebuked Coelho strongly and disposed of all of the military stock when he returned to Japan for his second visit in 1590.

The following portion of a letter written in the spring of 1588 by several leading Japanese Christians of the capital region and addressed to the Jesuit General, tells us eloquently of the troubled condition:

> In Miyako (Kyoto), the truth of this teaching (Christianity) had been promulgated and many daimyos had received baptism. While its roots were thus embedded deeply, the regent who rules Japan now has issued in the summer of 1587 the order to eradicate the teaching. Because of this, churches in many places have had to cease their activities suddenly, and all the padres and brothers have retreated to Hirado. . . .

> It is really tragic that since Gokinai (the capital area) is far from Hirado, the sheep who have been abandoned by the shepherd, wander here and there and will eventually become victims of vicious animals. Padre Organtino, who had been

the leader (of the Christians) in the Miyako region, has decided that it was not his desire to leave his sheep and move to Hirado with the other padres and brothers but to stay by himself in an isle to gather the scattered sheep together, give water to the thirsty, and warm those who are cold. He has been taking care of them in this manner until now. He is truly a pastor. In Kyushu as well, Padre Gaspar Coelho, the provincial of Japan, remains in hiding in remote mountains with all other padres and brothers. . . .

As stated above, for more than forty years since the departure of Master Francisco (Xavier), there has never been such a grave crisis as the one we have now, even though some disturbances have occurred from time to time. This man called regent is the most powerful man of the past five hundred years; he has gained control over the whole of Japan as he pleases, and the people fear him just as the grass bends before the wind. . . .

Harder tribulations may come, and even a time may visit us when we sow seeds of the blood of martyrdom in this country. Our spirits kindle when they are right, but when they are wrong, we are caught in deep fear. We beseech you to strengthen us with your compassion so that the churches which exist in different places of this country may flourish and the precious teachings may be spread for ever and ever. Amen.

As this heartrending letter indicates, the padres continued their pastoral work secretly instead of leaving the country as ordered, with the exception of three Jesuits who left for Macao for form's sake. Hideyoshi never attempted to ascertain whether or not all the padres had departed the country. Obviously, therefore, the edict was not strictly enforced. Not only that, but when Valignano returned to Japan for his second visit in 1590, though not as the Visitor but as the ambassador of the viceroy of Portuguese India, the regent received him warmly. Furthermore, Padre Dom Pedro Martins, who arrived in 1591 as bishop of Japan, was met with cordial greetings from him as well. Then in 1593, Hideyoshi gave the Spanish Franciscans permission to stay in the country. The Jesuits cautiously resumed their activities as well. Why then did Hideyoshi issue that edict in the first place?

### REASONS FOR THE EDICT

It is indeed difficult to explain why Hideyoshi had suddenly issued such a drastic edict. It was totally beyond comprehension, particularly on the part of the Christians. (Perhaps even Seyakuin himself was surprised, though happily so, to see what a strong effect his verbal instigation had on his boss!) Frois interpreted it to be due to Hideyoshi's drunken fury and not a premeditated plan (cf. his statements in the Jesuit Annual Report on January 22, 1588). There are, however, some indications which seem to point otherwise, as will be discussed below.

Avila Giron, a Spanish trader who stayed in Japan from 1594 to 1607 and wrote *Relacion del Reino de Nippon* (Accounts of the Kingdom of Japan), placed the blame for the whole problem on malicious intrigue on the part of the Buddhists against the padres who were "respected by the regent" and might have been able to convert him one day. He even stated that Hideyoshi was "like our father."

When Giron learned of the regent's death in 1598, "all of us were truly saddened. Except for mistreating the padres by confiscating their properties, he did no harm to us. He instead protected us and did not allow anyone to insult us. He even punished severely the Japanese who did so" (*ibid.*, chap. 10). Giron embraced a favorable view of Hideyoshi because of the latter's protection of trade with the Europeans. Many padres, however, called him a devilish tyrant because he opposed Christianity in favor of ideas which sounded blasphemous to them (which will be explained next).

### (1) Shinkoku ideology

Hideyoshi's issuance of the edict seemingly stemmed from reasons which were far more serious than simply a one-night drunken fury or some Buddhist slander. The first and perhaps most serious reason was a deep-seated suspicion in the mind of the regent that the padres' real intention might lie in the conquest of Japan. That which was underscored most emphatically in the edict is the point that Christianity was a totally alien religion which might undermine the very essence of the nation: "the country of gods (*shinkoku*)."

The "gods" of this epithet for the nation refers to the deities (*kami* or *shin*) of Shintoism. Shintoism is the native religion of Japan. It originated from ancient nature-worship, which gradually developed to represent the national life as its mythology expounded the birth of the country. From the sixth century A.D. when Confucianism was introduced to Japan, its original emphasis on ritualistic purity was reinforced with the Confucian notions of morality and filial piety, and then, from the eighth century onward, it was influenced by Buddhism.

These three religions were often highly syncretized particularly for the purpose of political legitimation. Hideyoshi was one of those political leaders who made use of such an intricately blended religious ideology to bolster his authority. The following statements from his diplomatic correspondence with the Portuguese viceroy in India and the Spanish governor of the Philippines cogently illustrate his view:

> Ours is the land of the kami, and kami is mind, and the one mind is all-encompassing. No phenomena exist outside it. Without kami, there would be no spirits or no Way. They transcend good times of growth and bad times of decline; they are yin and yang at the same time and cannot be measured. They are thus the root and source of all phenomena. They are in India under the name of Buddhism; they are in China under the name of Confucianism; they are in Japan where they go under the name Shinto. To know Shinto is to know Buddhism and Confucianism. (English translation cited in H. Ooms, *Early Tokugawa Ideology: Early Constructs, 1570–1680*, 1985, pp. 41f)

The idea expressed here is a characteristically Japanese form of pantheism. (The western concept of "pantheism" may not accurately describe the idea, however.) This *kami* (god) is not at all like the

Christian God who is the absolute and transcendent holy other, but rather is something like a consistent and all-pervasive creative power which resides and works throughout the ever-changing universe. Every existence in its very essence is, therefore, divine. The divine nature should be adored, in particular, in the benevolence and beauty of the natural world and also in the souls of ancestors. Life in accord with the way of kami is what one should pursue. Because of its universality, the shinkoku ideology claims, the way of kami is promulgated commonly by all three religions, with each retaining its own unique features.

A syncretism such as this, therefore, ignores the basic differences among these three religions. It is a self-serving nationalistic ideology through the use of these religions. Shintoism, above all, provides a convenient tool as it is indigenous to Japan, and also, because it originally had no structured doctrine, it has a pliable nature which can be used in support of the regime. The "ideology" of *shinkoku* (the country of gods) accommodates almost any religious, philosophical, and ethical notions as long as they can be amalgamated with itself; but if not, it refuses any intruders violently. Hideyoshi's edict exemplifies this.

Hideyoshi, who lacked any authoritative lineage, especially needed such an ideological assertion in order to legitimate his power. (He even claimed that he was a "son of the sun" because he was conceived in his mother's womb by the sun's rays, a power of *kami*.) He must have felt that Christianity would not be malleable enough to fit into the "shinkoku ideology." He was not at all an ideologue in any sense of the word nor even a religious man, but as a practical politician his judgment about Christianity as an intolerant religion led him to conclude that it should not be accepted, unlike Confucianism and Buddhism which also came from abroad yet had been conveniently Japanized.

Christianity, he feared, might even jeopardize the "shinkoku ideology" under his rule. It was, therefore, "a pernicious teaching," as he had called it in the first article of the edict. In the fifth article, moreover, he stated that "as far as those who did not disturb the Buddhist law" (which was an integral component of the shinkoku ideology), they were free to come and stay in the land. He, in fact, encouraged trade with the Europeans (cf. art. 4 and 5), but not the propagation of the Christian faith.

## (2) Suspicion of Jesuit political intention

Hideyoshi's denunciation of Christianity as a subversive religion was related to his suspicion of the Jesuits possessing some covert plan to topple his government and take over the whole country. The padres' attempt at evangelism was intended, in his judgment, to create a "fifth column" in Japan in order to achieve their aggressive colonial aim. The second article thus accuses the missionaries of "stirring up the rabble," and they "by their cunning teachings have gained supporters as they pleased, and thus violated the Buddhist law of Japan" (art. 3).

The aggressive colonization of, for example, the Philippines and Mexico by the Spaniards was already known in Japan. Hideyoshi had heard how the missionaries worked in cooperation with the army. There was, therefore, good enough reason why he became fearful of the padres' real intention. According to Padre Francisco Pasio, he was already quite suspicious of the Jesuits while he was still serving Nobunaga. The padre wrote in his letter of October 4, 1587: "In my judgment and also according to what the Japanese are saying, Hideyoshi believes that the padres did not come to Japan because of their spiritual zeal but out of the desire for conquest and rule. That is why he issued the edict of persecution. He once shared this view with Nobunaga; but Nobunaga, because he had a better understanding of the matter, answered him that it would be impossible to bring from a far-distant country a large enough army to carry out a campaign (against Japan)."

Not only Pasio but also some other padres who knew Hideyoshi personally appear to have sensed his concern. Padre Organtino, who adapted himself most effectively to Japanese society and worked many years in central Japan, attempted to switch the topic of conversation during a visit with Hideyoshi at his new castle in Osaka in 1586. This happened when Coelho, anxious to please the regent, offered to provide Portuguese armed ships for Hideyoshi's planned invasion of Korea. Coelho also told him that he would call upon the Christian lords to join in the campaign. Organtino knew too well that such an offer would most likely backfire. Ukon Takayama, who was also present at the time, reportedly tried as well to halt the subject from continuing any further. Valignano later admitted that Coelho caused the regent's suspicion to increase because of this incident.

On another occasion, Coelho appears to have made a similar error. Both Pasio (in his letter of October 4, 1587) and Valignano (in his report to the General of October 14, 1590) mentioned that Coelho visited Hideyoshi at Hakata in a Portuguese ship armed with several cannons. The Vice-provincial proudly told the regent who inspected the vessel thoroughly that it was a strong warship. Worried about any negative psychological effect which Coelho's move might have had on the regent, Yukinaga Konishi, a Christian lord, urged Coelho to donate the ship to Hideyosi. The padre, however, neither listened to the suggestion nor even understood Konishi's concern. Through these events, Pasio wrote, Coelho certainly aroused the regent's suspicion and jealousy toward the padres.

Valignano became aware of the Japanese misgivings of European expansionism during his first visit to Japan. Consequently, when Sumitada Omura offered the town of Nagasaki to the Jesuits, he first declined, partly because of his worry of possible misunderstanding by the Japanese. He was always careful to make sure that the Japanese knew that the Jesuit mission concerned purely spiritual matters and had not the slightest interest in political or military affairs. Nevertheless, he was obliged to accept Omura's offer a year after his initial hesitation. He also once helped another Christian lord, Arima, by providing weapons and funds.

Were there any other traces of evidence of Europeans attempting to ultilize military forces against Japan? As mentioned above, Vice-provincial Coelho was one of the padres who would not recoil from resorting to a use of force. As early as 1584 he appealed to the Spaniards in the Philippines to send troops to "support the Christians of Japan who were pressed by the heathens." Coelho's entreaty later reached even the Portuguese king. The Jesuit padre Alonso Sanchez shared Coelho's ideas. (The former mission superior, Cabral, also rendered strong support to Sanchez.) He wrote to the king from Madrid, Spain in 1587, referring to the two-year-old request (evidently that of Coelho) to send four galleons loaded with soldiers, guns, and food to Japan, and observed that if they would help the Christians in Japan who were guided by the padres, the king could then enter the land. Sanchez's proposal did not materialize, however.

When the padres encountered Hideyoshi's edict of expulsion,

Coelho, Frois, and others, despite the opposition of Organtino, schemed secretly to fortify Nagasaki intending to fight the despot. They sent messengers to the Philippines and Portuguese India asking for military enforcement.

This move, however, infuriated Valignano who was in Goa, India at that time. He rebuked Coelho in the strongest terms, calling the whole plan "dangerous and temerarious fancy" (cf. his letter of June 11, 1589 and of April 25, 1585, both from Goa). As soon as he returned to Japan in 1590, he liquidated all the military supplies accumulated by Coelho in Nagasaki and declared categorically to the Christians who were "frightened and agitated" by the Vice-provincial's measure that such action was strictly "against the order and direction of the Jesuit Society" (cf. his letter to the General on October 12, 1590 from Nagasaki). (It is wrong, however, to consider Valignano to be completely a pacifist. As mentioned earlier, he sent his military aide to Arima. In 1580 he, in fact, had thought of fortifying Nagasaki, though the plan was never carried out.)

The military adventurism was harbored not only by some of the Jesuits but also the missionaries of other orders. An example is afforded by the Franciscan friars in the Philippines. According to the Jesuit padre Luis Guzman, the Franciscans accused the Jesuits of owning a harbor (Nagasaki) and villages of that vicinity despite the fact that the lands should have rightly belonged to the Spanish king. If they were truly willing to prove themselves loyal subjects to the king, the friars insisted, they could easily make him the ruler of Japan, because numerous Christians there loved and respected the padres. They, therefore, could organize 30,000 fighters by recruiting the Christians in the region of Nagasaki alone. Once these men were trained in the Spanish military style, they and the Spaniards could conquer the whole country. The "king of Bungo" (referring to Yoshishige Otomo) and Don Augustin (Yukinaga Konishi) would help in this venture with all their power (cf. the last chapter of Guzman's history of the Jesuit missions in the east: *Historia de la Missiones de la Compañia de Jesús en la India Oriental, en la China y Japón desde 1540 hasta 1600*, Bilbao, 1891).

Against the Franciscans' censure, Guzman presented a strong rebuttal, pointing out that such an accusation came only from sheer ignorance about the real situation in Japan. It was total nonsense, he stated, to think that they could subjugate the Japanese who were well experienced in warfare. The Jesuits in Japan were so poor and helpless that they could hardly do anything of the sort the Franciscans were fancying.

From the foregoing observation, it is clear that the Jesuit policy in Japan embraced no intention of utilizing military force for their advantage. There were some exceptions to this, such as in the case of Coelho and others, but even to these this was simply a last resort out of desperation when faced with the edict of expulsion.

If Hideyoshi indeed had any fear about European aggression, it was therefore unwarranted. Most likely he did not seriously think that the Europeans would actually wage a wholesale war against his country, because he was confident (in fact, overconfident enough to invade Korea) about his military capability. However, his misgivings about the possibility that the padres would stir up the Christians against him were seemingly very real; as his inquiry to Coelho indicated, he was indeed concerned that the Christians might instigate another religious uprising like that of the Ikko sect with which he had had to engage in a long and bloody battle. Coelho, though well meaning, did unfortunately deepen the regent's suspicion.

### (3) Destruction of temples and shrines by the Christians

The second article of the edict specifically accuses the padres of instigating their followers to demolish Buddhist temples and Shinto shrines. This was also one of the questions which Hideyoshi demanded that Coelho answer on the night of July 24, 1587. Coelho insisted on the padres' complete innocence. He was, however, incorrect. Many padres encouraged and praised the Japanese Christians' violent actions against the idols and buildings of "the teachings of devils." Christian lords such as Otomo, Arima, Omura, and Takayama, among others, ordered the systematic demolition of the temples and shrines in their territories. A large number of Buddhists were exiled as well. This policy, in fact, created a considerable amount of social unrest, which proved to be one of the major reasons for the downfall of the first three of the aforementioned clans.

The very reason why Hideyoshi raised this matter as a part of his censure of the Christians was, precisely speaking, not really because he was a devout follower of Buddhism or Shintoism, but because he felt repulsed by the aggressive and intolerant nature of the Christian actions against the other religions which, in his view, could jeopardize the political unity of the nation he was anxiously creating. He stated in the second article of the edict that the lords were only temporarily entrusted with their fiefs conditioned upon their observance of "the law of the realm (*tenka*)." They, therefore, had no absolute and permanent right to do arbitrarily whatever they wished in their domain. To destroy temples and shrines, even if they were located in their own territories, was an action offensive to Hideyoshi's authority and to the nation as a whole.

*Tenka* means literally "all under heaven." It was often used throughout Japan's history to refer specifically to the land of Japan, though it could also allude to areas transcending the national borders, as was used in Hideyoshi's statement. "Heaven" stemmed from Confucian terminology indicating the ultimate principle of morality and order which was to be revealed through natural and social phenomena. The notion was Japanized and became a symbol for the supreme reality or power which combined the Confucian "heaven," Buddha, and the Shinto deities.

During the trouble-filled period of this civil strife, "heaven" was often conceived in a highly theistic (or even, in a broad sense, monotheistic) way. In some of the Christian literature written in this period, *ten* (heaven) or *tendo* (the way of heaven) was used to indicate the Christian God. (As mentioned in the first chapter, however, the padres came to realize the essential difference between *ten* or *tendo* and God, and they started using the Latin word Deus exclusively when referring to the Christian God.)

A person, according to this idea, became the ruler of the land by taking control over *tenka*. A good ruler was one who was able to put the mandate of heaven into practice effectively as he governed. An autocrat like Hideyoshi claimed that he was such a ruler. He therefore even called himself *tenka*. In the second article of the edict, in accusing the padres of instigating the demolition of the temples, he was, in effect, denouncing them for violation against the mandate of heaven which he was enforcing. Here we see that the concept of *tendo* was connected to the nationalistic ideology of *shinkoku* and used to legitimate Hideyoshi's authority.

Putting it very simply, Hideyoshi insisted that the padres were disturbing his rule—the execution of a heavenly mandate. This was the reason why the second question he directed to Coelho asked why the padres were not "conciliatory" toward the Shintoists and the Buddhists. The harmony of all under his rule was, he demanded, the will of heaven. From his point of view, therefore, the violent Christian opposition to the other religions was a disruption of the universal order, which consequently was bound to fail—a suicidal act on the part of the Christians themselves.

### HIDEYOSHI'S ERRATIC POLICY

We have thus far examined the several possible reasons for Hideyoshi's sudden order expelling the padres. These reasons, however, still fail to explain the timing. Evidence, though not overwhelming, points to the fact that this action came out of Hideyoshi's growing suspicion and displeasure as to the intolerant nature of Christianity rather than as the result of drunken fury. The intoxication and Seyakuin's instigation served simply as the trigger for him to release his cumulative feelings of irritation.

The edict was issued shortly after his successful campaign against Shimazu, which established his hegemony over the entirety of Kyushu. During his stay on this island, he found Christianity thriving, which seems to have caused him to feel it necessary to send the Christians warnings stiff enough to make them totally submissive to his rule. (It was his desire to make use of all religions to his advantage. He, following Nobunaga, fought to suppress the militant Buddhists, but once they showed complete obedience to him, he allowed and even helped to restore their temples and monasteries. He demanded the same from the Christians—they were to serve his authority in union with the other religious groups.) Ukon Takayama and the padres were victimized as a part of that "lesson." This edict, though not revoked, was nevertheless not really carried out either; and although a few Jesuits did leave as the community felt threatened, Hideyoshi never pursued the policy strictly.

As a matter of fact, when Valignano returned to Japan with the four young envoys to Europe, Hideyoshi met them in good spirits. The padre was careful not to use his title as the Visitor of the Jesuit Society but rather to call himself the official ambassador of the viceroy of Portuguese India. He presented a formal letter of good will from the viceroy, which was courteously accepted by the regent. The repeal of the edict expelling the padres was of course Valignano's ultimate aim as he met with Hideyoshi, which unfortunately he was not able to accomplish. The autocrat remained adamant on that issue.

The four Japanese youths, appearing in the clothes of black velvet and gold trim which Pope Gregory XIII had provided them, related to the regent their experiences. They sang the songs they had learned in Europe and played the musical instruments they had acquired there. Hideyoshi was so pleased with all of these presentations that he reportedly asked the youths if they would like to become his retainers. They, however, cordially declined his offer because of their religious vocation.

In writing a reply to the Portuguese viceroy, Hideyoshi initially insisted again on the prohibition of any padres' entry into the country; but at the suggestion of the interpreter João Rodriguez of the usefulness of the padres' presence for trade with the Portuguese, he decided to overlook this small number of the padres in Kyushu.

Valignano, after his friendly interview with Hideyoshi, evidently felt relieved, but yet was cautious not to stir up the situation in the capital area and went back to Kyushu to regroup the threatened mission. For this visit (which had been his second trip to Japan), he brought with him a printing machine, which enabled the Jesuits to publish many valuable books. Valignano left Nagasaki for Macao with Frois on October 2, 1592.

### ARRIVAL OF THE FRIARS

Hideyoshi's erratic conduct continued. Despite the edict, he not only did not expel all the Jesuits, but he even warmly accepted the Franciscans, who began their missionary work in Japan in the 1590s. How then did the despot deal with this new tide of European missionaries? Let us see first how this fresh wave rolled on to Japan and what kind of problems it brought.

The first Franciscan to come to Japan was Juan Pobre, a Spanish mendicant. On his journey from Macao to Manila, he stopped and stayed in Hirado for several months. During this short period of time, according to a report, he impressed the local Christians with his piety and honorable poverty so much so that they urged him to remain there the rest of his life. But instead he left for his original destination. Two years later, he did return to Hirado with three other mendicants: Franciscan Diego Bernal and two Augustinians, Francisco Manrique and Anri Bernal.

According to Diego Bernal's letter of October 7, 1584, the lord of Hirado, Matsuura, took pleasure in seeing a new brand of missionary and offered to build them a church. However, the real intention of Matsuura was hardly a religious one; his purpose was to reopen trade with the Europeans at his port of Hirado. Since he resented the Jesuits who caused him financial loss when they moved to the territory of his rival neighbors such as Arima and Omura, he saw a royal opportunity both to restore commercial ventures as well as to have revenge on the Jesuits. To promote this plan, he even wrote a letter to the Spanish governor in the Philippines, urging him to send merchants as well as friars to his domain. This, needless to say, greatly encouraged the friars who had been looking for a way to develop their mission in Japan.

### JESUIT CLAIM OF MONOPOLY OF THE JAPAN MISSION

The Franciscans' move to Japan did not please Valignano. As we have already mentioned in the previous chapter, after having consulted with his colleagues during his first visit, he confirmed the policy of the exclusively Jesuit mission in Japan. He reiterated the same contention in chapter nine of the report of his first visit to Japan (*Sumario de las cosas que partenecen a la Provincia de Japon*, 1583). There were seven points:

1. The Christian mission should present itself as a perfectly unified force (as the Jesuits have been doing) particularly in Japan where there are many different religious sects (which is a source of the people's resentment).
2. The teaching and practices of Christianity should be introduced to

the Japanese without causing any possible confusion. The Spanish friars might create this.

3. Any possible disharmony and accusations between different orders (as had happened in India, for instance) should be avoided.

4. The Jesuits have learned through years of experience the nature and customs of the Japanese which are quite different from those of the Europeans. The arrival of the inexperienced friars will likely hurt what is being done by the Jesuits.

5. One missionary society will suffice in training native clergy. Japan is the type of nation which cannot be ruled by any foreign countries, and Christianity in Japan should be eventually in the hands of the native people themselves.

6. The scarcity of financial resources cannot afford missionary activities by many orders.

7. An increase of missionary orders in Japan may worsen the suspicion which many feudal lords already have about the missionaries' political intention.

As clearly seen in these points of assertion, what was operative in the mind of Valignano and the rest of the Jesuit missionaries in Japan was the pride and conviction that none other than they were the founders and experts of Christian mission in Japan with the legitimate authorization by the Holy See. (Some Portuguese Jesuits like Coelho and the Spanish Jesuits were willing to allow the friars to work in Japan, however. The Italian Jesuits such as Valignano and Organtino were strong advocates of the Jesuit monopoly, though they had no national prejudices against the Spaniards.)

There was, as a matter of fact, good reason why they felt so. It was the era of so-called geographical discovery. A new world was just opened for the Europeans to explore which prompted fierce competition among them. In order to settle the conflicts over lands reconnoitered by Christopher Columbus and other voyagers of the late fifteenth century, Spain and Portugal, at Pope Alexander VI's decision, concluded the Treaty of Tordesillas in 1494. This agreement involved a demarcation of two halves of the eastern hemisphere, drawing a line from pole to pole at 370 leagues (one league was approximately three miles) west of the Cape Verde Islands. Portugal was given exclusive rights to the whole area east of the line and Spain to its west.

The Portuguese advanced southward along the west coast of Africa, went around its southern tip (the Cape of Good Hope), and reached India and East Asia. The Spaniards, by contrast, took a westward route, conquered the central and south Americas by going across the Atlantic Ocean, and finally arrived at the Philippines by way of the Pacific Ocean in the latter half of the sixteenth century. As far as Japan was concerned, the Portuguese believed that it was a part of the world which they discovered first and therefore legally belonged to their territory.

This was not only a political arrangement but also a religious matter, since the pope authorized and entrusted these two Iberian countries with rights and duties to carry out missionary activities as well as political and economic affairs of the newly discovered areas. The king was to ask the church for its blessing for his overseas ventures. Missionaries were, on their part, in need of permission from the king to engage in the evangelism in the new world.

For the Jesuit padres, Japan was exclusively their own mission land since the time of Xavier. The diocese of Macao, which included China, Japan, Macao and its neighboring areas, was formally recognized by the Vatican in 1576. It was administered by the Jesuits under the authority of the king of Portugal.

### THE COMMENCEMENT OF THE FRIARS' JAPAN MISSION

What about the Spanish side of the new world? The Spanish friars became very active in the Philippines during the 1580s. Their numbers increased considerably; there were Franciscans, Dominicans, and Augustinians, all of whom belonged to the mendicant orders. Their missionary zeal quickened them to envision the expansion of their work to Japan and China. This was the exact reason why Valignano voiced a strong defense of the Jesuit monopoly of the mission in these countries. Pope Gregory XIII listened to the Visitor's appeal and in 1585 issued a brief prohibiting missionaries other than Jesuits from engaging in the propagation of Christianity in Japan. In the following year the viceroy of Portuguese India, Don Duarte de Menzes, also gave an order of the same tenet in the name of King Felipe II.

In those days both Spain and Portugal were ruled by the Spanish king, Felipe II (1527–1598). (The Spanish annexation of Portugal took place in 1580 and lasted until 1640.) But as far as their colonies were concerned, they were administered separately as before the unification of the two countries, i.e. the Spanish colonies by the Spaniards and the Portuguese by the Portuguese. An ugly rivalry ensued between these two colonial powers. Felipe II, in accordance with the agreement at the time of the unification, kept intact the exclusive ministry of the Jesuits in the areas under the control of the Portuguese.

This official policy, however, did not deter the eager Spanish friars in the Philippines from attempting to develop their mission fields. They campaigned hard aiming at the repeal of the papal brief which they claimed to be a product of malicious intrigue by the Jesuits. Their criticism of the Jesuits involved their policy in general, their operation of silk trade, and their life-style itself. As noted in the previous chapter, Valignano's endeavor of sending the Japanese youths as envoys to Europe resulted in a severe denunciation of the Jesuits as well. Hideyoshi's edict of the Jesuit expulsion, in their view, resulted from the Jesuits' own errors.

All of these attempts, however, yielded no decisive results favorable to the Spanish friars. They thus decided to defy the official policy by sending missionaries to Japan even at the risk of the penalty of excommunication. This defiance took place in 1592, before which time, as referred to earlier, only a few of them visited there temporarily.

The friars' systematic entry to Japan was preceded by the commercial adventure of a Japanese tradesman by the name of Kiemon Harada. He advised Hideyoshi to dispatch an envoy to the Spanish governor of the Philippines, demanding the submission of the colony to Japan. The suggestion pleased the megalomaniacal taste of the regent so much that he immediately prepared an insolent letter, which Kiemon's nephew was ordered to carry to Manila. But the Haradas had a crafty scheme; instead of submitting Hideyoshi's letter, they told the governor that the real intention of the regent was the establishment of a peaceful and mutually profitable commercial relationship between the

Philippines and Japan. The friars' participation in this venture, they added, would be quite helpful.

In response, the governor sent the Dominican friar, Juan Cobo, to Japan with a cordial reply stating simply his interest in a friendly relationship with Japan. Cobo appears to have been warmly received by Hideyoshi, who sent him back with another letter to the Philippine governor. Cobo and the letter did not reach their destination, however, because of an unfortunate shipwreck near Taiwan.

Pursuing further the deceitful middleman venture, Kiemon Harada volunteered himself as an emissary this time. Hideyoshi entrusted him with another letter to the governor with the same message as the previous ones. Though politely welcoming the messenger, the Spanish official had already realized the true objectives of the Japanese despot. He was not ready either to submit himself to the Japanese or to fight off the arrogant demands. His letter to Felipe II of June 22, 1593 explained that his noncommittal way of dealing with the Japanese was contrived in order to buy time so that he could strengthen the fortification of Manila against a possible Japanese attack.

The governor returned Harada to his country with four Franciscan delegates: Pedro Bautista, Bartolomeo Ruiz, Francisco de San Miguel, and Gonçalo Garcia. Hideyoshi met them graciously, apparently because he took the Spaniard gesture as a sign of compliance with his will. He gave them permission to live in Japan officially as hostages but actually as free residents. This whole move by the regent was motivated by his anticipation of financial benefit from trade with the Spanish Philippines. It would also give the Portuguese in Japan competition, which would in turn provide him with the opportunity to exploit both of them. He was in need of money for his costly invasion of Korea.

The Franciscans, delighted with the strong man's friendly gesture toward them, commenced their religious task openly and soon built a church and monastery in Kyoto. The Jesuits, who were continuing their work quietly in Kyushu, advised them toward moderation, which was taken by the friars as a sign of cowardice. Their fearless efforts did indeed bear fruit; a lot of the local Christians who had been without pastors flocked to them.

### CONFLICT BETWEEN THE JESUITS AND THE FRIARS

The friars' approach was just the reverse of that of the Jesuits: the former placed their priority on the unprivileged class of the population, while the latter attempted to work from the upper class downward, as we have referred to earlier. The friars' constant model of practicing poverty was inspiring; they always wore their shabby habits and their feet were bare. They tended the sick and beggars. It was reported, for instance, that Pedro Bautista kissed lepers on their pus-covered sores. Profoundly impressed by all these meritorious acts of the friars, many local people were willing to enter the same faith and pledged their lifelong loyalty to them. Hospitals were opened in Kyoto and then in Osaka.

Friar Jeronimo de Jesus, who joined Bautista and others in 1593, wrote later as follows:

> It seems that God had revealed to comisario (Bautista), because he was always sensible and careful, that as far as the way to preach the teachings of the divine gospel in Japan, we should take the way opposite to the way of the Jesuit padres in order to move forward along a correct path. The Jesuits have sought after those who stood above, because once the head is caught, then his followers will be caught as well. As it has been proved through experience, however, once the head is lost, then his followers will be lost as well. We know that the Christians in Bungo and Takatuski of Justo (Ukon Takayama) have been lost after their lords died or were expelled.

> Our comisario sought after the poor and brought joy to them in accordance with the words of our Lord Christ who was sent to preach the gospel to the poor (Luke 4:18), as the God of heaven has sent us to preach to the poor. The Jesuits have huge commercial deals and merchandise while the barefoot friars live without money; the Jesuits go out riding on palanquins carried by men's shoulders while the friars walk without shoes; they ride on fine horses followed by retainers armed with swords and spears while [we] walk on foot wear-

ing rags—all this [contrast] has caused serious questioning among the Japanese. And the primary question concerns whether or not each one of us possesses one and the same God and seeks after the one and the same happiness.

The differences between these two orders were thus quite obvious in many ways. In sum, the Jesuits were more cautious and adaptational, while the friars were purist in their mission policy. Their purist position differed from the imposing and confrontational stance as represented by Cabral by its essential humility and friendliness toward the local people and culture, but it was similar to it in the sense that it tenaciously adhered to and insisted on its own beliefs and practices.

From the point of view of the Christian mission, it would have been greatly beneficial if the different orders worked in complementary fashion; it was indeed unfortunate that there was such grave animosity among the missionaries, particularly when they were in such a precarious situation under the rule of a despot like Hideyoshi. Concerted efforts on their part would have certainly lessened their trouble, though it is possible that even their best possible endeavor would not have altered Hideyoshi's adamant mind.

At any rate, the friars' presence in Japan was now a *fait accompli*. In 1586 the newly elected pope, Sixtus V, who was from the order of the Friars Minor, issued a bull authorizing the mendicants' work in East Asia, which was interpreted by the friars as a repeal of the prohibition declared by Gregory XIII. Then in 1600, Pope Clement VIII, yielding to the pressure from Felipe III, permitted all orders to engage in their activities in East Asia on the condition that they go under the Portuguese flag and by way of Goa, but these conditions were largely ignored. In the face of such daring toil by the friars, however, a tragic event happened.

### CONFISCATION OF THE CARGO OF THE SAN FELIPE

The drama of this rueful incident began with a Spanish ship called the San Felipe laden with valuable cargo including silver and gold. It set sail at Manila for Acapulco in July 1596. Set adrift by a violent storm, it was cast away on the shore of Tosa, Shikoku, the fief of

Motochika Chosokabe. The extant testimonies concerning what ensued vary; the sources originating from the Franciscan side are at odds
with those of the Jesuits. Information from the Japanese side is unfortunately indecisive.

### (1) The Franciscan view

Let us listen first to what the Franciscan camp had to say. According to Friar Juan Pobre who was aboard the San Felipe, this is what
happened next (cf. his testimony cited in C.R. Boxer, *The Christian
Century in Japan*, pp. 420–424). Lord Chosokabe, upon receiving the
news, immediately examined the ship and sent a report to Hideyoshi's
government. He apparently suggested to the captain of the ship that he
send an envoy to Kyoto with a gift so as to gain favorable treatment
from the government. Thus three friars who were on board went to
Kyoto to negotiate directly with Hideyoshi but failed even to obtain the
opportunity to have an audience with the regent.

Bautista, therefore, sent Br. Gonçalo and João Rodriguez with a
gift of one hundred pesos to Genni Maeda, the commissioner of the
city of Kyoto, anxiously hoping that Maeda could do something to help
the Spaniards in Tosa. The commissioner did write a letter on their
behalf to Nagamori Masuda, Hideyoshi's special commissioner of investigation. But almost ten days before the letter reached Tosa, the
regent had already ordered confiscation of the cargo.

As instructed in Maeda's letter, Masuda told the Spaniards of the
ship that they would not be harmed because they were neither pirates
nor spies, though some Jesuits and Portuguese merchants had so informed the regent. In return for this favor, he demanded gold, despite
the fact that they had already given him gold and silver amounting to
about 30,000 pesos. Nonetheless, ten days later Masuda took the goods
anyway.

Masuda then summoned the pilot of the ship and asked him how
the ship came to Japan. To answer the question, the pilot showed him a
chart, which astonished the Japanese official because it depicted his
country as "smaller than a thumb," compared to all the other immense
lands and seas which belonged to the Catholic king. The next question
Masuda asked concerned the purpose of the padres' presence on the

ship. The pilot's reply was that it was twofold: first to heed the religious needs of the crew and second to gain converts in the lands they visited.

Masuda's third question was about the Spanish king. He insisted that the Portuguese had told Hideyoshi of two sovereigns, Spanish and Portuguese. To this, the ensign by the name of Cotelo firmly answered that both countries were under the power of one ruler, the Spanish king.

According to Pobre who was the affiant of this testimonial story, "he (the ensign) further suggested that he and some other Spaniards should be sent for an investigation into the truth of the matter before the Emperor (meaning Hideyoshi), and that if they could not prove that they were right, they should all be killed as pirates, since this was what they were accused of being with the design of spying out Taikosama's (Hideyoshi's) ports—whilst on the other hand, if the Portuguese and the Jesuit padres were proved to be liars, that they should suffer the death penalty as perjurers." In response, Pobre went on to state, Masuda said to him, "Whether you lie or whether the Portuguese and the padres lie, nobody will be killed for it, since although you ask me to kill them, yet they did not ask Taikosama (regent) to kill you, but only to confiscate your cargo and send you away."

From Pobre's affidavit, it is clear that the Spaniards and the friars placed the blame for Hideyoshi's maltreatment of them squarely on the malicious slander by the Jesuits and the Portuguese in an attempt to drive them out of Japan and also on the corruption (double crossing and solicitation of bribes) on the part of Masuda and Chosokabe. (Giron also mentioned Masuda's deceptive maneuver in order to obtain the cargo.)

## (2) The Jesuits' view

What then do sources other than those of the friars have to say about this event? We have an affidavit of Rui Mendes de Figueiredo, captain-major of the ship which brought Bishop Dom Pedro Martins and another six padres to Japan a little more than two months before the San Felipe was stranded in Tosa (cf. Boxer, *ibid.*, pp. 415–418). According to this captain, Chosokabe "did not allow any of the cargo to be touched until he had given news of the event to Taikosama." The captain of the San Felipe thereupon sent some men to the friars in Kyoto in order to negotiate with Hideyoshi. Although Bishop Martins offered help, the friars declined it.

"The friars did not negotiate properly," Figueiredo continued to testify, "and covetousness gradually took hold of Taikosama, together with some distrust he already had because the pilot-major of the same ship had said something very thoughtless to one of Taikosama's governors whom he had sent there concerning the conquests of the Castilians (Spaniards) and their method of proceeding therein, adding that they sent religious ahead to make Christian converts who afterwards joined with the invading Castilian forces. He therefore ordered all the ship's cargo to be confiscated, which was done even to the very clothes which the men wore.

"When the said governor (Masuda) returned from Tosa to Kyoto and gave Taikosama an account of what the pilot had said about the conquests and the sending of religious abroad, the friars were likewise accused of having been sent for this purpose and of having built a church in Kyoto against his edict, and of preaching and converting Christians publicly—Taikosama at once said that they should all be killed. . . . He finally ordered the crucifixion of six friars, and three Japanese brothers of the Company (the Jesuits) along with them, besides another seven Japanese Christians."

Mendes de Figueiredo's report indicated several serious errors on the part of the friars and the pilot of the ship which brought disaster— the execution of eventually in all twenty-six Christians. These mistakes included the refusal of aid from the more experienced Jesuits, a misunderstanding of the affair, and the pilot's thoughtless blabber of the Spanish plan for aggression with the cooperation of the missionaries. (Pobre admitted that the pilot was "a little careless" and "thoughtless," but tried to defend him by saying that "he was not to blame . . . because he was well-intentioned.")

The Jesuit padres, as expected, insisted on their total innocence in the whole affair. Bishop Martins, for example, stated categorically in his letter to the king (dated November 17, 1597) that it was "a big lie" that the Portuguese had caused the confiscation of the ship and its cargo, that they had denied the Spanish king, and that they had spread the rumor that the Spaniards had come to conquer Japan. The Portuguese could not have done any of those things, Bishop contended, because none of the Portuguese were in Kyoto when the San Felipe reached Tosa.

Lack of objective evidence hinders us from reconstructing exactly what happened. But as many modern researchers acknowledge, there is no historical source which can substantiate the possible slander of the Jesuits against the Spaniards and the friars, nor is there irrefutable evidence to suggest greed or improprieties on the part of the Japanese officials serious enough to bring such disastrous results.

### (3) The pilot's blabber

The available sources indicate, as we have observed in the testimonies of Pobre and Mendes de Figueiredo, that the conversation between Masuda and the pilot (ensign?) of the ship played a vital role—a major factor in damage to the cause of the friars and the Spaniards. It seems very probable that the Spaniards of the ship did boast of the military might of their country out of vengeful fury when faced with a confiscation of their gold and expensive merchandise. (Incidentally, Frois noted in his report to Rome dated March 15, 1597 that it was a traditional Japanese custom for a lord to claim any ships which might stray into their area along with its cargo. This information was inaccurate, however. It was Hideyoshi's policy to defend the shipowner's rights.)

In fact, Hideyoshi's order for the execution of the twenty-six Chistians was issued just about a week after Masuda made an official report to the regent concerning what he had discovered in Tosa. Unfortunately it is beyond our reach to verify the content of Masuda's affidavit. But it seems most likely that Masuda recounted what the pilot had told him (or what he thought the pilot had told him) which included the Spanish (and the friars') colonial intention.

The fact that the pilot (and perhaps some others on the ship also) made some seriously offensive remarks to the official investigator is confirmed by the sworn statements made by several crew members of the San Felipe. The navigation officer, Juan Lorenço de Silva, is recorded to have said, for example, when asked how Spain obtained Peru, Mexico, and the Philippines: "A Spaniard at present answered that the king sent first the monks of all orders to propagate the holy gospel, and when the people of these countries converted, the Spaniards advanced to take over the countries. That is how they were conquered." The testimonies to the same effect were also made by some other crew members.

The concern about possible Spanish aggression against Japan seems to have been real in Hideyoshi's mind. It is manifested in his own statement. In August 1597, when the Spanish governor of the Philippines sent him a special envoy requesting the return of the confiscated goods and the bodies of the martyrs, Hideyoshi wrote a reply in which, immediately after brief introductory remarks, he underscored first the "shinkoku ideology." He then insisted that the padres' propagation of "the teachings of foreign devils" jeopardized the shinkoku, which prompted him to forbid this religion, but the missionaries from the Philippines, instead of returning to their countries, continued preaching to poor serfs. Therefore, he, Hideyoshi maintained, was forced to execute them.

"It was done," he stated, "because I learned that the promulgation of this religion was a part of the scheme of your country to conquer other nations. If some Japanese preachers and laymen come from Japan to your country, preach the teaching of Shinto, and create disorders by leading your people astray, are you as the ruler pleased with it? You would not be. So, can you blame me for that?" Hideyoshi went on to explain that the confiscation of the ship was done because the Spaniards violated the law of his country; nonetheless he was ready to return the goods. Commercial trade, he added, would be welcome as long as no "false preaching" was done.

The letter closed with his thanks for the gift of a black elephant (which was tremendously appreciated by him), mention of his return gift to the Spanish governor, and an assurance of the safe return of the crew members of the ship.

This letter was written in the summer of 1597, just about a year before Hideyoshi died. His invasion of Korea was then running into a serious quagmire after an initial triumph. (Some of his generals, such as Yukinaga Konishi and Mitsunari Ishida, were secretly attempting to negotiate a truce with the Koreans and the Chinese.) The regent was in deep anxiety for his own declining health and the future of his infant heir (who was then only four years of age). To make his emotional instability worse, a terrible earthquake hit the country in the summer of 1596, causing extensive damage in many areas. Hideyoshi himself, in fact, barely survived the disaster. Hence the orders which the frightened dying despot issued in the midst of such turmoil were senseless and cruel, and the twenty-six Christians became victims.

### THE TWENTY-SIX MARTYRS

On December 11, 1596 Hideyoshi ordered the execution of all the Franciscans in Japan. His troops immediately surrounded the Franciscan residence in Kyoto and arrested Bautista and other missionaries as well as their Japanese followers, totaling about one hundred and sixty. (Some of them were arrested in Osaka. Giron reported that when Hideyoshi's order was publicized, approximately three thousand Christians stepped forward to identify themselves as Christians.)

Mitsunari Ishida, commissioner of Sakai and close aide of the regent, felt the number of persons was too high and cut it down to forty-seven. He then eliminated further about half of them thereby making the final number twenty-four. He did this without getting his sovereign's approval because of his sympathy toward the Christians. (He was a close friend of the Christian lords such as Yukinaga Konishi and Ukon Takayama. Because of their influence, he himself almost became a Christian.)

The twenty-four executed included the following:

† six European Franciscans
—three padres (Pedro Bautista, Martin de la Ascencion, Francisco Blanco),
—three brothers (Francisco de la Parrilla, Gonçalo Garcia, Felipe de Jesus),
† eighteen Japanese
—a Jesuit brother (Paulo Miki),
—two Jesuit dojukus—João Goto, Diego Kisai,
—fifteen lay followers of the Franciscans (Paulo Suzuki, Gabriel [dojuku], Juan Kinuya [silk merchant], Tome Ise ["preacher"], Francisco Kusushi [pharmacist], Tome Kozaki [dojuku], Joachim

Sakakibara, Ventura [dojuku], Leon Karasumaru, Mathias, Antonio [dojuku], Luis [dojuku], Pablo Ibaragi, Miguel Kozaki, Cosme Takeya [bamboo merchant]).

The background of most of these prisoners is unknown, and even the full names of some of them are unclear. Evidently all the Japanese prisoners were rather poor commoners. It is possible that the three Japanese Jesuits were included by mistake. There were young boys: Tome Kozaki (fourteen years old), Antonio (thirteen years old), and Luis (twelve years old). On December 31 they were thrown into jail in Kyoto.

On January 3 of the following year, after a part of the ear of each prisoner was cut off, they were forced to parade through the streets of Kyoto. As they were pulled on foot, they sang Te Deum, and Bautista and Paulo Miki took turns preaching to the huge crowd of onlookers. Many of those who came out to watch them were Christians, who joined them singing and praying. Some of them even cried out, expressing their desire to partake in martyrdom themselves. There were also Buddhists among the crowd, who abused the prisoners verbally.

The site of their execution was Nagasaki. The prisoners had to travel a month's journey on land in cold winter, but en route were treated with care by the local people, partly because of their pity and sympathy and partly for the fear of penalty should the prisoners be harmed for some reason while they were in their territory. At each station they prepared a place for the prisoners to stay, and sometimes they even provided warm clothes and a means for transportation (e.g. horses, etc.).

The prisoners were allowed to write letters, some of which have been preserved either in copies or in translations. Bautista, for instance, sent his fellow friar Rodriguez a note of spiritual triumph by stating: "We are now in great joy." He also extended deep concern for the well-being of the patients in the Franciscan hospitals in Kyoto and Osaka. Blanco likewise mentioned in his letter "a miraculous comfort" that he was feeling within himself and said that it put him to shame to see so many Japanese Christians who had come out to greet them, expressing their sincere desire to join them in martyrdom.

The following is a letter of Tome Kozaki, a fourteen-year-old dojuku, to his mother:

> By the grace of our Lord, I wanted to write this letter to you, dear mother. According to the written sentence, all of us will be crucified along with the padres in Nagasaki. We are twenty-four in all. Please do not worry about father Miguel and me, for we will be waiting for you in paradise. Should you fail to find a padre who could officiate the last rite for you, please remember a contrition for your sins, and keep profound the faith. Remember also the innumerable blessings bestowed by the Lord Jesus Christ.
>
> As everything of this world can be lost soon, even if you might become poor and have to beg for food from people, please take care not to lose the glory of paradise. No matter what people may say to you, please forbear with patience and love to the end. It is important that my brothers Mancio and Felipe will not fall into the hands of the pagans. I will pray for them to Deus. Please pray to him for us all. Consider, I beg of you, one most important thing above all others. I ask you again to immerse your heart always in contrition for profound sins. As the padres have taught us before, Adam's soul was able to gain salvation only through the contrition for his sin. Even when no padre is available for confession, your sins will be forgiven through contrition.
>
> May Deus protect you.
>
> > Tome

En route also, two more prisoners were added. One was a certain Christian called Pedro who claimed that he was sent by Padre Organtino from Kyoto to give some money to the three Jesuits and some other Japanese prisoners, and the other was Francisco Gayo, a carpenter by occupation, who decided to follow the Franciscan missionaries. The total number of the prisoners became, consequently, twenty-six.

### THE MARTYRDOM

On February 4, the party finally reached its destination, Nagasaki. Since the commissioner of the city, Terasawa, was absent at that time, his brother by the name of Hanzaburo Terasawa took charge. This man, though not a Christian, was apparently sympathetic to the Christians, perhaps because of the influence of his brother who was a confessed Christian. Hanzaburo felt pity particularly on Luis who was only twelve years old (ten years old, according to Giron), so much that he repeatedly urged him to abandon his faith, and he promised him his safety and even employment in exchange. The boy resolutely declined his offer, however.

The site of the execution was a hill overlooking the town of Nagasaki. In describing it Avila Giron mentioned, by quoting Juan Pobre who was apparently at the scene as a spectator, that several Portuguese felt the place was not appropriate for a Christian martyrdom because it had been used previously for executions of common criminals, and asked the overseeing official that the site be moved to a little lower part of the hill facing the sea. The official was willing to consent to it and said quite remorsefully that he wished he could have avoided killing these prisoners, though he was "one of the most cruel pagans I have ever met" (*op. cit.*, chap. 8).

Giron also described the shape of their crosses. Each cross consisted of one vertical slab of lumber with two crossbars fixed on it, the upper and longer bar to tie a prisoner's arms and the lower and shorter bar to tie his feet. There was also a small piece of wood attached to the middle of the vertical lumber to support his weight. Twenty-six such crosses were erected in an area which was encircled by a makeshift fence.

According to Leon Pagés (*Histoire des vingt-six martyrs Japonais*, Rome, 1862), the officials allowed two Portuguese to enter within the fence to accompany the prisoners; they were João Rodriguez, the interpreter, and Francesco Paez, the captain of the Santa Cruz, both of whom were sent from Vice-provincial Pedro Gomez to console the prisoners. Bautista, the leader of the twenty-six, thanked them and told them that he would forgive the Jesuits and the Portuguese for their malice toward the friars. (This also indicates how deep the love and hate relationship was between the Spanish Franciscans and the Portuguese Jesuits.) Jesuit Bishop Martins was not allowed to attend there, but he stayed at a nearby village house.

Bautista asked the executioners that he be crucified with iron spikes in the same way as Jesus Christ was, but the request was denied. He was instead tied to a cross with ropes, and the same was done to the other victims. Bautista was in the middle; on his right were Martin de la Ascencion, Felipe de Jesus, Gonçalo Garcia, Francisco Blanco, Francisco de la Parrilla, Mathias, Leon Karasumaru, Ventura, Tome, Joachim Sakakibara, Francisco Kusuki, Tome Ise, Juan, Gabriel, and Paulo Sazuki; and on the left of Bautista were Antonio Luis, João Goto, Pablo Ibaragi, Paulo Miki, Diego Kasai, Muguel Kozaki, Pedro, Cosme, and Francisco Gayo. Hymns and prayers were on the lips of the martyrs and the Christian spectators. It was late afternoon; the red sun was setting on the horizon of the strangely dark sea.

The executioners approached, one on both sides of each cross. On command, each of them pierced the side of the victim's body with a long spear. Cries of agony hardly effused from the martyrs, but they echoed loudly among the onlookers. So prodigious was the impact that the people could no longer contain themselves but rushed to the crosses, pushing the fence down, with the guards unable to restrain them. They touched the blood flowing down from the martyrs' bodies; pieces of cloth or paper were used to soak it up to save it.

Many people tried to obtain some fragments of their clothes as holy relics. In fact, according to Giron, by the time the Spanish governor of the Philippines formally requested the return of bodies of the martyrs from Hideyoshi, they had long since been removed from the site by the Japanese and European Christians. (The head of Martin de la Ascencion, for example, was procured by a Frenchman who carried it eventually to Goa, India.) The governor's envoy, therefore, failed to discover even a piece of one cross.

In 1627 these martyrs were beatified by Pope Urban VIII, and then in 1862 they were canonized by Pope Pius IX.

### CONCLUDING REMARKS

It is quite ironic that the Christian mission prospered more in these less stable social conditions than in the settled situation in pre-modern Japan. Before Hideyoshi gained a firm control over the whole nation, the missionaries were able to choose warlords who were willing to accept and help promulgate the Christian faith. Many of the lords were anxious to invite the Europeans to their territories with an eye toward commercial benefits. The Jesuits, intentionally and unintentionally, took advantage of the competitions among the lords. There were several lords, nonetheless, who understood correctly and believed sincerely in Christianity. Sumitada Omura and Ukon Takayama were, among others, good examples.

Once Hideyoshi established his hegemony, however, the Christians were at this despot's mercy. Compared to his predecessor, Nobunaga, Hideyoshi does not seem to have embraced a warm respect toward the padres. As has always been the case with dictators, he too was cruel and egoistic, and, worse still, he was a megalomaniac who was not satisfied with gaining power over Japan alone but dreamed of subduing Korea and China. His senseless invasion of Korea as a step toward the conquest of the entire Chinese subcontinent eventually failed, however.

To this man's eye, Christianity appeared pernicious because of its foreign and intolerant nature. Hideyoshi was not a religious man by nature but was not particularly against religion either. In his mind, religion, like everything and everyone else, was supposed to serve his own wish. He mercilessly destroyed the militant Buddhists, but once they became submissive to him, he was willing to forgive and restore their religious facilities.

Hideyoshi was not an ideologue, but used the "shinkoku ideology" to bolster his own authority. This "ideology" was not a well-thought-out philosophy, but a logically vague and basically emotional syncretism forcefully combining Buddhism, Confucianism, and Shintoism. Christianity, which confessed one absolute God, could hardly fit into this conglomerate. The large-scale attacks on Buddhist temples and monasteries by the Christians in the fiefs of the Christian feudal lords, as Hideyoshi saw it, illustrated the essentially alien, aggressive, and subversive character of Christianity. If that was the case, he decided, it should be eliminated—thus the edict of explusion of the padres was issued and the twenty-six Christians were martyred.

How then did the missionaries respond to this critical situation?

There were three distinctive approaches: first, the adaptational approach, which was carefully thought out, discussed, and to a large extent successfully practiced by the padres like Valignano and Organtino. This method intended to cautiously evaluate the local tradition, culture, and social conditions and skillfully adapt Christian evangelism to these given factors.

The opposite of this approach was the confrontational approach. It attempted to impose Christian teachings and practices on the people of the mission land, ignoring their peculiarities. It asserted resolutely the absolute supremacy of Christianity and European culture over the rest of the world and its religions. Padre Cabral represented this view. Such a "no-buts-and-no-ifs" stance was shared by the third approach, which can be termed purist. It was uncompromising as far as its own religious styles were concerned, since it believed that they were an expression of its religious integrity. The intransigent nature of this approach, unlike the second approach, did not stem from a sense of cultural superiority, however. The friars' mission policy belonged to this third category. It hated to make any compromise with the local conditions but was willing to contribute to them.

Which of these three approaches was more successful in Japan? Judging from what Torres, Valignano, and Organtino and others accomplished, it seems reasonable to say that the first approach seems to have been better than the other two. Cabral alienated many of the Japanese who came to know him personally. The use of military force in support of the Christians in Japan as planned by Coelho and him (and even, out of desperation, by a Japan expert like Frois) was categorically rejected by Valignano. The enthusiastic friars, despite their self-sacrificing work of charity, met tragedy in its magnitude. Did this happen because of their overzealous actions which provoked the tyrant's wrath? Or was it an inevitable event which the Christians had to face regardless of what approach they took?

A unified endeavor was basic to Valignano's mission policy. He was convinced of its efficacy and hence insisted on the monopoly of the mission by the Jesuits. Under such a difficult condition as that in which they found themselves, close coordination among the Christians was of absolute necessity. The mutual animosities and denunciations among the missionaries and the different nationalities (the Portuguese versus the Spaniards, and later both of them against the Dutch and the English) did considerable harm to the Christian cause.

The Christian mission under Hideyoshi's reign closed on a dark note. The death of the despot, however, brought an end to his lunatic invasion of Korea and a temporary halt to the persecution of the Christians. After his death, new political leadership stepped forward in the person of Ieyasu Tokugawa. How did the Christians fare under his rule? This is the subject of our next chapter.

# 5

# Persecution by the
# Tokugawa Bakufu (1)

Despite Hideyoshi's desperate hope, his young son, Hideyori, was unable to succeed his father's throne. Instead, the one who grasped the nation's hegemony was Ieyasu Tokugawa (1542–1616) who was the strongest economically and militarily of all the feudal lords at the time of the death of Hideyoshi in 1598. Within five years Ieyasu eliminated those who opposed him and became the autocrat of the whole country. The imperial court granted him the title *Seii-taishogun*, an old term for the supreme commander in war, which came to designate the highest ruler of the nation.

Ieyasu's government was established in Edo (contemporary Tokyo); it was hence called the Edo Bakufu. Retired as the shogun in 1605, Ieyasu passed the title to his son Hidetada, thereby creating the hereditary rule of the country by the Tokugawa clan. By contrast the Toyotomi family was destined to destruction; after losing in battle to the Tokugawa forces, Hideyori and his supporters perished in flames at the Osaka castle in 1615.

What kind of man was Ieyasu Tokugawa? He was born in 1542 as a son of a small warrior chieftain whose domain lay near the territory of the Oda clan. All through his young life he lived under the shadow of the neighboring strong warlords. By allying himself with Nobunaga, however, he succeeded in increasing his power steadily. Because of the hardship of his young days, he had learned to be cautious and patient.

147

He grew to be a man who knew how to bide his time. While Hideyoshi was alive, though formally obliged to be a subordinate of the regent, he never regarded himself as his retainer. He, for example, declined Hideyoshi's request to send his troops to Korea. To honor his special status, Hideyoshi allowed him a fief far larger than any other feudal lord.

His far-sighted determination was indeed rewarded when the "tenka" came under his authority. The first task he accomplished was the careful redistribution of fiefs to the warlords in order to secure his absolute control over them. Those who had been serving him before Hideyoshi's death (they were called *fudai daimyo*) were assigned in strategic areas with rich rewards, while those who had recently joined his camp (i.e. *tozama daimyo*, those who had no hereditary ties with him) in places far away from Edo, his capital. In an attempt to curtail their economic potency so as to prevent any possible rebellion, the *tozama* lords were frequently called upon for expensive public service, such as the construction of the streets of the city of Edo, repair of the Edo castle, and other projects.

The territory which Ieyasu personally owned increased in size tremendously as he confiscated a huge amount of land from his enemies (the fiefs of some ninety clans were confiscated). Ieyasu also imposed on the daimyos limits on the size of their castles and the capacity of navigation in coastal regions. These measures were taken so as to prevent these lords from gaining too much economic and military strength.

Second, Ieyasu appointed reliable bureaucrats to be commissioners of the important cities throughout the nation. This move solidified the efficient communication between the capital Edo and each local area. Third, a survey of the farm lands was undertaken as it had been previously by Hideyoshi.

Fourth, Ieyasu laid down three sets of rules to be observed: one by the daimyos and their retainers, another by the nobles in the imperial court, and the last by all Buddhist priests and monks. They were intended to place each of these three groups of people under rigid control by the Edo government within the feudalistic social scheme. The structure of the society comprised four classes: the warrior, the farmer, the artisan, and the merchants. Each individual was inherently tied to his or her family, which constituted a hereditary unit of respective social classes.

The stabilization of the whole nation in this manner marked a culmination of the process which began with the policy of warrior domination by Nobunaga and Hideyoshi by means of the land survey and the confiscation of weapons from the non-warrior classes. The establishment of such a rigidly structured society, unfortunately, left little room for the Christian mission because it was supported ideologically by the traditional religions: Shintoism, Buddhism, and Confucianism (or, more exactly speaking, a combination of these three).

It is not without significance for our interest to mention the fact that Ieyasu, in order to formulate such a social policy, relied particularly on the following three religious people as his trusted aides. First, there was Tenkai (1536–1643), a chief abbot (*dai-sojo*) who belonged to the Tendai sect of Buddhism. He acted as an influential counselor for the three successive shoguns (Ieyasu, Hidetada, and Iemitsu) especially in regard to religious policy-making. He was entrusted to write a draft of the rules concerning the shrines, temples, monasteries, and the personnel attached to them. Many temples and monasteries of his sect were built or restored because of the enormous political power he possessed.

Second, we should mention Konchiin Suden (1569–1633), a monk of the Rinzai sect of Zen Buddhism. He served Ieyasu closely by drafting diplomatic and other political and legal documents. Third, Razan Hayashi (1583–1657) was a brilliant Confucian scholar who functioned as an advisor and tutor in Confucian teachings for four shoguns (Ieyasu–Ietsuna). He worked hard to promote Confucian thought by influencing the shoguns and other important people in the bakufu government and also by opening a school for the study of Confucianism in Edo.

Though these three persons belonged to their own respective religious sect and tradition, they all shared a syncretic religious thought— a nationalistic ideology of Japan as a shinkoku. They played a vital role in creating *pax Takugawae* by providing it with an ideological basis. As far as the Christians were concerned, however, this state of "peace" proved to be none other than an arena for their martyrdom.

### IEYASU'S POLICY TOWARD THE CHRISTIANS

Ieyasu's attitude toward the Christians was basically the same as that of Hideyoshi, i.e. anti-Christianity. And like Hideyoshi, his interest in foreign trade seems to have overridden his antipathy toward the "teachings of the Namban." However, economic concerns prompted his foreign policy to adopt a conciliatory course unlike his predecessor's high-handed approach. He took the initiative to open several channels of trade with various countries. First he reestablished diplomatic relations with Korea which had been severed due to Hideyoshi's senseless aggression. Commercial exchange with China was a great enticement to him, but China was too suspicious about Japan's intention to recommence formal trade.

In the situation where direct exchange was impossible, an indirect way (i.e. through middlemen) had to be sought. That was where a significant function of European traders lay. The Portuguese had been playing this role and had received huge benefits from it. Chinese silk, in particular, was the most profitable commodity which they sold to the Japanese. The participation in this trade constituted the principal financial source for the Jesuit missionaries in Japan as well. In fact, annually close to ten percent of the Portuguese trade with Japan went to the Jesuits.

### (1) The Jesuits

Recognizing the important role of the padres in the Portuguese trade, Ieyasu attempted to make use of them. In 1603, for example, he appointed Toan Murayama and several other Christian officials to supervise trade matters at Nagasaki and asked the best Japan experts, Padre João Rodriguez and Vice-provincial Pasio, to act as their consultants. Responding to the shogun's request, Rodriguez, who was excellent not only in the Japanese language but also in diplomacy, became involved deeply in the political and economic affairs as the *procurador* (procurator).

The Jesuits' involvement in these quite secular matters seemingly went too far, however. A conflict of views and interests was inevitable; some serious complaints arose against the Jesuits both from the Portuguese merchants and from the Japanese. Deputy Murayama, disenchanted with the Jesuits, turned to side with the Spaniards, newcomers to Japan. There were also criticisms raised by a number of the padres themselves. Organtino, for instance, made a strong plea to Rome that a directive be issued prohibiting each and every Jesuit from participating in secular affairs. The General did send orders to that effect, in fact, repeatedly in 1593 and 1612.

The bakufu's intention was to make use of the padres for the sake of commercial diplomacy but eventually to take over the whole business into their own hands. They, in fact, did so when they imposed a governmental monopoly on the sale of imported raw silk in 1604. This lessened considerably the degree of participation of the Portuguese merchants and the Jesuits in this commercial dealing. The decline of Portuguese influence in East Asia was accelerated by an increase in the power of the Dutch. The latter eventually shut the former out of Japan; after the bakufu banned the Portuguese in 1639, the Dutch became the sole European trading partner of Japan. When the commercial and diplomatic usefulness of the padres was reduced to nothing, their mission was doomed.

*(2) The Franciscans*

In ruthlessly pursuing profitable trade, Ieyasu's interest turned toward the newcomers to this part of the world—the Spaniards and the Dutch. They were quite anxious to expand their market. For this reason alone, Ieyasu apparently saw some usefulness in the Spanish misssionaries, and he, therefore, did not oppress the Christians until the very last years of his life. He, for instance, even attempted to employ the Franciscan friar Jeronimo de Jesus.

This priest had escaped from arrest at the time when Hideyoshi ordered the execution of the twenty-six Christians and remained underground in Kyoto to take care of the Christians there. But he was finally captured and expelled to Macao in March 1597. This hardly deterred him from continuing his mission to Japan. In the beginning of the following year he succeeded in reentering the country secretly. Having heard of his return, Ieyasu sent a summons for him to come forward to talk with him. When the priest appeared from hiding, the shogun offered him a deal which would allow him to build a church in Edo in exchange for his help in promoting trade with the Philippines. The ecstatic Jeronimo immediately embarked upon both projects. A church was completed and blessed on May 30, 1599.

In order to fulfill the other part of the deal, Jeronimo de Jesus returned to Manila. He was successful in this matter as well; the Spanish governor acceded to a resumption of trade with Japan. In May 1601 he was able to come back to Japan with the Franciscan priest Louis Gomez and Br. Pedro de Burguillos. They were permitted to open a mission house in Fushimi, a castle-town of Ieyasu. Thence until the outbreak of the general persecution in 1614, the friars continued to arrive in Japan regularly at the rate of from three to five every year.

Jeronimo de Jesus died in Kyoto in 1601, and Alonso Muños took over leadership. Ieyasu again urged him to work hard on trade with the Spaniards. He, in fact, even sent the priest as a trade envoy to Mexico in 1610.

Meanwhile the missions prospered under Ieyasu's policy of toleration of Christianity in exchange for the missionaries' contribution to the trading enterprise. According to Pagés, in 1606 there were 750,000 believers with an average annual increase of 5,000 or 6,000. (Don Rodorigo, a Spanish trader who came to Japan in 1607, reported that the number of the Christians in Japan in 1610 was 300,000, most of whom were devout believers. It is difficult to ascertain the exact number.)

The most thriving commercial port city, Nagasaki, was also a "Christian" town; Bishop Cerquiera once called it the "Rome of the Far East." The adventurous trader Avila Giron wrote that he saw in 1607 the missionaries of four different orders (the Jesuits, the Franciscans, the Dominicans, and the Augustinians) openly engaging in missionary activities at their churches in various major cities in Japan.

## LUIS SOTELO AND ENVOYS TO EUROPE

Ieyasu's keen interest in foreign trade encouraged his feudal lords to seek opportunities for overseas commercial exchanges as well. A well-known example was Masamune Date who ruled over a large fief in the northern part of Honshu. He became acquainted with a Franciscan friar, Padre Luis Sotelo (1574–1624), in Edo where the latter was the superior at the Franciscan mission house. The lord's favorite lady attendant received medical treatment at the clinic attached to the house. Through this connection, the priest entered the lord's good graces and was invited to come to his fief. Sotelo happily obliged and began vigorously evangelizing the people of that part of Japan. By his and other missionaries' labor, churches were formed in many different places in that region and a considerable number of people received baptism.

Masamune's real interest lay in commercial benefits, however, and Sotelo had to satisfy this desire. They then jointly came up with the grand plan for sending an emissary to Spain and Rome in an attempt to promote diplomatic and commercial relations with Spain by way of Mexico (which was a Spanish territory then). The chosen envoy was Masamune's retainer by the name of Tsunenaga Hasekura (1561–1622).

Hasekura and a large entourage, guided by Sotelo, set sail on October 29, 1613, carrying with them the lord's official letters to Pope Paul V and the king of Spain. They reached Mexico by going across the Pacific Ocean on January 25 of the following year. The Spanish viceroy of Mexico received them with due honor. Sixty-eight Japanese from the party were reportedly baptized with the exception of Hasekura himself, who was to be baptized after arriving in Europe. (If this mass baptism indeed took place, it seems to have been diplomatically motivated.)

In October of the same year they set foot in Spain. King Felipe III welcomed them in Madrid, where Hasekura received baptism. Their next and final destiny was Rome. There again the party enjoyed a great reception, though not as magnificent as the time when the four youths visited there in 1585. Honorable citizenship of Rome was granted to Hasekura. It was the end of 1615 when they left Italy, and in the spring of the next year they went back to Spain.

Notwithstanding the warm welcome in Europe, their mission was not really accomplished. The king of Spain did not show any willingness for trade with Japan by way of Mexico. There were several reasons. First, the Spanish government was apprehensive about jeopardizing the trade between the Philippines and Japan by commencing another route of commercial exchange. The Spaniards in the Philippines, including Sotelo's fellow Franciscans, campaigned against it vigorously.

Second, the Jesuits in Japan also raised strong objections, contending that it might cause suspicion in the mind of Ieyasu as to a possibly pernicious alliance between Masamune Date and the Spanish government. This might undermine, they indicated, not only the political power of Masamune, a friend of the Christians, but also the security of Christianity in Japan itself.

The Jesuits also advised Rome of the undesirability of Sotelo's deep involvement in commercial and diplomatic business. Padre Jeronimo Angelis wrote on November 30, 1619 that the whole venture of sending the envoys was intended to fulfill Sotelo's personal ambition to become a bishop in Japan. It was claimed that he had talked Masamune into his scheme by enticing him with the possiblity of extravagant financial gain from the trade with Mexico. (Angelis also made negative mention regarding this lord's status, his faith, and his moral behavior.) Masamune, blinded by this greedy plan, allowed Sotelo to write "whatever he wanted" in the official letter in his name to the pope and the Spanish king.

The third negative reason came from a recent report from Japan that the Tokugawa bakufu had begun a new policy which was even more oppressive toward the Christians than before.

### TRAGEDY OF SOTELO

The failure of the mission meant personal defeat for Sotelo. As clearly stated in Masamune's letter to the pope (Sotelo played a major role in producing this letter), it was Sotelo's vision to make the northern part of Japan a Christian (Franciscan!) country, which he could lead as the bishop or archbishop. He was, in fact, nominated as bishop by Pope Paul V but was never consecrated.

The disheartened party returned to Japan in 1620, but Sotelo alone stayed in the Philippines. The homeland the others had left behind seven years before had changed drastically from the open and forward-looking country which had enthusiastically sent them abroad to a closed and insular land which hardly welcomed their homecoming. The Tokugawa bakufu, by issuing an order totally prohibiting Christianity in 1614, had launched a systematic crackdown on the Christians throughout the nation. The trade with the Portuguese and the Spaniards was no longer an enticement to the shoguns in Edo. And Masamune Date had to comply with the national policy.

Hasekura died in total disappointment two years after he had returned home. Sotelo, who remained in Manila, was not able to forget Japan. In 1622, he attempted to enter the country by disguising himself as a merchant only to be captured and thrown into jail in Omura. While imprisoned, he sent to Rome a long letter on January 20, 1624 describing his situation with a sharp censure of the Jesuits. This letter was presented to the ecclesiastical authorities by his friend and colleague in Japan, the Dominican provincial, Diego Collado, who was also bitterly critical of the Jesuits.

This highly emotional letter revealed his unshaken confidence in an eventual rescue by Lord Date. (He had been delivered by Masamune from prison once before. But this time this formerly independent-minded and capable warlord was compelled to enforce anti-Christian measures because of the bakufu's pressure.) The priest never abandoned his vision of his bishopric in the Date fief until the very last day of his life.

The primary message of Sotelo's letter concerns his bitter criticism of the Jesuits. He repeatedly denounced them for their various attempts to undermine and disrupt the missionary activities of the other three orders (the Franciscans, the Dominicans, and the Augustinians). Evidently it was his firm conclusion that the trouble which the Christians were experiencing stemmed largely from the Jesuits' vice and failure. He pleaded with the pope that four bishops be appointed to lead each of these four orders in Japan.

By submitting Sotelo's letter as evidence, Collado campaigned hard in Rome on behalf of the three orders, while criticizing the Jesuits. The Jesuits did not sit back quietly, however. The Vice-provincial of Japan, Sebastião Vieira (1574–1634), in particular, countered by presenting the Jesuit case. His attempt was successful; the pope gave approval to the Jesuits' work in Japan. Sotelo's letter was apparently considered as a spurious product by Collado. Vieira went back to Japan to tell his colleagues the triumphant news. There, however, he subsequently, but unflinchingly, faced a martyr's death. Sotelo met the same fate on August 24, 1624 while still dreaming of his bishopric in the Date domain (as detected in a letter he wrote on the day before the execution).

As illustrated by his blind trust in the friendship of Masamune Date, Sotelo does not seem to have had a good grasp of the political and social climate of Japan. His judgment of various matters betrayed his naiveté. Although he embraced a strong personal ambition, he was indubitably a venerable Catholic and an undaunted laborer of the church. He believed that the single-minded propagation of what he understood to be Catholic teaching would solve every problem in the world. He criticized harshly the Jesuits' adaptationist ways.

The animosities between the Jesuits and the Spanish friars certainly did much damage to the Christian cause in Japan. But their conflicts were not the only ones; when the Dutch and the English arrived in Japan, the strife among the Europeans was greatly intensified.

### THE ARRIVAL OF THE DUTCH AND THE ENGLISH

Just as the first Portuguese drifted ashore by a storm in 1543, the first English and Dutch men reached Japan when pushed ashore by violent weather in 1600; for them, however, unlike the Portuguese, Japan was their intended destination. They were on board the Dutch vessel, the Liefde, which was wrecked on the shore of Bungo. The ship and its cargo were immediately confiscated at the order of the bakufu, but the surviving crew members were treated hospitably. Among them was the pilot of the ship, an Englishman by the name of William Adams (1564–1620), who was able to enjoy the personal favor of Ieyasu because he considered him useful as a source of knowledge concerning shipbuilding and navigation.

Holland, which became independent of Spanish rule in 1581, allied itself with England and was competing with the Iberian countries to secure the command of the sea. Both the English and the Dutch were newcomers in the east, and they aggressively sought to expand their commercial and military influence there. The English East India Company was founded in 1600 and a Dutch counterpart in 1602.

Ieyasu, who had been frustrated with the Iberians for the slow progress in gaining from them necessary technological knowledge and skill as well as the commercial benefit, was pleased to find a new European source. Furthermore, the fierce competition between these new and old Europeans could be exploited to his advantage. The

Japanese, in fact, found out soon that this competition stemmed not only from the political and economic affairs but also from religious discord. When interrogated, Adams declared unequivocally that his faith in the creator God was different from what the padres had been preaching and that he would not seek to convert the Japanese to his faith.

Adams informed Ieyasu that both the Dutch and the English were keenly interested in trade with Japan, which was exactly what the shogun had been looking for—trade with a new European country without religious ties. And thus a solely commercial relationship commenced between the Japanese and the Protestant Europeans. Two Dutch vessels arrived in Hirado and a trading house was erected in 1609. Owing to Adams' efforts as well, an English trading firm was also constructed in Hirado in 1613.

Adams became an interpreter and a trusted aide, working closely for Ieyasu. He was given a small fief, adopted a Japanese name, Anjin (meaning pilot) Miura, and married a Japanese woman, by whom he had two children. He died in Hirado in 1620.

The Catholic missions in Japan, now facing new and formidable opponents from Europe, entered a period of horrendous persecution. The following event was one of the incidents which triggered the systematic oppression against the Catholics by the bakufu officials.

### THE AFFAIR OF THE MADRE DE DEUS

Just several days before the two Dutch vessels arrived in Hirado, a Portuguese ship called Madre de Deus brought the captain general of Macao, Andre Pessoa, to Nagasaki. He came to Japan to officially negotiate with the bakufu concerning problems arising from a fight between a band of the retainers of Lord Harunobu Arima and some Portuguese residents in Macao. The strife resulted in the deaths of some forty Japanese. Pessoa's task was to explain to the Japanese government what had actually happened and how he had handled it. In Nagasaki, however, he was subjected to a tragic fate.

Sahyoe Hasegawa, the commissioner of the city of Nagasaki, treated Pessoa coldly because he had already been influenced by the understandably biased account of the Japanese survivors of the Macao event. Despite his repeated requests, the commissioner would not even transmit the Portuguese plea to Edo. The situation became even worse for Pessoa as soon as the Dutch arrived in Hirado, because they vilified the Portuguese, their rival, in the strongest terms. When Ieyasu heard all of these reports, though initially not willing to treat Pessoa harshly, he finally decided to order Arima to seize Pessoa and his ship. This measure the shogun made was indicative of his determination to steer the course of his foreign policy in favor of the Dutch and against the Portuguese.

Arima immediately took action. Pessoa, refusing to surrender, fought bravely, but, realizing there was no possibility of escape, blew up the ship, himself and his men included. Arima's aggression was not only to avenge his retainers' deaths in Macao but also to please Ieyasu.

Anxious to further ingratiate himself with the powerful man in Edo, Arima let his son, Naozumi, marry the granddaughter of Ieyasu by forcing him to divorce his wife, who was a devout Catholic and the daughter of the late Yukinaga Konishi. Pleasing Edo for the sake of the security of his own fief overrode his Catholic faith totally at this point.

### DOWNFALL OF THE ARIMAS

By carrying out faithfully all of these matters in accordance with the bakufu's desire, Arima felt himself to have risen high in Ieyasu's favor. This confidence led him to take measures to attempt to regain an ancestral territory which had been lost. Hoping to receive help for his cause, he sent a bribe to a man by the name of Daihachi Okamoto, a retainer of Lord Masazumi Honda who was an influential official of the bakufu. Okamoto, though he gladly received the money, had no intention of doing anything on behalf of Arima. Arima grew impatient and finally brought the case directly to Honda.

Now the whole affair became public. When Ieyasu heard what had happened, he was infuriated, condemned Okamoto to death, and deposed Arima. Harunobu Arima was later ordered to take his own life, but declined to do so by saying that suicide was forbidden by the church. He was consequently executed on June 5, 1612.

This whole incident brought the Christians great tragedy: the beginning of systematic persecutions. Harunobu Arima was well known as a Christian, and Okamoto was found to be also a Christian. Ieyasu hence commanded the discovery and expulsion of Christians from the governmental offices. According to Padre Pedro Morejon, fourteen officials (six of whom were high in rank) had to meet this fate.

Harunobu Arima's son, Naozumi, was ordered by the bakufu to banish all the Christians from his fief, which was one of the areas where the Christian population was highest in the nation. Naozumi, though nominally a baptized Christian, consequently launched the systematic oppression of the Christians. Since his second wife, Ieyasu's granddaughter, was a devout Buddhist and fanatic foe of Christianity, she actively supported her husband's anti-Christian campaign. The padres were ordered to leave the domain. (They continued working there secretly, however.) The churches, seminario, colegio, and other facilities were confiscated.

To carry out further the policy of the eradication of Christianity, Naozumi issued an order that every Christian in his fief should abandon the faith. Some did so out of fear of severe punishment, while many others resisted. Those who disobeyed were deprived of their homes and property. Embarrassed by the open disobedience of many of his subjects, the feudal lord decided to execute eight of those who were rather prominent among his Christian retainers, including their families, as a warning to all other Christians.

The victims were burned alive on August 16, 1613. The annual report of the Society of Jesus for that year made mention of more than 20,000 people who came out to witness this solemn moment. Surprised by the unexpectedly large number of spectators, many of whom were Christians, the officials, contrary to their initial intention, had to change the site secretly in order to avoid any possible riot. They even set up a high fence preventing the crowd from seeing the sight of the execution, because they realized that martyrdom served to encourage the people's faith.

In addition to this well-publicized martyrdom, several other executions of Christians were also done by the order of Lord Arima. Despite all these bloody anti-Christian measures taken in order to demonstrate loyalty to the Edo bakufu, the Arima clan was transferred by the shogun's order to another fief in Kyushu in 1614.

### DECREE AGAINST CHRISTIANITY

As mentioned earlier, Ieyasu, a serious Buddhist, never took any interest in Christianity, but overlooked the activities of the Christians because of the diplomatic significance of the padres in connection with the trade with the Portuguese and the Spaniards. Through a series of events (observed in the previous sections), he became more and more openly antagonistic toward the Catholic Christians. And when he heard that many of the Christians in the Arima territory tenaciously resisted the official order of a renunciation of their faith, he finally issued a decree prohibiting the practice of the Christian faith.

The shogun entrusted the Zen monk, Konchiin Suden, to write a draft of the decree. The fanatically anti-Christian Buddhist gladly carried out the order overnight. It was made public at the end of January 1614. This marked the beginning of the horrendous periodic persecutions wrought nationally during at least the subsequent two centuries.

The decree opened with a statement used often by the rulers: "Japan is a divine country (shinkoku)." It then proceeded to denounce Christianity by saying: "But bands of the Christians have come to Japan by trade ships not only to exchange commodities but also to spread an evil teaching and to beguile correct doctrines so as to subvert the government of the nation in order to take over the country. This is an omen of great disaster, and thus it should be suppressed."

The decree then returned to the theme of Japan as "the country of gods and Buddha," which, it asserted, possessed a clear standard of adjudication of good and evil. However, it continued, "all of that band of padres have violated the national command, questioned the way of the gods, slandered the right doctrine, undone the righteousness and corrupted the goodness. When they see a criminal (referring to Christ), they rejoice and run to him, worship him and pay reverence to him. They hold it as the essence of their belief. If this is not an evil teaching, what else is it? It is indeed an enemy of the gods and Buddha. There will surely be a peril to the nation unless they be prohibited. . . ."

The content of this decree was a rehashing of Hideyoshi's edict expelling of the padres; the reasons for the suppression of Christianity and the ideological basis (the shinkoku ideology) were identical. But this time the central government evidently concluded that the eradication of the Christians should override the diplomatic usefulness of the padres.

This decision stemmed from the following two major reasons. First, the bakufu wanted to consolidate its absolute authority over the whole nation as any reminiscence of the former regime (the Toyotomi family in Osaka) was dying. The Christians were regarded as a potential threat to national unity. Second, the Dutch traders were offering a convenient alternative means for commercial exchange with the Europeans without religious involvement.

Ieyasu took this action just two years prior to his death (1616). As noted before, he had always looked the other way regarding the activities of the Christians because of his interest in international trade. In this, he was identical to his predecessor, Hideyoshi. But now as he approached the final stage of his life, the security of his clan apparently became the most vital point of his concern. After all, he was personally involved in the downfall of two of the preceding ruling families. He decided to ensure at any cost the *pax Tokugawae* which he had worked so hard to establish throughout his life. An ideological control over the citizens seemed to him to be a crucial step to create and uphold the absolute rule of the nation. Christianity, as a result, became the victim of his political scheme. From a long-term historical viewpoint, this move meant a retreat to a kind of national cocoon. By snuggling in its own little nest, Japan missed a golden opportunity to move steadily forward to the modern age.

## CLOSING THE COUNTRY

During the era of Ieyasu's immediate successors, his son Hidetada and his grandson Iemitsu, the policy of the self-exclusion of Japan was firmly established. These shoguns and their aides promulgated a series of decrees attempting to minimize foreign influence on Japan. This involved not only the total expulsion of the missionaries and an annihilation of the native Christian population but also a strict limitation of trade with Europeans. A few months after Ieyasu's death, Hidetada ordered the enforcement of the suppression of Christianity even more harshly than before and also the prohibition of any foreign ship from arriving at any Japanese ports excepting Hirado and Nagasaki. (There was also another exception: Chinese vessels were able to come to port any place to engage in commercial business.)

The edict specifically noted that this restriction was to be applied not only to the Portuguese and the Spaniards but also to the Dutch and the English, because all of them belonged to the same faith. (It sounds as if the shogun was indeed suffering from a paranoia about Christianity!) In reality, however, the religious issue was not the only reason for concern, for the government's monopoly of trade was also an important consideration. The edict would serve a double purpose: it would enrich the shogun's own treasury, while it would weaken the feudal lords financially. The lobbyists for the Japanese traders, closely allied with the government, must have worked vigorously behind the scene for the bakufu to issue this order as well.

To pursue the policy of restriction, the bakufu gave out another edict in 1620. It demanded that all the Portuguese were to leave. If they were married with Japanese women and had children, they were to leave taking only their sons and not their wives and daughters. Second, no Japanese citizen was allowed to leave the country for Manila. Third, no Japanese ship owner was to hire Portuguese pilots. Lastly, Portuguese merchants were permitted to visit Japan and spend nights only at non-Christian homes.

When Iemitsu, the third shogun, took hold of the supreme power following his father's death in 1632, the exclusion policy was intensified even more. Between 1633 and 1639, five edicts were issued, the contents of which were all similar: neither a ship nor a person without a valid license was allowed to leave Japan for a foreign country. Should anyone leave secretly, he or she would be put to death. The Japanese subjects who had lived abroad should also be put to death, should they return to Japan, except for those who had stayed less than five years and returned for unavoidable reasons (but should they attempt to go abroad again, they were to be put to death).

The edicts then declared the prohibition of Christianity. The commissioners in Nagasaki were to investigate those who were accused of practicing the forbidden faith. Informants as to the whereabout of padres would be granted a good amount of monetary reward. Anyone who attempted to propagate illicit religions was to be imprisoned. All vessels should be thoroughly searched in order to ensure the absence of padres. Several more items concerning the restriction of foreign trade were also included in these edicts.

In 1636 the bakufu orderd the children and grandchildren of Europeans by Japanese mothers to leave the country (287 of them left for Macao in that year). In the same year also, all European residents were told to move to houses prepared in Dejima, a small land filled in at the head of Nagasaki bay. This order was applied initially only to a few remaining Portuguese, but they were expelled from Japan shortly afterward (1638). Dejima thus became the residence of the Dutch merchants alone, the only remaining Europeans in Japan. (England lost in the commercial competition with Holland in East Asia, and their trading firm in Hirado was closed in 1623. Trade relations between Japan and Spain were terminated in 1624.)

In order to minimize the possibility of any Dutch influence on the local people, the bakufu attempted to confine them there as much as possible and added further restrictions such as a prohibition of their mediation of letters and gifts between the Japanese in the homeland and abroad and their observance of Christian liturgies during their stay in Japan.

The bakufu was also extremely sensitive about the importation of foreign books. Books considered even slightly connected with Christian topics were confiscated and destroyed. This measure was taken particularly after some Christian books written in Chinese (such as Matteo Ricci's books) were discovered in the imported cargo of a Chinese ship in 1630. The ban became even more stringent as years went by. Even European books on astronomy, mathematics, and literature were prohibited, because they were regarded as somehow subversive to the bakufu feudalism. Such a paranoid isolationist policy regrettably curtailed the intellectual horizon of the people.

Thus Japan became a closed country. This, however, did not mean that Japan had no contact with any foreign country. Though disturbed at times, the trade with the Dutch and the Chinese continued.

Later during the reign of the eighth shogun Yoshimune (1716–1745), the study of European-style science and technology was encouraged. Some intellectuals took a keen interest in European culture through books acquired from the Dutch merchants (the so called *rangaku*, Dutch learning). The hitherto strict ban on foreign books became somewhat relaxed. Many books including ones on astronomy, the calendar, mathematics, and geography which were written in Chinese by European missionaries and their native disciples were imported. As far as Christianity was concerned, however, contact with Christian countries was cut off; a few Catholic missionaries did try to smuggle themselves into the country only to be captured and subjected to hellish torment.

CHRISTIAN LORDS AND MISSIONARIES

The main target of the bakufu's oppression of the Christians was the Christian lords and the missionaries. The feudal lords who were baptized or sympathetic toward Christianity were strictly ordered to abandon any association with Christianity under the threat of the confiscation of their fiefs and sure death for them and all the members of their families.

Ukon Takayama, as mentioned already, gave up his fief and went into exile. His close friend, Yukinaga Konishi, was beheaded when he and his allies lost a war with the forces of Ieyasu. (The warriors were expected to commit suicide instead of submitting themselves to be captured and executed. But he chose not to commit suicide because it was against the Catholic law. Harunobu Arima took the same course, as referred to before.)

Other daimyos who became serious Christians died from old age. Their heirs, such as the sons of Omura, Arima, Kuroda, Gamo, and some others, all left the faith and even turned to become vicious persecutors, anxious to prove their submission to the bakufu's order. The central government thus effectively eradicated the protectors of the Christian mission.

Important also to the government's plan of Christian oppression was the annihilation of the missionaries. According to Pagés, in 1612 there were one hundred and twenty-two Jesuits, of whom sixty-two were priests (including six Japanese) and the remainder brothers (including twelve Europeans), fourteen Franciscans, nine Dominicans, and four Augustinians. The bakufu ordered in 1614 that all of these missionaries and lay leaders be expelled from the country. As a result, twenty-three Jesuits, two Domincans, four Franciscans, and two Augus-

tinians were sent to Manila, and sixty-one Jesuits to Macao. Among
the deposed dignitaries on board was Ukon Takayama who had been
hitherto protected by the Christian sympathizers. Shortly after he
landed in Manila, he died from sickness.

The remaining clergy went underground in order to continue
their work. Pagés mentions twenty-nine Jesuits, six Dominicans, six
Franciscans, and one Augustinian. Despite extreme danger, these padres survived with the help of their Japanese faithful. A padre's life of
secret missionary activity was quite vividly illustrated in the following
letter by Padre Mateus de Couros, the then Vice-provincial, written in
Takaku, Kyushu in 1626:

> Recently the commissioner has sent his men to search (for
> the padres) systematically by examining every house, hut,
> enclosure, and cave; they inspected in order to ascertain that
> nothing is concealed even under the mats on the floor. One
> who came to confiscate the items left by Padre Baltazar de
> Torres, who was burnt alive for the sake of Jesus Christ,
> happened to discover a hiding place in that house. They,
> therefore, figured that more such devices might be found and
> thus checked every corner. The Christians were so discour-
> aged that they advised me to leave immediately by a boat so
> that I might find a safe place. In order to set their minds at
> ease, I told them that I would leave the following night. The
> owner of the house, nonetheless, dug a hole without letting
> anyone know. The size of the hole was twelve palms by four
> palms. The sun shine never came in and there was no light.
> I crawled into it with a dojuku and a servant in the dark of
> night. Nobody knew it except for the owner of the house. We
> lived in the darkness night and day, but we got light only
> when we ate, did religious duties, and wrote letters.
>
> The food was given through a small crevice about the size
> of a roof-tile. The crevice was located inside a small hut
> where an old man was working. It was covered by straws
> except when the food was inserted. We opened the entrance
> of the hole every three days in order to let the bad air out.
> The food was little, because the owner could not obtain

much food for fear that someone might suspect that he was hiding us. We stayed in that hole thirty-five days, during which time we came out of it only on Saturday of Halleluya, Easter, and the eighth day prior to it in order to celebrate mass.

Since then until now, the end of September, we have been hiding in the similar holes here and there which the same owner of the house made for us. I am carrying the necessary equipment for celebration of mass. There is a storage for instruments for farming above this hole (where we are now). The entrance to the hole is very small and is covered with straws and straw mats so as to avoid any suspicion. When the night comes, we go out of the hole to prepare a table for mass, and we crawl back into it with the robes and other utensils before sunrise.

When I get a little sunray during the daytime through a crevice, I write. One day when the dojuku and the servant were sitting in the kitchen, a spy came. They barely escaped to the woods and I managed to crawl into the hole. Since then, he has come back from time to time. The spies are stationed scattered around in this territory. Their only aim is to find me. The commissioner guessed an area where I might be hiding, and ordered that the inner walls of every house in the area be destroyed so that the inside of each house could be surveyed at one glance upon entering.

My servant departs in the middle of the night once every week to go to Nagasaki carrying my letters. Incoming letters are delivered to a reliable person, who hands them to the owner of this house at an appointed place. This is the only means of correspondence. In the manner I described in this letter, a handful of padres continued to take care of their sheep.

Provincial Valentin de Calvalho who was expelled to Macao also in 1614, reported that there were still 300,000 Christians in Japan in that year. (The total population of Japan was estimated to be twenty million then.) Many of these Japanese Christians were either forced to recant or perish by execution or deadly imprisonment. A considerable number of others pretended apostasy.

In addition to such savage measures as sadistic torture, inhuman imprisonment, and cruel execution, the bakufu adopted a systematic program by which the Christians were forced to convert to Buddhism. It started locally after 1614 and then became a nationwide requirement by the middle of the 1630s. Every citizen was required to register as a member of a Buddhist temple, which would guarantee his or her religious status. In other words, the Buddhist clergy were called upon to function as inquisitors, so to speak.

Lists of parishioners were made in order to ascertain that there were no Christians in each local area. As early as 1614, for instance, such a catalogue of names was prepared in Nagasaki. It recorded 24,693 residents indicating each person's name with his or her seal, his or her temple and its sect. They were undoubtedly forced converts because this thriving town had earlier consisted almost entirely of Christians.

Such catalogues were usually prefixed by a statement vowing that the families enrolled in the catalogue had indeed left Christianity completely and would never return to it. The following is an example:

We were Christians for several years. But as we learned the teachings of Christianity, we came to realize that it was a doctrine of the devil. It concerns first of all one's afterlife. It teaches that should one disobey the padres' orders, he will be excommunicated only to fall into hell. How can a human drive another into hell? Having realized that the padres are plotting to take over a foreign country by telling such things, we decided to convert to Buddhism (here the head of each family entered the name of the Buddhist sect).

This is to notify the honorable commissioner as well that we will never return to Christianity and even within our hearts we will never again harbor a desire toward Christianity. Should we diverge from this even slightly, we will receive punishment from God the Father, the Son, and Holy Spirit, Santa Maria, and all the saints, will lose the grace of Deus, forfeit his mercy like Judas, without any penitence, will make a laughing stock of ourselves, and eventuate in an undue death. As a result, we will suffer in hell and will never be saved. Such is the denunciation of the Catholic church.

It is not known who the author of this document was, but it is indeed puzzling that a vow of apostasy was made in the name of the Christian God, Mary the mother of Jesus, and the saints. For a converted Buddhist, no punishment by the God of the holy Trinity would supposedly be efficacious. The document sounds as though the person was still a strong believer in Christianity.

Perhaps some officials deliberately composed this peculiarly styled document in order to prevent fake conversions. (A serious Christian could not do so if he or she used the name of the God of Christianity.) Apparently there were a considerable number of those "pseudo converts" throughout the country. It is not known how widely the conversion document with the invocation of the Christian God was used. But it is certain that it was not the standard formula, because other extant documents of the same kind refer to Buddhist authority.

### NEIGHBORHOOD ASSOCIATION AND CONFRARIA

In addition to this system of religious registration at local Buddhist temples, the bakufu created a structure of neighborhood associations aimed at making the residents of the same neighborhood watch one another. Just as Buddhist parish priests were used as "governmental spies," neighbors were expected to function in the same way. Usually five families in the same neighborhood block formed one unit, which was presided over by an elder. They were to help one another much like an "extended family" as well to keep the whole block "safe" from such a "subversive" religion as Christianity. Should any traitor be found in a unit, all of its members were to be responsible and subjected to punishment.

It is interesting that the Christians themselves had such a "cell" system. It was called *confraria* (a Portuguese word for confraternity) or *kumiko* (its Japanese equivalent). This was not a device which the Christians invented to counter the government-ordered anti-Christian neighborhood association. It instead antedated the governmental counterpart.

The Christian ideal of a community can be traced back to the era of the early church. In the Acts of the Apostles 2:43–47, for example, we read that "all who believed were together and had all things in common, and they sold their possessions and goods and distributed them to all, as any had need. And day by day, attending the temple together and breaking bread in their homes, they partook of food with glad and generous hearts, praising God and having favor with all the people." Under the padres' direction and encouragement, the Japanese Christians formed such groups as the one mentioned in this biblical passage. In some cases, they apparently even lived communally. Those communities were called "confraria."

It is not known exactly when the first confraria was founded, but reference to a misericordia by Padre Cosme de Torres in Br. Fernandez's letter of December 1, 1560 seems to be the earliest information we have. Br. Almeida who contributed greatly to the medical missions must have played an important role in forming many charitable groups. Visitor Valignano was instrumental in organizing the system of confrarias. Not only the Jesuits but the Spanish friars were also quite active in creating their own "confradia." (It was unfortunate but there were some instances of ugly competition between the Jesuit sponsored confrarias and the friars' confradias.)

Based on the virtue of Christian brotherly love, some confrarias were devoted to charity works. They were called *confraria de misericordia*. Their benevolent activities of medical care and of aiding the poor, orphans, and widows were particularly helpful at the time of military conflicts and feudalistic exploitations. Such charitable actions certainly contributed greatly to the tremendous success of the Christian mission.

The annual report of the Jesuit Society of 1583 mentioned the erection of a "house of misericordia" in the area of Nagasaki, which had one hundred members led by one overseer (called *provedor*) and twelve officers (*mordomos*). They followed a set of regulations similar to that observed by the Portuguese in Macao. This confraria consisted only of males, but a female counterpart was soon organized. In 1596, for instance, a group of ladies from the upper class families in Kyoto formed a sisterhood by taking vows of poverty, chastity, and obedience under the direction of Padre Organtino.

The structure and scale of confrarias expanded gradually; the difference in terms of gender disappeared and each small confraria was coordinated into a larger unit (*confraria mayores*) and further into a conglomeration of a large geographical area (*confraria universais*), thereby creating a hierarchical structure.

There were two sets of seven commandments of charitable actions mentioned in a document called *Mizerikorujia no shosa* (Practice of Misericordia). The first group concerned physical needs:

1. Feed the hungry.
2. Quench the thirsty.
3. Cloth the naked.
4. Care for the sick and the imprisoned.
5. Lodge travelers.
6. Give custody to refugees.
7. Bury the dead.

The second group concerned spiritual needs:

1. Give good counsel to others.
2. Instruct the way to the ignorant.
3. Console the distressed.
4. Encourage the remonstrated.
5. Forbear shame.
6. Forgive the mistakes of neighbors.
7. Pray to Deus for the living, the dead, and those who trespass against us.

The Christians were instructed to recite these commandments alongside the Lord's Prayer, the Apostles' Creed, the ten commandments, and other prayers. They passed them on from one generation to another.

During the era of persecution, the confrarias functioned as underground cells of the Christians. The government-ordered five family neighborhood association was sometimes used as a cover for a Christian confraria, when a whole neighborhood was Christian. The well-structured and tightly knit confrarias were so strong that they often withstood even tough official inquisitions and savage persecutions. An example of such a confraria was the Confraria of St. Joseph which was formed during the persecution in Arima by the children younger than fifteen years old. The members pledged in writing that "even if our nails and teeth may be plucked out, our bodies may be tortured by water and burnt with fire, we will never abandon the teachings of Christ which we have decided to believe in."

The leader of a confraria functioned as the elder of a neighborhood association. He was often called *jiji-yaku* (officer of the elder), which was perhaps transformed from the original *jihi-yaku* (officer of charity). He acted as a lay pastor of his group and a teacher of Christian doctrines for the youngsters. The rule of the confraria of Santa Maria of Holy Assumption written by Padre Jeronimo Rodriguez in 1617 instructed the jihi-yaku not only to take care of the spiritual as well as physical well-being of the members but also more specifically to prepare them for their giving confession, receiving holy communion, making sure dying persons received last rites, and so on. He was also responsible for the discipline of the members.

There was also a person who fulfilled the duty of performing baptism. He was called *omizu-kata* (officer of water). When a baby was born, for instance, he was responsible for christening it. In this way the Christians tried to continue to practice their faith under horrendous oppression without padres or churches or any external help.

### CHRISTIAN SYMBOLS AND FUMIE

One other device used by those "underground Christians" was the concealment of Christian symbols in statues of Buddha. A crucifix was often engraved in the back of a Buddha's wooden statuette. The madonna and child were sometimes painted or engraved disguising a Kannon Buddha (merciful Buddha) holding a baby. Other times, three Buddhistic images (representing the Trinity) were placed in a family shrine. The word Deus or Christ was inscribed inconspicuously somewhere in these images. Adroitly modified forms of the cross were

Crucifix concealed in the back of a statuette of Buddha.

usually incised on Christian tombstones. A round stone was occasionally used to indicate the Virgin Mary, because the Japanese word for round was *marui*, which sounded similar to *Maruya* (Mary). These and many other devices showed the desperate ways they found to express their faith under the eagle eyes of the officials.

Having discovered the Christian adoration of holy objects, the official inquisitors began using them in their search of Christians. They made people trample upon plaques of the madonna and/or Christ. This method of inquisition proved very effective. It was called *fumie* (literal meaning: to trample on a picture). Even those who pretended to have abandoned the Christian faith, when demanded to commit such an act of sacrilege, could no longer hide the true belief they embraced deep within themselves. This measure began to be employed around 1620 and from then on widely spread in investigatory practice throughout the country. In the following sections we proceed to observe several notorious cases of persecution resulting from such tactics by the investigators.

### PERSECUTION BY KIYOMASA KATO

Kiyomasa Kato (1562–1611) was one of the bravest generals under Hideyoshi Toyotomi. For example, his military prowess was well demonstrated in the battlefields during the Japanese invasion of Korea. His single-minded aggressiveness, however, failed to be supplemented by political discretion. Yukinaga Konishi who also distinguished himself as a general in the same war was excellent in diplomacy as well and therefore became a formidable rival of Kiyomasa.

After the downfall of the Toyotomi clan, Kiyomasa turned to serve Ieyasu, who gave him a sizable portion of the former fief of Yukinaga. He was a fanatic follower of the Hokke sect of Buddhism, and as such he launched attempts to systematically eradicate the Christians in the former territory of his old political and religious rival. By virtue of Yukinaga's strong support, Christianity had flourished in this domain; there were reportedly 50,000 Christians there when Kiyomasa took over.

The new ruler tried on the one hand to force the Christians of his domain to renounce their faith by threatening them with the confiscation of their land and property. On the other hand, many temples and monasteries of the Hokke sect were built, and the retainers were ordered to listen to lectures on the Lotus sutra (which the Hokke sect valued more than any other of the Buddhist scriptures). These attempts proved to be ineffective, however; many of the Christians steadfastly clung to their faith, and others simply left their homes for areas of the country where Christianity was not suppressed.

Kiyomasa, out of frustration, ordered the arrest of their leaders, who were sentenced either to long-term imprisonment or immediate execution. This took place in December of 1603. Oppression ensued; it extended from the retainers to the merchants and peasants. And even after the death of this cruel lord, the persecution continued, owing to the anti-Christian policy of the central government.

### MARTYRDOM IN NAGASAKI

In 1622 fifty-five Christians were martyred in Nagasaki. Among them there were nine European padres. Twenty-five of them were burned at the stake. There was also a woman eighty years of age, Lucia de Freitas, who was the widow of a Spanish man by the name of Felipe de Freitas and was respected by the Christians in Nagasaki as the "mother of confraria." She was always helping the poor and the sick as well as providing food and lodging for Christian refugees including some padres. But hiding padres meant the death penalty, and for this "crime" she was burned alive.

As was sometimes done to prolong the victim's pain, the fire was deliberately kept less intense. It took four hours for the victims' bodies to be consumed by the fire. Such a scene of horrible suffering, in the persecutors' expectation, would discourage those Christians who were among the spectators. It did not work always; it oftentimes inspired them instead. Even some jailers were so impressed by the martyrs' ardent faith that they became Christians.

The thirty other victims were beheaded. This group included thirteen women and even seven young children. Maria Murayama was one of them. Even though she was a niece of the commissioner, she was not spared. Leon Pagés commented as follows: "In the history of Japan, it had been regarded as inhuman and barbaric to involve the

Martyrdom in 1622.

youngsters in the arrest of their parents who were convicted for execution for the charge of treason. It had also been told that arresting officers greatly hesitated to put hands on these young victims. . . . But now the executioners killed these children without mercy. They cut them as if they were lambs."

All the martyrs' bodies were burnt to ashes, which were scattered in the ocean. This was done in order to prevent any remains from being taken by Christians as holy relics, as had often happened. The officials gave out the order prohibiting any reverence toward the victims' corpses or even prayer at the site of the execution. Offenders were to be punished, males to be beheaded, and females to be exposed naked to the public.

### MARTYRDOMS IN KYOTO AND EDO

The Christian mission was tenaciously kept alive in the capital city of Kyoto and in the bakufu's capital Edo despite severe oppression. Pagés recorded the martyrdom of fifty-two people in Kyoto in 1619. They were the residents of a section called *Daiusu-machi* in Kyoto. (*Machi* means a section of town. An old map of Kyoto shows a block named *Daiusu-cho* or *Daiusu-no-tsuji,* meaning Deus block.) This section was inhabited solely by the families of above-average warriors, who were, as the name of their area indicated, mostly Christians. Thirty-six of them were arrested and their properties confiscated and sold at auction. Others fled and hid themselves in other sections of the town or in nearby mountains. The Christians, including several padres, were nonetheless working clandestinely to encourage one another to keep the faith.

Then in the summer of that year, Shogun Hidetada visited the city. When he heard that the Christian community was still alive and operating, he ordered that all the Christians be burned alive. Fifty-five of them, young and old, male and female, fell as victims. According to Pagés, the commissioner of the city, though he wanted to set them free from prison, had to carry out the shogun's order.

The third shogun, Iemitsu, was even more cruel than his father, Hidetada, in suppressing Christianity. In contrast to his grandfather Ieyasu, in particular, he seems to have been paranoid about a possible

European invasion. François Caron mentioned that at one time when he showed the shogun a world map, "he was greatly surprised (at the smallness of his country compared to others) and heartily wished that his land had never been visited by any Christian." (Old maps made by the Europeans in those days tended to exaggerate their lands.) Such a national inferiority complex drove him to inflict an even more savage attack on the Christians whom he considered to be subversive traitors. The persecution of helpless Christians was one way he could satisfy his fragile ego. He encouraged local commissioners to redouble their efforts to hunt, torture, and punish the Christians in each of their territories.

As soon as he became a shogun in 1623, Iemitsu commenced a systematic hunt of the Christians in his town of Edo. As a result many were imprisoned (one source says four to five hundred), and fifty of them were burned at the stake. Arrests and executions ensued; more than three hundred presumably perished.

BRUTAL TORTURE

We have mentioned thus far savage incidents of persecution in Kyushu, Kyoto, Edo, and the northern part of Japan. There were numerous other events in these places as well as in many other areas in the rest of the country. Boxer counted 2,128 people including seventy-one Europeans who were martyred during the period from 1614 through 1650 (cf. a list of martyrs' numbers in his *The Christian Century in Japan*, appendix XIV). This is the total number of the recorded cases. But there were many more martyrs who have never been documented. These victims suffered not only a horrendous death but also brutal torture which often preceded their slaughter. There were also a considerable number of those who recanted their faith because of the threat of monstrous pain of torture.

It seems instructive to quote Caron's account here in order to illustrate the atrocity of the torture. As referred to previously, Caron was a Dutch trader stationed in Hirado from 1626 to 1641. (He was the head of the Dutch trading firm from 1639 to 1641.) Being a Dutch, he was a fierce foe of the Iberians and a militant Protestant. His report was therefore first hand and motivated neither by glorification nor by romanticization of the Catholic martyrs.

The people who came to believe in Christianity because of
the teachers of Romists, were first beheaded and then crucified. It seems to us quite a serious event, but they died with
satisfaction, singing, laughing, and rejoicing. They were
slaughtered by thirty, by fifty, and by a hundred in many
towns and villages; nonetheless their faith was not perturbed
but kindled even more greatly.

In order to change this laughter, singing, and satisfaction
to crying and tears, they decided to tie the followers to stakes
to burn them alive, and killed a few thousand of them. The
officials were perplexed, however, at the failure to attain
their purpose by the execution of so many people. They
hence devised another method to force them to recant. As a
result, they inflicted terrible and loathsome torture.

They stripped lovely girls and women in public, forced
them to crawl on their fours, twisted their bodies, and dragged
them. Next they let ruffians molest them. They then confined
them nude in wooden tubs filled with hundreds of snakes until
they died. . . . Some (of the victims) were wrapped with
sunokos (sunoko used in this case was a mat of bamboo or other
rods laced together) and poured boiling water on them. As the
boiling water passed through the sunokos ceaselessly, the victims died after two, three days. . . .

A group of the old and young were put in a cage on the
seashore so that they were either immersed in the water or
dried under the hot sun. Most of them lasted twelve or thirteen
days because the food and water were provided in order to
barely sustain their lives thereby prolonging their pain.

They blinded some parents and inflicted pain on their
young children who were placed nearby. As the youngsters
shed tears and blood crying to their parents, "Daddy, Mommy,
help me, please take away the pain. Unless you convert, I
suffer from pain. Mommy, Mommy, help me," the hearts of
the parents were broken as they could hardly tolerate to continue listening to their children's cries and entreaty. Some of
them indeed died heartbroken.

There were those whose nails were plucked off and those

whose limbs were pierced by pipes. . . . Finally, one device was invented: a victim was hung in a pit upside down by securing his feet to a fixture. In order to prevent the blood to flow out too quickly, a cross-shaped cut was made slightly on his head; thus his blood would be gradually let out. Today this method is no longer used, but he is hung without a cut on his head. He certainly lasts nine to ten days without losing consciousness until the last moment. Two years ago, a girl died after fourteen days, which is rather long and unusual. The reverse hanging causes an indescribably terrible pain. Many Christians could not help but abandon their faith. They say that no human can bear the pain of hanging upside down, and I think so, too. I talked sometimes with people who apostatized after having hung upside down for two, three days; they all declared that it could not even be compared with any other torture such as one by fire.

Caron also mentioned that he actually saw children as young as eight to thirteen years old refusing the officials' exemption of the death penalty by saying that they had no fear of death but wished to join their parents. But some other children who were afraid of death were told by their parents that they could go with them to the precious and beautiful land where all of them could live together with joy eternally. Caron eyewitnessed the deaths of all of them together.

Caron was totally horrified at these atrocities, but according to the persecuted Catholics, the Dutch and the English in Japan exercised the same amount of cruelty toward the padres as the Japanese inquisitors had done not only by cooperating with the Japanese but also by torturing them themselves.

### EXHORTATION TO MARTYRDOM

In order to encourage the Christians against such horrendous persecutions, various writings were produced by Christian leaders. It is of interest to consider a notable example in the following.

The document we observe here has been called *Maruchirio no susume* (Exhortation to martyrdom). It was most likely written by a

Torture by Hanging (picture drawn in 1675).

padre with the help of a Japanese Christian, because it contains many accurate citations of scriptural passages as well as numerous references to church fathers and European martyrs. There is only one mention of a martyrdom which took place in Japan: the death of Juan Doju at Sumpu in 1614. This date suggests the date of composition as a little later than 1614.

There are six sections. The first section discusses the reasons why the Christians had to endure persecutions and suffer martyrdom. The author attempts to answer these questions by stating that Deus has wisdom beyond any human understanding and wants to discipline the believers to let them win the final glory in heaven by providing them with travail on earth.

Then five more specific reasons are stated. First, suffering will distinguish who are true Christians and who are not. Second, Deus will reveal his power through plight. The author promises that one or two thousand people will become Christians by eyewitnessing the martyrdom of one Christian.

Third, the literature goes on to instruct that Deus gives us hardships in order to manifest the truth of the Christian teachings. The truth can be proven by surviving difficult tests, while falsehood cannot endure. Fourth, Deus allows persecutions as a punishment for not accepting the missionaries from abroad just as Jesus lamented over Jerusalem for its refusal to listen to him. The fifth reason for persecution is because the Christians can learn to follow Jesus through various tribulations in order eventually to reach the glory of paradise.

The second section deals with the answers to these questions: Why are the persecutors not punished? Why does Deus not protect his followers against the oppressors? These questions must undoubtedly have bothered many Christians. The author condemns such questions by saying that they are as nonsensical as insisting on the non-existence of the sun in the cold weather.

The writer continues to assert that Deus' plans are indeed inscrutable to every sentient being. It is wrong to be impatient. It is his merciful desire to give non-believers opportunities to repent of their sins. But in the end he will punish the persecutors severely by throwing them into hell's fire. The Christians, therefore, should endure the hardships of the moment. St. Peter and St. Paul could not have gained the crown of glory without the horrible oppressor, Emperor Nero. The grace of Christ was given through the treacherous act of Judas. Deus thus uses evil to accomplish his righteous plans.

The third section strongly warns against apostasy. The sin of apostasy is far more grave than sins committed by those who have not known of Deus. Renegades will suffer the following. First, the merits accumulated since becoming a Christian will be annulled. Second, divine grace, charity, and the gifts of the Holy Spirit will be lessened. Third, their hope and will shall be lost only to be driven by carnal desires. Fourth, their conscience will torture them.

Fifth, the renegades will have no power to protect themselves from temptations. Sixth, they will become targets of resentment not only from the faithful but also from non-Christians. Seventh, they will be mocked by the whole world for their cowardice. Eighth, they will become servants of devils. Ninth, they will be abhorred by the angels, the saints, and especially by their guardian angels. Tenth, they will have to suffer eternally in hell.

The author attempts to inculcate repeatedly that the hardships of persecution can be overcome not by one's own self but only by the power of Deus. Apostasies take place when one's mind is still attached to wealth, family, friends, and sovereign, all of which are temporal and earthly existences. Fidelity to the faith, on the other hand, concerns eternal and heavenly matters.

This section also admonishes strictly against the idea of a temporal or pretended departure from the faith. There were evidently a considerable number of the Christians who resorted to this compromising way; some of them pretended publicly that they had abandoned the Christian faith but kept it privately, hoping that the persecution would soon end, and others decided to defect until the end of the official prohibition of Christianity.

The author strongly renounces these courses of action, indicating that a pretended apostasy is still an apostasy, which harms the Christian cause. Since no one knows what will happen the next day, a "temporary apostasy" is wrong. A "gimmickery desertion" of any kind is foolish, asserts the author, because it can be likened to a suggestion that a sick man should commit suicide when the availability of a physician is uncertain.

The relatively short fourth section praises an unshaken loyalty to the Christian faith. By citing as an example Abraham who was, at God's command, willing even to sacrifice his son Isaac (Genesis 22), God will reward those who are faithful to him to the end. The fifth section makes references to the many saints who had become martyrs and acclaims the priceless merit of martyrdom.

The sixth section constitutes the last segment of the book. It instructs the Christians to prepare themselves for martyrdom in the following five respects. First, it recommends that they pursue the virtue of humility. Deus will bestow grace on those who are humble in spirit. Second, the virtue of purity is urged. The soul should be kept pure by staying away from all earthly desires.

Third, the Christians should offer prayers constantly so that they may receive a great spiritual encouragement. Fourth, they should teach others, including their families, goodness and faith. Finally, it is stated that in martyrdom one should think not about oneself but about the glory of Deus alone. Keep reflecting, inculcates the author, only on the wisdom, mercy, grace, and sovereignty of God. The whole book closes with a pious prayer.

Martyrdom is the ultimate way of witnessing to the glory of Deus! Submit to it with neither compromise nor resistance. That is the basic message of this document. This writing seems to have been widely circulated, taught, and taken very seriously by the believers.

As taught in literature such as this, no attempts of revolt against the bakufu were to be made by the Christians, not only because the power of the Tokugawa regime was so overwhelming, but also because they sincerely believed in non-resistance. It was their firm conviction that punishment and reward belonged to Deus alone. There was, nevertheless, one event quite exceptional to this belief—a rebellious war in Shimabara. This uprising is the subject of the next section.

## REVOLT IN SHIMABARA

### (1) Background

A small peninsula, originally an isle which had been attached to Kyushu by a volcanic eruption in time immemorial, was Shimabara.

It, together with several other zigzagging peninsulae and many rugged islets, formed the craggy coast of western Kyushu. Because of its geological makeup, the whole region was quite barren. Peasants managed to till a little ground suitable for farming, and fishermen sought after what the clear water of the surrounding sea provided. They were always at a barely subsistent level.

Shimabara had belonged to the Arima family until the Tokugawa bakufu transferred the clan to another part of Kyushu. The population, because of Arima's influence, consisted heavily of Christians. There were also a number of Christian refugees from the territories of the anti-Christian lords; they found a haven there. But when a new feudal lord arrived, their plight became quite serious.

The bakufu appointed Shigemasa Matsukura to take over the domain. He was one of the worst rulers; not only was he a merciless persecutor of Christians but he was also a cruel exploiter of his subjects. He enforced a series of oppressive measures to raise funds, which he spent simply to ingratiate himself with the shogun and the high officials in Edo. He, for example, volunteered to reconstruct the stone walls of the Edo castle, though it was too costly a job for a minor daimyo like himself to undertake. Heavy taxes were imposed on the already poor peasants.

Worse still, there was a series of serious crop failures for several years after 1634. Instead of trying to improve the rueful condition of his fief, Matsukura added more burdens on his subjects by levying fresh taxes including even taxes on new births and deaths in the family. A failure to pay the taxes resulted in either starvation or cruel penalties. A number of his subjects were tortured and executed, and their wives and daughters were humiliated and sold to brothels. The horrible situation continued after Katsuie Matsukura succeeded his father as ruler of the fief.

The same condition existed in the neighboring territory of the Amakusa islands, south of Shimabara. Since, like Shimabara, Amakusa was once governed by the Christian lord, Yukinaga Konishi, it was an overwhelmingly Christian region. Now under a fiercely anti-Christian overlord, Katataka Terusawa, the residents had to bear horrendous persecution. The economic exploitation in Amakusa was as hard as in Shimabara.

## (2) Revolt

In the autumn of 1637, the farmers both in Shimabara and in Amakusa finally rose up out of sheer desperation. Since there were a number of former warriors (mostly Christians) who settled in the farmlands there, the rebels were led by those who had had actual experiences in battle. The local magistrates were unable to suppress the angry insurrectionists and barely escaped into a fortress.

The news soon reached Edo. The bakufu officials thought it was one of those discontented farmers' revolts which had taken place from time to time in various parts of the country. A commissioner was sent to quell the problem with the help of the troops from the neighboring fiefs. The rebels' resistance was unexpectedly strong; the bakufu army had to suffer a disastrous defeat and the commissioner-general was killed during the conflict.

Terribly alarmed at this shameful loss, the bakufu dispatched 120,000 men against the rebels, who numbered only 27,000 including women and children and were very poorly equipped. (The number of the insurrectionists indicates that more than eighty percent of the entire population of the region participated in the rebellious war. The close network of confrarias was able to produce such a mobilization of the population.)

They chose as their leader a young man, sixteen years old, by the name of Shiro Tokisada Masuda (usually called Shiro Amakusa), the son of a former retainer of Lord Konishi. Both the father and the son were devout Christians. In addition to his spiritual strength, Shiro was endowed with a handsome face and an impressive physique. His fellow rebels apparently believed that he was sent by Deus to destroy the oppressors.

Knowing well that they could not possibly cope with the overwhelming number of bakufu troops in the open fields, the rebellious fighters chose to defend themselves in an old fortress called Hara-jo located on a promontory surrounded by the sea on three sides and with muddy rice paddies on the open side to the west.

The natural formation as well as the morale of the defenders presented a formidable foe to the bakufu army. The initial attack on the fortress was repulsed. A Dutch ship was then requested to shell the fortification from the sea, an action which was soon cancelled because of strong criticism voiced from both sides, the attackers as well as the defenders, that the bakufu had had to resort to calling on a foreign power. The alternative offensive strategy was a tight besiegement in order to starve the defenders.

The strategy worked; Hara-jo fell after a ninety-day holdout. The punitive action was most savage—all the people, including women and children, were slaughtered save less than twenty people who somehow managed to escape. Thus ended the revolt. The casualties on the part of the bakufu side were also heavy: 1,992 dead and 10,656 wounded.

The bakufu put Katsuie Matsukura to death for the gross mismanagement of his fief and confiscated the land. A big portion of Terasawa's fief was confiscated as well. He later took his life out of remorse and humiliation. The severe penalty inflicted on Matsukura was meant to be a warning to all other feudal lords. (Daimyos were not usually executed because it was considered to be a terrible dishonor, but they were ordered to commit suicide.) The bakufu also directed all the feudal lords of the nation to treat peasants with care.

The government's policy toward Christianity was a totally different matter, however. The bakufu considered the revolt to be an open attempt by the Christians to take over the country. The search and destroy mission against the Christians was intensified even more thoroughly than before. A total prohibition of the arrival of any Portuguese vessels was decreed. This completed the political course of isolation of the country as pursued by the bakufu.

### (3) The nature of the revolt

Was this revolt really a war waged by the Christians with a political aim against the government as the bakufu claimed it to have been? As we have observed, what triggered the uprising was basically the economic oppression and cruel treatment of the peasants. In this sense, it was not a religious war. Many modern historians judge the incident so. As indicated previously, the Christians in Japan had never tried to use force in defending themselves against the persecutors. The padres strictly admonished them against any physical resistance even when faced with bloody torture.

Nonetheless, the revolt was not a purely economic and political event either. The immeasurable pain and outrage caused by the horrendous persecution did, in fact, drive the Christians of those regions to seek religious freedom. The banners flown in their fortress carried explicitly Christian symbols. They chose a leader, attributing to him a messianic quality.

They fervently believed in the imminent coming of God's judgment upon their oppressors and the final rescue of the faithful. This belief was emphatically expressed in the secret letters circulated among the villagers, urging them to join in the uprising. One of those letters, written on October 25, 1637, included a statement: "This is the time of the judgment of Japan as a whole." This "judgment" was meant to be the final judgment by God, as another letter referred to "the judgment of fire by Deus."

The same religious idea continued being mentioned in the messages to the attackers attached to the arrows which were shot from within the fort during the siege. Such an eschatological fervor erased any fear of death on the part of all the besieged. (There was only one defector and this person was said to have been executed some years later on the charge of preaching Christianity to his neighbors.)

We may well conclude, consequently, that the revolt was indeed deeply motivated by religious aspirations, and certainly not simply for purely economic and political reasons. The nature of this whole event comprised a mixture of both religious and economic struggles. It was a desperate outcry of deprived peasants who were inspired by the Christian eschatological hope.

But, alas, to no avail—they all perished. And their deaths, which they had hoped would be counted as martyrs' deaths with the promise of eternal bliss in paradise, were not recognized as such by the Catholic Church because of their use of physical force. There was not a single padre among them to guide them. The terrible tragedy called the Shimabara revolt was the only recorded military uprising by Christians against the authorities throughout the history of Japan.

### CONCLUDING REMARKS

The oppression of the Christians, which commenced with the order of Hideyoshi Toyotomi, was intensified to the greatest magnitude during the reign of the second and the third shoguns of the Tokugawa bakufu. Both Hideyoshi Toyotomi and Ieyasu Tokugawa, though basically anti-Christian, overlooked the practice of Christianity because they recognized the significant contributions made by the padres to the trade with the Iberians.

However, such a stance, open toward the outside world, was replaced by a policy of isolationism under Hidetada and Iemitsu Tokugawa. The bakufu's basic concern was its own self-perpetuation. Not only foreigners but also native Japanese who had any contact with the outside world became automatically suspect. Above all, the Christian teachings were regarded as subversive to the Tokugawa Japan.

The conflicts between the Jesuits and the other missionary orders unfortunately militated against their supposedly common purpose, the evangelization of Japan. The arrival of the Protestant Europeans made the situation even worse. The Catholic and Protestant Europeans brought their fight in Europe to Japan, and, as a result, the Christian cause suffered gravely.

The bakufu's persecution of the Christians became savage and monstrous. Hundreds of the victims, including the padres, lay followers, and even young children, were inhumanely imprisoned, tortured, and killed. Except for those in the Shimabara revolt, none of them resorted to physical resistance, and they meekly submitted themselves to the sadistic violence of their persecutors.

For the Christians, martyrdom was one way to follow the Christ who himself had suffered and died for the sake of everyone. It was to them an ultimate means of witnessing to the truth of the teaching of Deus, thereby glorifying Him. A submission to pain and death without resistance, no matter how terrible the torture might be, guaranteed him or her an eternal reward in paradise. The victims would be sanctified both in the body and in the soul by dying for such a righteous cause. The believers therefore venerated martyrdom and cherished the physical remains of the martyrs as holy relics.

Such a spirit as that of Christian martyrdom was rather incomprehensible to the non-Christians in Japan. There had been some Buddhist priests and their followers who were persecuted and even suffered death because of their beliefs and teachings. A branch of the Hokke Buddhist sect (usually referred to by the name of *Fuju-fuse-ha*, meaning literally "the sect of non-receiving"), for example, was suppressed because of its intolerant nature throughout the Tokugawa era.

The Buddhists, however, generally never attributed any doctrinal significance to their religious suffering, nor glorified their painful experiences. No stories had ever been written in praise of martyrs; no literature was circulated among the followers instructing them to prepare for suffering and eventual glory. They had no doctrine of eternal reward and punishment. As Konchiin Suden's anti-Christian document exemplified, the Japanese non-Christians regarded the Christian honor of martyrdom and martyrs' relics as a worship of devils.

The Christian spirit of martyrdom consequently constituted a diametrical divergence from the Japanese religious tradition. There seems to have been one possible area of similarity, however. That is, the spirit of martyrdom, in one sense, agreed with the strong sense of loyalty which was often considered to be a most acclaimed virtue of the warriors (samurai)—the so-called *bushi-do* (the way of the samurai). The good samurai was supposed to have no fear of anything, including death for the sake of what he valued supremely such as the "name" (a symbol of the esteem and honor) of his overlord, his family, and himself.

Such a native mentality appears to have militated in favor of the Christian spirit of martyrdom on the part of the many Japanese Christians not only of the samurai class but also even of peasant origin. In both cases of spiritual aspiration, the sense of loyalty was essential, and death constituted a threshold to enter a higher glory, in which one's old small self would lose its significance and his or her bigger and new self was to triumph.

This apparent similarity was superficial, nonetheless. The spirit of the samurai was concerned after all only with oneself (or extension of oneself to the group one belonged to), whereas the Christian spirit was focused on the salvation of the whole world. In the former case, moreover, one would live only in the memory of others after one's death, while for the latter there was a promise of future glory. Lastly, the *bushido* demanded death to be a final reality which should be taken at one's own hand. In other words, suicide was a honorable way of dying, while an execution would bring him shame.

By contrast, the Christians believed that life was a gift of God, and that, therefore, suicide was a sin. No matter how painful it might be, they had to bear any persecution without resistance. This was the reason why many of the Christian warriors never chose to take their own lives as warriors were supposed to do.

Martyrdom, consequently, marked a culmination of the life of faith of the Christians under the hellish persecution. For those Christians, martyrdom meant, in reality, a spiritual victory over the devilish power of this world. Victory promised them eternal bliss in paradise. That was the reason why those Christians who were condemned to death called one another "*kahomono*" (a lucky one). Such a religious conviction seems to have been the ultimate reason why even the bakufu's systematic and ferocious persecution was not able to annihilate the Christians entirely.

There were, however, many who left the Christian faith. It is the task of the next chapter to observe the circumstances, the happenings, and the results of some notable cases of apostasy as well as martyrdom.

# 6

# Persecution by the
# Tokugawa Bakufu (2)

The priest bowed his head in silence. Then raising it his eyes
met those of the old man who was sitting in the middle chair
of the five. A kind smile playing on his lips, the old man
watched the priest with the curiosity of a child who has been
given a new toy.

This is the scene described by the modern Japanese novelist,
Shusaku Endo, about the first encounter of Padre Giuseppi Chiara
(Rodriguez, in the story) with Masashige Inoue, inquisitor general
during the height of the Christian persecution by the Tokugawa
bakufu. Endo, a Catholic writer, deals in this novel with the subject of
the apostasies of the padres. This book, entitled *Chinmoku* (Silence),
became a best seller and was made into a movie in Japan. It was
originally published in 1966 in Tokyo and translated into English by
Fr. William Johnston in 1969.

As seen in the passage quoted above, the author attempted to
underscore the impression of a gentle Japanese official: contrary to the
padre's expectation of meeting a fearsome sadist the inquisitor always
behaved mildly and even sympathetically toward the captured European. This characterization of Masashige Inoue, though an imaginary
reconstruction by a modern novelist, seems to illustrate rather cogently

191

the approach this infamous inquisitor adopted in treating the Christian prisoners.

Inoue (1585–1661), although the lord of a relatively small fief, was an influential official of the bakufu who enjoyed the great trust of Shogun Iemitsu and also of his close aides. He held the position called *ometsuke*, attorney general, for many years (from 1627 to 1658 when he retired at the age of seventy-four). His effective participation in resolving the revolt in Shimabara prompted the bakufu to entrust him with additional responsibility as the inquisitor general in charge of religious affairs. Thus for all intents and purposes he came to assume complete authority over matters regarding the Christians. As Endo described in the novel, Inoue must have been regarded as the very source of devilish terror as far as the Christians were concerned.

The tenacious and fearless fight the rebels waged in Shimabara apparently convinced Inoue and other governmental officials that they must ban Catholic Europeans totally from Japan. Within a couple of years following the revolt, the bakufu issued a formal decree prohibiting Portuguese arrivals in the country. This left the Dutch as the lone European traders in Japan. Inoue was also in charge of overseeing the Dutch, whom he moved from Hirado to Dejima, a tiny port area in Nagasaki.

As fiercely anti-Portuguese as he was, yet he was not an ignorant persecutor of Catholic Christianity. He, in fact, seems to have seriously studied Christian teachings when he was younger. (Some modern historians suspect that he was once even a believer.) His interest in European culture was genuine; he actively protected trade with the Dutch and promoted the importation of science and technology which they could offer his country.

This enlightened official knew well that simply harsh treatment would not make the Christians give up their faith. The bloodier the persecution, the more unyielding they became. They were taught by the padres and believed sincerely that the blood of martyrs became the seeds for planting Christianity. As soon as one was crucified or burned alive, a hundred more lined up and anxiously awaited their turn. They had no fear of pain and death, which they rather deemed their glory. Recognizing this, Inoue made a change in basic policy when he assumed the office of inquisitor general. The massive imprisonments and public executions, which had been the usual practice, were altered; instead concentration was placed on the leaders and there was vigorous and ceaseless coercion of them to encourage apostasy.

This hardly meant that the tactics of oppression became more gentle or civil, but they did become more patient and shrewd. As Endo pictured in his novel, Inoue talked to the prisoners sympathetically, attempting to break down their mental guard. His pity may have been, in fact, truly genuine, though he did not hesitate to resort to cruel torture when it was deemed necessary. According to his successor, Ujinaga Hojo, Inoue told him that Christianity, though "pernicious" to the national interest because of its foreignness, did offer "some reason for people to believe." Hojo did not elaborate on what kind of "reason" his predecessor meant. Inoue, a loyal servant of the bakufu, evidently shared the government's concern about the Christians as a subversive group potentially inimical to the security of the country.

As will be discussed in the following sections, Inoue was indeed successful in achieving his goal; many Christians, including some prominent padres, did fall victim to his tactics. He used his own estate in Edo for their interrogation and imprisonment.

### CHRISTOVÃO FERREIRA

Christovão Ferreira became the first victim of Inoue as far as the padres were concerned. He came from his native Portugal to Macao in 1600, where he completed theological training and was ordained. After arriving in Japan in 1609, he studied Japanese in Arima for two years, and then moved to Kyoto to work as the minister, consulter, and admonitor for the Rector at the Jesuit residence there. When Provincial Carvelho was expelled by the bakufu in 1614, the responsibility of the mission's superiorship for the Kami district fell to Padre Ferreira.

In 1617, when Padre Mateus de Couros assumed the post of Provincial, he called Ferreira to Nagasaki to work with him as the secretary. Because of de Couros' poor health, Ferreira assumed much of the Provincial's job. Meanwhile he took the final vows as a Jesuit, which, along with his formal philosophical and theological education, put him in the elite ranks of the priesthood, so to speak. According to Pagés, Padre Ferreira "was blessed with grace and a rare genius," was "trusted like an angel" by the Japanese Christians, and "heard confessions for 1,300 people." "He performed his spiritual duty while walking on sea shores during the night."

Upon the death of de Couros in 1632, Padre Sebastião Vieira took over his office, only soon to be arrested. As the most senior in line, Ferreira succeeded Vieira, and his assignment became official by the end of that year. The formal notice of his appointment as Vice-provincial, however, failed to reach him before he was arrested in the following year.

Ferreira was taken to Inoue for interrogation. The padre's stubborn refusal to apostatize led him to be tortured; he was suspended upside down with his head in a pit. After agonizing five hours in that state, he gave in. He was released from prison and was given a house in which to live in Nagasaki. Inoue also arranged that Ferreira be given the Japanese name of Chuan Sawano and that he be married to the Japanese widow of an executed Chinese merchant. He had one son and two daughters by this woman. Collaboration with Inoue became his new occupation.

This transformation of the former Vice-provincial was a great prize to the inquisitor general; it afforded tremendous publicity against Christianity. He often employed the ex-padre as his interpreter during negotiations with the Europeans. Sawano, alias Ferreira, was also useful as a translator of various European books and documents. And above all, however loathsome to him it may have been, during interrogation and torturing he was forced to help the inquisitors by urging the Christian prisoners to desert their faith. Available evidence points to the fact that he performed all of those tasks efficiently.

Ferreira was in fact an excellent interpreter and translator. At Inoue's request he rendered into Japanese a science textbook which was being used at the Jesuit school in Macao. The scientific information contained in this book came from a Jesuit mathematician and astronomer, Christopher Clavius (1538–1612), known particularly for his revision of the calendar under Gregory XIII.

Since Ferreira was not able to write Japanese, he wrote his translation in Latin script. This version was transcribed into Japanese by Kichibyoe Mukai. The book, with Mukai's commentary, was published in 1652(?) with the title *Kenkon Bensetsu* (A Critical Explanation of Heaven and Earth). It dealt with cosmology (chap. 1), the earth: its size and components (chap. 2), and astronomy (chap. 3). Ferreira's work constituted the first publication of western scientific theories in Japan, which subsequently exercised significant influence on Japanese intellectuals for many years.

Did Ferreira really renounce Christianity? Was his apostasy the unfortunate result of a temporary mental state caused by an extraordinary afflux of blood from having been suspended upside down for five hours? Did he indeed become a Zen Buddhist as recorded in the registry? No one but Ferreira himself could answer these questions. The records available show that he never tried to explain what was really going on in his mind. Only a few Europeans were able to talk personally with him, but they apparently failed to pry into his inner thinking. He perhaps felt too numb to express his candid feelings. A later story had it that he confessed his original faith on his deathbed, but there is nothing to substantiate this.

### KENGIROKU

There is a monograph entitled *Kengiroku* (A Disclosure of Falsehood) which carries Ferreira's name as the author. (An English translation was published by G. Elison in his *Deus Destroyed*, pp. 293–318). The author claims in the postscript that the literature "presents a summary of the secrets of the Christian religion. It discloses truth and falsehood and discusses right and wrong." The following six topics are dealt with: the creation of the universe, the immortality of the human soul, the ten commandments and the church laws, Christ, the sacraments, and the last judgment. Each of these subjects is explained as a padre would do, and then is commented on negatively. The date of publication indicated in the book is September 29, 1636, but the original work seemingly had been revised a few times before this date.

The portions containing doctrinal explanations in this piece of literature must have come from Ferreira. But the paragraphs denouncing Christianity seem to betray a composite provenance. In criticism of the Christian teachings of the divine creation of the universe, the Greek philosopher Aristotle is quoted as saying that heaven and earth had no beginning. This most likely originated with an ex-priest who was acquainted with Aristotelian philosophy.

Immediately following this reference to the Greek philosopher, however, a Confucian idea is mentioned: yin and yang are portrayed as the principles which affect earth, water, fire, and air—the basic elements comprising the universe with no beginning and no end. Refutation of Christianity is done, therefore, basically from a Confucian standpoint, which does not seem to have been that of Ferreira. The author rather calls himself one who "converted" from his religion to become "an adherent of the Zen sect," though a Zen flavor is not apparent at all throughout the book.

The author demonstrates his sure knowledge concerning the laws of the Catholic Church and papal authority, while he also complains, much like a disgruntled Catholic layman, about the money-hungry clergy. There is, however, one other peculiar fact found in this document. That is, the author's views concerning the sacraments sound more Protestant than Catholic. For example, his understanding of the eucharist is highly symbolic, which is not consonant with the theory of transubstantiation, a Catholic teaching emphatically endorsed at the Council of Trent. He calls this sacrament simply a metaphor. This fact has prompted some modern scholars to assume the influence of the Dutch Protestants (traders at Dejima) on the production of this writing; this, too, however, is difficult to substantiate.

All in all, we should conclude that *Kengiroku* is a literary work composite in origin. It did not come directly from Ferreira. It was written in Chinese. Perhaps a Confucian scholar wrote it in Ferreira's name in order to reconvert the Christians. (Chinese was the usual literary language in use by literati at that time.) Ferreira most likely supplied the information concerning Christianity. It is beyond our reach to ascertain how closely they collaborated, but Ferreira, in all probability, played a significant role in producing this anti-Christian monograph. This indicates that his apostasy was neither simply a nominal nor a spurious action on his part. He spent the rest of his life playing an active role in the religious inquisitions in Nagasaki, where he died in 1650.

### OTHER VICTIMS

When Ferreira was suffering in deathly agony in the pit, there were seven others who were also being exposed to the same horrendous treatment. They were five Jesuits (the three priests including Julian Nakaura, Joseppe Mateo Adami from Sicily, Antonio de Sousa from Portugal, and the two Japanese Jesuit brothers called Pedro and Mateo), and two Dominicans (Padre Lucas del Esposito Santo from Spain and a Japanese brother named Francisco). They all died in their pits. (Surviving the longest was Padre Santo who lasted nine days.)

Julian Nakaura, the reader will recall, was one of the four youths who visited Europe in 1584–1585 as envoys representing the three Christian lords of Kyushu. After having left Europe, he was ordained a Jesuit priest in Macao in 1603 and returned to his home country in 1605. Until such time as he was discovered and arrested, he vigorously performed his apostolic ministry in Kyushu. It was reported that he said aloud as he was about to be suspended in the torture pit, "Watch closely this splendid scene for the sake of the greatest glory of the Lord in heaven!" This was indeed his battle cry as he entered the last fight with the oppressive power in his life.

(Only a few facts are known of the lives of the other three former envoys. Mansho Ito became a Jesuit priest but died from illness in 1612; Miguel Chijiwa, after joining the Jesuit Society in 1591, recanted the Christian faith and left the order in 1603; Martino Hara joined the order in 1600 and worked as a priest in Nagasaki until he was expelled to Macao in 1614.)

The incredible news of the apostasy of Padre Ferreira shook Catholic Europe. It "gave an extreme pain to the Society of Jesus and other orders," wrote Pagés. Many Jesuits volunteered to be sent to Japan "for the purpose of reparation of the sin of the colleague with their own blood." Thirty-four Jesuit padres were selected for this task with the financial support by King Felipe IV; they, led by Padre Marcello Mastrilli, set sail from Lisbon in 1635.

When the party reached Manila, however, they encountered stiff objection from the Spaniards there, who forced all but Mastrilli to return to Macao. A Spanish ship carried the lone padre to Kyushu. Within only a few days after his arrival, he was spotted and thrown into

74

P. Iulianus Nacaura Iappon, Societ· IESV, olim Romam legatus ad Sumū Pontificem, pedib' sulpēsus, & in foueā cingulo tenus depressus quarta die moritur Nāgasachi 21. Octob.152? in odiū Filiei.

Martyrdom of Julian Nakaura in 1633.

jail. After three days of cruel torture, including being hung upside down in that infamous pit, his life was ended by decapitation.

### PEDRO KIBE

The European Jesuits were not the only ones anxious of ascertaining the truth about the apostasy of Vice-provincial Ferreira and of doing reparation for it. A Japanese priest by the name of Pedro Kibe affords a Japanese example. It is of interest to look into his life, which was full of adventure.

His family lived in the territory which was once ruled by the Christian lord Yoshishige Otomo. As we observed earlier, this lord's personal influence and official directives produced numerous Christians in his domain; among them was the Kibe family. Pedro Kibe, after training at the seminario in Arima for six years (1600–1606), became a dojuku and worked in the Christian communities in Nagasaki and Arima. In 1614 he was arrested and expelled along with other Christians by the Tokugawa bakufu to Macao.

His life in this Portuguese colony was spent at the seminario, but it was not an enjoyable one to him. His desire was to become a priest but the superior would not allow it. Out of sheer frustration, the strong-willed young man decided to go to Rome all by himself, where he hoped to be ordained. He was brave enough to journey through Persia and Arabia, and reached Jerusalem in 1619 to become the first Japanese to step on the Holy Land. From Palestine, pilgrim ships carried him to his final destination in the following year.

Though he possessed no recommendation letter to legitimize his status, the Jesuit General's office in Rome took this stranger under its wing. By the hand of Bishop Raffael Initiatum, Pedro Kibe was ordained. After spending two years in Rome and a year in Portugal, Kibe set sail, heading home in 1623. Secret entry into Japan was, needless to say, a most difficult task; he had to stay in Southeast Asia for a few years, waiting for an opportunity. In 1630 a small old boat brought him finally back to his home country.

From 1630 to 1639 (the year of his arrest), Kibe's strenuous priestly labor continued under incessant and extreme danger and covered an area stretching from Kyushu in the south to the northern tip of the island of Honshu to the north. But finally a poor villager, enticed by ten pieces of gold, informed on him to the authorities. He was taken to the court of inquisition in Edo. This was where a matter which had deeply troubled him for many years became clear—the apostasy of Padre Ferreira. One of the interrogators who appeared in front of Kibe at the court was none other than his former Vice-provincial, Christovão Ferreira. The one who deliberately set up their encounter was, needless to say, Inoue, the inquisitor general.

Clad in a native garment, Chuan Sawano, alias Ferreira, advised his former colleague to save his life by leaving the faith, even if he did so only nominally. Padre Kibe's response was a resolute and emphatic "no," with the desperate plea that Sawano return to the church. The utterly embarrassed inquisitor had to leave the court. The interrogation was held four times to no avail. Inoue, according to court records preserved in the document entitled *Kirishito-ki* (Record of the Christians), even arranged an unusual meeting of inquiry between Shogun Iemitsu and Kibe and two other captured padres (Giovanni Battista Porro and Martino Shikimi). The interview ended in futility.

The failure of the attempt to convert the padres had the inevitable finale—suspension in the pits. The agony in the pits produced what Inoue intended; Porro and Shikimi apostatized. Kibe, however, did not. *Kirishito-ki* tells us of the last moment of the ordeal:

The aforementioned three padres were interrogated concerning the teachings of Christianity for ten days at the court of Chikugo-no-kami (Inoue). After ten days, Chikugo-no-kami sent his retainer to the prison to submit the three padres to torture. Juan of Compania (Porro) and Martino Ichizaemon (Shikimi) apostatized and invoked Buddha's name. Afterwards they were brought to Chikugo-no-kami and imprisoned for two years until both died of illness.

Kibe Pedro did not apostatize, and hence died from the suspension. He was tortured and allowed to die because until then (the time of his death) he had been so insolent and he continued even then encouraging the two dojukus who were also suspended in the same pit. After Kibe expired, however, both dojukus apostatized. They were lifted out and sent to prison, where they remained for years.

## RUBINO GROUPS

At hearing the news of the martyrdom of Padres Mastrilli, Kibe, and others, the fervor to reconvert Ferreira increased even more intensely among the Jesuits in Europe and in Southeast Asia. The leader of a brave group of aspirants was Padre Antonio Rubino (1578–1643). This Italian Jesuit had been working for many years in India and became the Visitor General in 1639. With this authority, he organized two groups with a plan for them separately to enter Japan secretly for the purpose of meeting the apostatized Vice-provincial personally and to persuade him to return to the Catholic fold.

The first group consisted of the following five padres: Francisco Marques (the son of a Portuguese father and a Japanese mother), Diego de Morales (a Spaniard from Mexico), Antonio Capece (from Naples), and Albert Mecinski (a Pole). They were accompanied by three laymen: Pascal de Souza (Portuguese), Thomas (Korean), and João (Japanese). The personal background of these individuals is not known.

They set sail in a Chinese boat from Manila and arrived in Kyushu in 1642. While hiding in a cave near the shore, according to *A History of Nagasaki*, they were spotted by some hunters, who immediately informed the local authority. They were thus arrested soon and interrogated in Nagasaki. Chuan Sawano, whom the group was so anxious to meet, served as an interpreter. Pagés tells us that Sawano, at Rubino's sharp denunciation, had to excuse himself from his task.

The same gruesome scenario ensued: water torture and suspension. They died one by one—Thomas, Mecinski, João, and de Souza. The remaining three survived as long as nine days; on the tenth day they were lifted out of the pits and beheaded.

The second group which Visitor Rubino organized consisted of the following four padres: Pedro Marques (Spanish), Alonzo Arroyo (Italian), Francisco Cassola (Portuguese), and Giuseppe Chiara (Italian). They were accompanied by the Japanese brother Vieyra and four dojukus (two Japanese and two Chinese). Padre Marques was the leader of this group.

According to an historical record preserved in Japan, on June 27, 1643 the party, all disguised as Japanese, approached the northern part of Kyushu by boat but were soon suspected to be strangers. Their attempt to escape failed; all of them were captured and sent to Nagasaki for interrogation. Their identity was easily determined by the officials, who then deported them to the prison at Inoue's estate in Edo.

In an attempt to convert them, Inoue put forth his best effort. The result was the apostasy of every single member of the second Rubino mission team. The leader of the group, Padre Marques, became a collaborator of Inoue and so served for fifteen years until he died at the age of eighty. He was called Heitaro (Pedro) by the Japanese. Padre Arroyo died in prison not long after he again confessed his faith following a temporary apostasy.

Padre Cassola was put in a *joro* (which meant literally a women's prison, but it actually was a prison where a male prisoner was seduced by female agents to submit to the officials' desires). Inoue's shrewd device worked quite effectively in this instance as well. Cassola apparently, however, did not live long afterward. After forsaking his faith and mission, Padre Chiara adopted the Japanese name Saemon Okamoto, married a local woman, and served the office of inquisition for forty-two years. He died in Edo when he was eighty-four years old. The rest of the team followed the same fate as Padre Chiara.

The second Rubino group thus ended in a disastrous failure. The effect of the apostasy of these padres on the lay Christians who were hiding was drastic; many of them were so demoralized that they gave up their faith. Padre Vieira (martyred in 1634) was right on target when he stated during the deadly interrogation: "Even though you kill the Christians, Christianity will survive. It will never die out unless the padres apostatize."

There were, nonetheless, a number of those who remained faithful to Deus and Christ. From time to time, those hiding Christians were discovered and many of them perished, refusing to apostatize. The following list of 1658 dramatizes the extent of the tragedy:

|                | Omura | Nagasaki | Saga | Hirado | Shimabara | total |
|----------------|-------|----------|------|--------|-----------|-------|
| execution      | 131   | 123      | 37   | 64     | 56        | 411   |
| death in prison | 26   | 10       | 24   | 9      | 9         | 78    |

| release | 44 | 15 | 17 | 19 | 4 | 99 |
| imprisonment | 8 | 12 | 0 | 0 | 0 | 20 |
| total | 209 | 160 | 78 | 92 | 69 | 608 |

The faithful were usually located in these areas of northern Kyushu, but surprisingly there were many others who secretly preserved their Christian identity in various other places throughout Japan, though their actual number and locations cannot be accurately determined.

Thus far we have observed the cases of apostasy which were induced by torture and other uses of force. There were, however, those who voluntarily left the faith as well. In the following section, we will examine a notable example, a former brother who called himself Fabian Fucan.

## FABIAN FUCAN

### (1) The life of Fabian

Little is known about Fabian's early life, including even his original name. He was born in 1565 and educated to be a monk of Zen Buddhism. Around the age of eighteen he became a Christian and adopted a new name, Fabian Fucan. Again details of the motivation behind his conversion elude us. After one year of general education at the seminario in Takatsuki near Kyoto, he was enrolled as a dojuku in Osaka in 1584. His spiritual and academic excellence apparently impressed the padres, who accepted him as a brother of the Society of Jesus in 1586.

He received further theological training and worked for the missions in the northern part of Kyushu. He was the youngest participant present at the general conference presided over by Visitor Valignano at Kazusa in 1590. In 1592 he was asked to be a teacher of the Japanese language at the collegio in Amakusa, where he stayed until 1603 when a new assignment was given to him to assume a more important responsibility in Kyoto. While teaching at Amakusa, he edited and published in the Latin script the *Heike Monogatari*, a work of Japanese classic literature about the strife between the two powerful clans, the

Heike and the Genji, of the twelfth century. The book was used as a text of Japanese for the European missionaries.

Though the details are not known, Fabian's activities in Kyoto seem to have been quite outstanding; he was a useful colleague of the beloved Padre Organtino and was an "excellent preacher" as the padres so commented. He was a great success in debates with many Buddhists. His intellectual and speaking excellence was widely recognized. For instance, in 1604 he reportedly presented a lecture on the recent European astronomical theories in front of Hideyori Toyotomi (the son of Hideyoshi). He was deemed so superb a preacher that he was invited to deliver a eulogical homily at the funeral of Josui Kuroda, an influential feudal lord in Kyushu and one of the strong patrons of the Christian missions.

In 1605 his book *Myotei Mondo* (Dialogue between Myoshu and Yutei) was published. As will be considered in the following section, it dealt with a systematic comparison of Christianity with the Japanese religions. It was a treatment of a kind written for the first time in history. Discussed from a Christian perspective, it demonstrated very well the author's acumen as well as his wide range of knowledge with regard to all of these religions. He also wrote another Christian apologia against the Japanese religions, which he presented to Masazumi Honda, a respected aide of Shogun Ieyasu Tokugawa, when he enjoyed an audience with him as a companion of Vice-provincial Pasio in 1607. Reportedly Honda was quite impressed by this book. Unfortunately it is not extant.

The next incident in Fabian's life worthy of noting was his debate with Razan Hayashi and his associates in 1606. Razan (1583–1657) was a brilliant scholar of Neo-Confucianism (especially the teachings of Chu-Hsi, a great thinker of twelfth century China who revitalized traditional Confucianism). He served as a close aide to the initial four shoguns of the Tokugawa bakufu, and wrote the official laws regulating the warriors. Being a then young and energetic Confucian, he challenged Fabian, a famed Christian intellect, at the Jesuit house in Kyoto.

A record of this encounter is found in Razan's short essay entitled *Hai-Yaso* (The Contra Jesuits). (An English translation was published by G. Elison in his *Deus Destroyed*, pp. 149–153.) The discussion between the two seems to have been unproductive. It began with Razan's question about "the portrait of Deus." (A picture of Jesus was probably hung on the wall of the room in which they met.) Fabian's "response was evasive: Fucan evidently feared the exposure of his shallowness and did not elaborate." They then exchanged their views about the shape of the earth. Fabian, based on the recent European science, stated its roundness, while Razan countered by quoting Chu-Hsi's theory: "half of heaven rotates about the earth's bottom."

Razan then criticized Matteo Ricci's assertion that heaven, the earth and the spirits had beginnings but no ending, and insisted that if there was a beginning, there should be an end as well, and if there was no beginning, neither should there be any end. To this, according to Razan, Fabian could not answer.

The report of the debate, written by Razan, is one-sided. The conversation was at any rate totally unfructuous, as both sides held on to their personal presuppositions and made no attempt to seek the truth together open-mindedly.

One curious fact we may detect in Razan's essay is that Fabian, albeit his fame as an excellent preacher, does not seem to have been eager to evangelize these Confucians. Instead of acting like an older and experienced missionary, he appeared to have shown emotional irritation; as Razan put it, "the color of rage and the airs of jealousy appeared upon his countenance." Was this indicative of Fabian's spiritual instability at that time? It may very well have been the case. About a year after this incident, in fact, he made a drastic move. This elite Christian suddenly decided to abandon the Christian faith.

His apostasy was not the result of any external coercion. The bakufu's persecution of the Christians had not yet begun. He, of his own free will, left the Jesuit Society one day with a novice of the sisterhood of the same order. Henceforth for several years they lived privately, because, according to him, he was afraid of punitive actions by the Jesuits.

Why did he apostatize? The real reason remains a matter of conjecture, since no historical document is available for clarification. A few years after he left the Jesuit order, he sent to his former superior, Padre Pedro Morejon, a letter which was apparently filled with invective toward the padres. But this letter has been lost. The only extant writing produced by him after the apostasy was a book entitled *Ha-Daiusu* (The Contra-Deus).

In the preface to this book the author stated, "Then one day I clearly perceived that the words of the adherents of Deus were very clever and appeared very near reason—but in their teaching there was little truth." This is the only explicit reference to his recantation. But toward the end of the treatise, his fury against the padres burst: "Being so arrogant, they do not even regard the Japanese as persons. . . ." "Henceforth, they do not let Japanese become *bateren* (padre)!—we all felt terribly nonplussed by this principle of operation. But you can guess what kind of a feeling it is to know that one's real purpose can never be attained."

Some modern scholars consider this emotional statement as indicating the real reason for his apostasy. As a capable brother who had contributed so much to the Christian missions, it was Fabian's ardent desire to become a priest, which was for some reason denied. Feeling totally dejected and angry, he decided to leave the church. The letter he wrote to Padre Morejon most likely contained many protests and diatribes written out of frustration.

This may well have been the case. Not only Fabian but many other Japanese brothers appeared to have experienced the same disappointment. Pedro Kibe, whom we have referred to previously, was another notable example. We have also before noted Padre Cabral's policy rejecting native clergy, which caused considerable antagonism on the part of the Japanese Christians. Despite Visitor Valignano's effort to nurture native leadership, the suspicion persisted thereof among the European padres. There were many Japanese aspirants for the priesthood who failed to be qualified intellectually and/or spiritually. Fabian, for some reason, apparently fell into that category. (There were only about ten Japanese padres at that time.) And he took it personally.

More than ten years after the apostasy, Fabian published *Ha-Daiusu* in 1620. This book, a systematic refutation of Christianity, was the first of its kind written in Japan's history. The author's intention seems to have been twofold: reprisal and self-vindication. That is to say, it was, on the one hand, aimed at the padres, denouncing them for what he deemed the "inhuman" treatment of him for not allowing him the status of priesthood. On the other hand, it was to prove his innocence by rebutting "the false teaching of Deus." The then intense persecution of Christianity most likely quickened the latter motive for the publication of the book.

(According to the Dominican friar, Iacinto Orfanel, Fabian wrote this book for Shogun Hidetada at the request of Heizo Suenaga and Gonroku Hasegawa, both commissioners of Nagasaki and cruel persecutors of the Christians. Padre Orfanel arrived in Japan in 1607 and was martyred at Nagasaki in 1622. He wrote a history of the Christian missions in Japan during the period of 1602 through 1621, *Historia Eclesiastica de los sucessos de la Christiandad de Japon, desde el ano de 1602, Que entro en el la Orden de Predicadores, hasta el de 1620,* Madrid, 1633.)

The impact of Fabian's book on the general public was considerable and was indeed deadly for the Christian community, which desperately attempted to counter the negative effect it caused. The padres called the book a "hellish pest." Let us then examine next Fabian's two, very different, books, *Myotei Mondo* and *Ha-Daiusu* more closely.

## (2) Myotei-Mondo

*Myotei-Mondo* consists of three parts: (a) criticisms of Buddhism, (b) criticisms of Confucianism and Shintoism, and (c) explanations of Christianity. Fabian wrote this book apparently for the ladies of the upper echelon who, though eager to learn Christian teachings, had a limited amount of freedom to attend a church or to talk with the missionaries because of social restrictions. For this reason the author chose to use a literary style of a dialogue between two noble ladies: Yutei (a Christian) and Myoshu (a Christian sympathizer).

### (a) On Buddhism

The first part which deals with Buddhism had been long lost until Professor Anesaki identified this document, which was preserved together with other old manuscripts. (Some fragments of the portion of this book on Shintoism were also found among them.) Since it is narrated as an ordinary essay, instead of a dialogue, it must have been a rewritten version of the original.

The author begins presenting his views on Buddhism by talking about the meaning of Buddha: the enlightened one. What kind of enlightenment does one gain? Fabian's answer is that it consists in an inner self-realization that every existence is, in the ultimate sense, nothing, i.e. there is nothing in the world which is permanently substantial. The author denies this view and says that it is particularly deplorable that the Buddhists refuse to believe in an afterlife, which affords a proof for the substantiality of one's existence.

Fabian then points out that all these great Buddhas, including Guatama Siddharta who initiated this religion, were humans, and that they, therefore, cannot guarantee life after death. It is a serious mistake on the part of the Buddhists, he contends, that they attribute to Buddha eternal glory. Gautama Siddharta never preached the existence of an afterlife; ordinary people, however, have been told by Buddhist preachers that there is a paradise in the western extremity of the world. Because the world is round, our Christian critic determines, such a paradise cannot exist.

The Buddhist view of nothingness, Fabian also insists, entails a serious confusion in one's thinking. Ethical standards, for example, cannot be established firmly, if there is no permanent and absolute norm. Without a supreme master who is able to judge right and wrong, people will do whatever they please. Likewise, in Fabian's opinion, the Buddhist practice of the invocation of the Buddha is pointless, since Buddha himself is non-existent as well.

Fabian's censure of Buddhism as mentioned above, though it demonstrates his wide scope of knowledge thereof, contains some serious distortions. The most blatant of them lies in his understanding of the Buddhist notion of nothingness (*mu* in Japanese, *shunyata* in Sanscrit). As we have discussed previously, it does not indicate the non-existence of things as Fabian interprets it to mean. (He seems to have distorted the notion deliberately for the sake of argument.) It rather signifies the undefinable, ultimate nature of reality which from eternity to eternity is in an ever-changing state of flux. It is a delusion to think that things can retain their own identity permanently. This position, however, does not necessarily cause confusion in thinking or moral judgment as Fabian alleges.

Fabian is right in asserting that Buddhism originally did not teach a belief in the afterlife, since the individual's identity was deemed temporal. The belief in the Buddha's land of bliss in the west, a religious image developed later, is total nonsense as far as Fabian is concerned, because of the geographical information which he learned from the padres. This seventeenth century Christian convert is quite rational in his criticisms of Buddhism. The same rationalism, however, fails to permit him to really appreciate (even though he may disagree with) a valuable Buddhistic insight into reality. It would have been extremely interesting if he had known and could have compared Christian mysticism (e.g. Meister Eckhart and John of the Cross) with the Buddhist wisdom of *mu* (no-thingness rather than non-existence).

### (b) On Confucianism

The first half of the second section of *Mytei Mondo* comprises Fabian's discussion concerning Confucianism. The first subject he takes up is the Great Ultimate (*taikyoku* in Japanese). This notion indicates the ultimate reality which contains the actual and potential principles of all existences. It is operative in actuality through two mutually complementary ways: *In* (*Yin* in Chinese) and *Yo* (*Yang* in Chinese). The former represents the female and passive principle, while the latter represents the male and active counterpart. Every existence in the world functions owing to a combination of these two forces.

By way of illustration, Fabian compares the Great Ultimate to a medicine box. Just as the box opens by separating the lid from the container so that the medicine will become accessible, *taikyoku* works its way by "opening" itself as *In* and *Yo*. After explaining thus the fundamental Confucian notions, Fabian raises several questions criticizing Confucianism. First, how can the box open without someone to open it? The box, the Ultimate, has no will of its own. That is to say, unless some outside force is available, the Great Ultimate and *In* and *Yo* would not commence their actions. It follows that the outside operator, Deus of Christianity, is necessary.

The second major point of Fabian's argument against Confucian ideas concerns the nature of the Great Ultimate. He, invoking Lao-tzu, the eponym of Taoism, considers it the principle of nothing.

(Confucian and Taoist ideas were often admixtured.) Consequently, according to Fabian, the Great Ultimate is non-existent. Since it is also the ultimate principle of each person, every individual's core is also empty. (Chu-hsi saw a correspondence between the universe as the macrocosm and the individual as the microcosm.) The idea of non-substantiality of self is in consonance with the Buddhist view. So, then, Fabian returns the verdict: all three religions see commonly non-existence as the core and source of everything including human be-ings, which, however, does not make sense.

Fabian's argument is so forced that it is not at all persuasive, however. As in his criticisms of Buddhism, here again his understand-ing of "nothing" is a distortion. None of these religions advances the assertion that the physical world originated from non-existence unlike the Christian teaching of God's creation of the world out of nothing (non-existence), and the core of existence is nothing (blank).

It says in *Tao Teh Ching* (chap. 1), for example:

> The tao that can be expressed is not the unchangeable Tao.
> The name that can be named is not the unchangeable name.
> The nameless is the origin of nature (heaven and earth). . . .

Likewise, the great Taoist master, Chuang-tzu (fourth century B.C.) says in *Chuang tzu* (chap. 12):

> The concept of nothingness existed before the beginning of the universe; it is nameless, undefinable in its nature. The concept of oneness is inextricably entwined with nothing-ness. All things derive their existence only in terms of the One from which they derive their reality. I call this the Teh.

As seen in these quotations, "nothingness" constitutes the ultimate real-ity encompassing all existences and is thus not the opposite of existence. It is called "nothingness" because it is undefinable and absolute.

The third major area of Fabian's censure of the Confucian teach-ings concerns the understanding of human existence. According to

Confucianism, since human beings originate from the Great Ultimate just as do all other things (grass, trees, animals, birds, etc.), there is no fundamental uniqueness in the human essence. Against this view, Fabian contests that the almighty Deus bestowed each person with a unique soul, which distinguishes him or her from all other creatures.

Despite these problems, Fabian adds, Confucianism is better than Buddhism and Taoism because of its emphasis on morality, though even here it lacks something when compared to Christianity. (A higher estimation of Confucianism on account of its ethical orientation was also held by Valignano and Ricci. This seems to have been the view about Confucianism commonly held by the Christians at that time, though some padres were apparently quite impressed by the Zen Buddhist monks' austere life-style and their meditative spirituality.)

Fabian closes his discussion of Confucianism with cynical remarks about an ancient Chinese legend concerning the origin of the universe. The tale says that in the beginning heaven and earth were in a state which could be compared to the contents of an egg in the sense that the earth was like the yolk in the white which was heaven. A king by the name of P'an-ku appeared in the midst of this universe and established a dynasty. His throne lasted 84,000 years.

Fabian states that the rationale of the story is so absurd that serious Confucians refuse to take it as credible. He adds the following mockery: "It is a shame that P'an-ku's cry, 'cock-a-doodle' is missing in the story!" He then turns and comments in a serious vein that this story in essence symbolizes a sexual view of the origin of the universe, an idea similar to that which is found, Fabian points out, in early Shinto mythology, as will be mentioned in the following section on Shintoism.

### (c) On Shintoism

An account of the genesis of the land of Japan is the first target of Fabian's attack on Shintoism. Claiming itself as the national cult of the country, Shintoism cherishes a mythological story. It is recorded in the Japanese classic called *Nihongi*, the oldest historical book compiled in the eighth century. With fiction and fact combined, it covers Japanese history from its mythical origin to the end of the seventh century.

According to this tale, the male deity Izanagi and his consort Izanami, standing on a heavenly bridge, lowered the spear, by which they churned the sea below. There appeared above the tide the letters *dai nichi* (meaning great sun). The drippings of water from the spear fell and hardened to form the land of Japan. The letters which had appeared became the name of the country.

Fabian points out the obvious sexual connotation of this myth— the participation of the male and the female, a spear (male organ), the sea (female organ), the drippings (semen), and the letters. The letters write 大 日, the shape of which depicts, Fabian says, "a person lying down with arms and legs spread out. This again is something I need not explain in detail." Therefore, he concludes, "the real teaching of Shintoism boils down to the way of *In* (female) and *Yo* (male), intercourse between a husband and wife." Fabian rather uncourteously demythologizes other stories recorded in *Nihongi* as well. All the Shinto deities are, he excoriates, deified people or natural objects. As they were made divine by the priests, they came under the control of the priests who were human.

To drive home his contention, Fabian makes mention of the fact that Japanese ancestors immigrated from China instead of having been created by Izanagi and Izanami. They possessed no written language until the fifteenth year of Emperor Ojin. Here again the critically-minded Fabian lays bare what the people naively believed about their country. His information is basically accurate: the Japanese ancestors did come from several different parts of Asia (including China), and the Japanese writing system was imported from ancient China (the date Fabian gives is found in *Nihongi*, which is highly legendary. The introduction of the Chinese writings most likely took place in the early centuries A.D.).

Contending thus, Fabian's aims are clear: (a) to denude the "embarrassing" nature of the Shinto doctrine; (b) to indicate the fact that Shintoism, like Buddhism and Confucianism, lacks an adequate explanation as to the origin of the world, which, in turn, (c) leads one to the true answer—the Christian teaching of a transcendent creator; (d) to criticize the assertion of Japan as a divine country (*Shinkoku*), an ideology which was used to persecute the Christians. With the discussion on Shintoism, Fabian concludes his censures of the Japanese religions and proceeds to his explanation of Christian doctrines.

## (d) On Christianity

In this section, Fabian discusses the following four major topics of Christians teachings: (1) the existence of a creator God as the provider of the natural order, who is formless and without beginning and end; (2) the existence of the immortal rational soul bestowed by the creator on human beings alone; (3) the existence of an afterlife, which makes every person liable for his or her deeds before God's final judgment (in paradise located beyond the sky or hell beneath the ground); (4) God's salvation through his Son. All of these subjects are familiar ones; Fabian faithfully follows what the padres had taught him. His understanding of the basic items of Christian doctrine is in agreement with the teachings given in Valignano's *Japanese Catechism*.

As for the subject (4) of God's salvation of men and women, some comments are in order. Needless to say, this theme is supposed to constitute the heart of the Christian doctrine. In Fabian's treatment, however, it obtains no special emphasis but comprises a rather brief and general mention of the hereditary sins of Adam and Eve, the suffering and death of Jesus Christ, and the uninterrupted apostolic succession from Peter to the Roman pope. (Deus, according to the author, sent the Son to save people because Adam and Eve deeply repented. This is not mentioned in the Bible. The *Japanese Catechism* lacks such a statement, too.) Fabian goes on to state that "the way people today, like you and I, can be saved" is by receiving baptism, keeping the ten commandments, and revering Deus. Doing these three things will guarantee the security of life in this and the next world.

It is true that not only Fabian but the other Christian teachers also spent much effort discussing such topics as the origin of the world and the existence of the rational soul, and thus sometimes failed to place much emphasis on individuals' sins and Christ's redemption. This tendency largely stemmed from the Christians' apologetic endeavor against the Buddhists and Confucians. It was also the sequence usually followed in traditional Catholic theological education.

This hardly means that the Japanese converts possessed little comprehension of the atonement of their own sins by the savior. There is ample evidence that many of them did in fact experience a Christian conversion in a genuine sense. Fabian's writings, however, fall short of such a profound awareness of sin or an existential appreciation of divine grace. Also, there is no mention of such an important doctrine as the Trinity. Fabian's apparent failure of any real appropriation of the central message of Christianity seems to be one of the basic reasons why he later abandoned this faith. His understanding of Christianity, in other words, remained to the end basically on an intellectual level.

Fabian's chapter on Christianity concludes with remarks clarifying several practical problems. The first question concerns the taking of oaths. This was a serious action particularly for warriors (samurais) who were expected by their sovereigns to pledge their absolute loyalty to them. The Christian samurais were often suspect in this regard because of their allegiance to Deus. As a matter of fact, some of them were either expelled or executed for their refusal to take fealty oaths in the name of Shinto deities or Buddha.

Fabian takes up this issue by citing the third commandment of the decalogue: "Thou shall not take my name in vain." He interprets this law as a general prohibition against the taking of empty oaths in God's name. (The catechisms used in his day taught the same.) He first underlines the loyal and reliable nature of Christian samurais when they take oaths in the name of Deus, the true and immutable God, rather than in the name of the false Shinto gods or Buddha. But he concedes that there are some Christians who, on account of their weak faith, have broken their oaths. Ironically, he himself would fall under his own reprimand when he apostatized later.

The second practical question Fabian discusses concerns the issue of a Christian's loyalty to his or her country. This is a criticism Japanese Christians had to deal with again and again. There was a deep-seated suspicion that the Christians might form a "fifth-column" working for a European colonial invasion by undermining the security of the land. The accusation was so widespread that Fabian too felt it exigent to refute it. His argument is largely the same as that of many other Christians to which we have previously referred.

To recapitulate, Fabian avers that Christianity will bring about peace and order, and that it teaches the virtue of obedience to the sovereign. That is the reason, he says, why there has never been a war or rebellion for the past thousand years in the Christian countries(!). By contrast, numerous incidents of fighting and disorder have occurred in China and Japan, the lands of Buddhism and Confucianism.

There is, according to Fabian, one more fact to consider, that is, the Christian countries in Europe are so far away from Japan that even if they wanted, they could never send enough warships and troops to conquer Japan, a country which has substantial military power and has been experienced in warfare for many centuries. Besides, the padres are monks who have completely renounced worldly desires.

The last question Fabian attempts to answer is also a familiar one which the padres had oftentimes to explain to the Japanese. That is, why did not Deus let the Japanese know of him much earlier? Is he not a respecter of persons? This is, of course, a difficult question to answer, since it involves God's will itself. Fabian replies by indicating three forms of God's self-revelation. First is, the "teaching of nature" (i.e. God reveals his ways by giving each person the wisdom to discern between good and evil). The second is the "teaching of scripture," and the third, the "teaching of grace" (help provided by the divine incarnate). It is not a serious disadvantage, the author tries to console the readers, to learn of these teachings later than others.

Thus ends Fabian's exposition of Christian teachings. *Myotei Mondo* is concluded with the words of Myoshu, the inquirer, expressing her ardent desire to join the church.

The intelligence and knowledge Fabian demonstrated in *Myotei Mondo* is quite impressive. His critical mind proves to be of a rare quality for his time. His Christian faith sounds unshakable. Nonetheless it met with total bankruptcy in 1607 (or 1608). As referred to earlier, he wrote the monograph *Ha-Daiusu* (The Contra Deus) denouncing Christianity later (1620) in his life. What did he have to say in this writing? We will deal with this question next.


(3) Ha-Daiusu

The purpose of this writing is clear: the point by point refutation of the Christian apologia in *Myotei-Mondo*. The content, which consists of seven sections plus one addition, follows almost exactly the development of argumentation found in the author's earlier book.

### (a) On the Creator

The tract begins with a discussion of the creator God. Rejecting the assertion in *Myotei Mondo* that the Christian God alone is the transcendent being who made the world, Fabian now claims that in the Japanese religions as well, the notion equivalent to such a creator God does exist. Buddhism, for example, teaches the transcendent Buddha (*hosshin* in Japanese). Furthermore, the Buddha is believed to have assumed the form of the deities of Shintoism.

Fabian's argument, however, presents a half-truth. Indeed, the *hosshin* Buddha represents Buddha of transcendent quality, but it is not a willful creator like the God of the Bible. Furthermore, the Shinto deities do not possess a transcendent nature, as Fabian indicated in *Myotei Mondo*.

Fabian then laments over the Christians' lack of an understanding of the Buddhist concept of nothingness (*mu*). This "ignorance" is that which Fabian himself evinced in his previous work, which we pointed out in the preceding subsection. In *Myotei Mondo* he perhaps chose to distort the concept deliberately in order to use it against Buddhism (and also Confucianism). Here he praises the superiority of the notion of *mu* over *yu* (being or existence) which the Christians emphasize, since *mu* represents a quality beyond any definition, transcending *yu*.

### (b) On the rational soul

The question of the existence of the immortal rational soul, which is, according to Christianity, the unique possession of human beings, was also a hotly debated subject between the Christians and their opponents in Japan. It was strongly defended by Fabian in *Myotei Mondo*. Here in *Ha-Daiusu*, however, Fabian raises the following two points against the Christian contention: first, the fact that human beings alone are endowed with the capacity of making rational and ethical judgments has been long and universally known, and thus it is not a view unique to Christianity. Both Confucianism and Buddhism have taught the profound wisdom thereof. Second, however, the suggestion that the soul is essentially different from other forms of existence cannot be taken seriously. Every existence in this world should be understood as rather the same in essence but different only in kind.

### (c) On paradise and hell

Because of the position mentioned above, Fabian rejects the Christian teaching of the existence of paradise and hell. He asks a question which the padres had to answer numerous times: Why did Deus create Lucifer and Adam and Eve in such a way that they would fall into sin? Is it not indicative of defective workmanship? If so, then he must be either extremely cruel or simply incompetent and not omnipotent. It is thus totally arbitrary for Deus to punish people who commit sins because of the weak character which Deus gave to them.

### (d) On original sin

Just as the rational Fabian demythologized the Japanese religions in *Myotei Mondo*, in *Ha-Daiusu* he attempts the same with Christianity. The story of the fall of Adam and Eve recorded in Genesis, chapter three, according to Fabian, furnishes an example of the arbitrary nature of Deus. Not only did Deus create Lucifer and the people in a defective way, but also the supposedly all-merciful God let Lucifer seduce Adam and Eve in his own garden without protecting them. The whole story, the apostate critic contends, betrays the terribly contradictory character of Deus, and thus makes no sense.

As a result of the first parents' sin, every one of their descendants must suffer from its consequence. Fabian mocks the Christians who give thanks to God, the ultimate trouble-maker. Fabian fails to see the significance of individual freedom of choice which is the main thrust of the story of Genesis, chapter three. He does not seem to have studied the scriptures very well. The curriculum of the seminario, in fact, placed no emphasis on a detailed exposition of biblical passages.

### (e) On Jesus Christ

On this subject, Fabian first raises a question: Why was Jesus Christ born five thousand years after the creation? (The padres taught

the Japanese that the date of the genesis of the world was 5000 B.C.
Fabian questions also the accuracy of this date, which does not seem to
him ancient enough.) Is it a merciful thing, he asks, for Deus to leave
millions of people without a savior? Many of them, Fabian says, must
have fallen into hell "like a heavy rainfall!"

This question is not new either; it was asked by many Japanese,
particularly those who genuinely worried about the "whereabouts" of
their ancestors—in hell or in paradise? (He makes no mention of
purgatory and limbo, though he must have learned about them.) Fabian, who did not provide a convincing answer to this question in
*Myotei Mondo*, uses it here as a criticism of Christianity. He perhaps
never found a persuasive answer throughout his lifetime.

Fabian's second question concerns Joseph and Mary, whose marriage, he avers, was never consummated because of Mary's eternal
virginity. This seems to him in contradiction to what a marriage is
supposed to be, and is therefore wrong. Fabian does not question the
virgin birth itself, which is somewhat unexpected for this rational
critic, but he regards Christ's resurrection and ascension as nothing but
a "magical trick."

The suspicion we raised earlier as to Fabian's dearth of understanding of Christ's redemption from sin seems to be confirmed, because in
this section which deals with his criticism of the Christian teachings on
Christ, he never refers to the subject in any meaningful way. It may be
safe to conclude, consequently, that he, even when a Christian, did
not really gain an existential comprehension of the meaning of Christ's
death. He, as a foe of Christianity, needless to say, comes up with no
serious argument against it either.

### (f) On the decalogue and baptism

Fabian's shallow understanding of Christ's saving work apparently caused him to describe in *Myotei Mondo* Christian salvation
simply as the receiving of baptism and the keeping of the ten commandments. In *Ha-Daiusu*, the same superficiality is found in his
attack on Christianity.

He takes up first the ten commandments, of which he says several
are identical to the Buddhist five commandments: the prohibition of

killing, stealing, adultery, lying, and drunkenness. The ninth and tenth commandments, in Fabian's interpretation, concern restraining reckless desires of the mind. The commandments, therefore, are tantamount to the Buddhist fifth commandment, a prohibition of drunkenness (the uncontrolled mind). The point of his argument is that there is nothing unique or superior about the Christian commandments.

According to Fabian, there is, however, one biblical stipulation which marks an indismissible difference between the Christian commandments and the Buddhist counterpart, and that is the first of the decalogue. It demands an absolute loyalty to Deus alone, which, our detractor insists, will undermine the security of Japanese society. He says, "The first commandment urges disobedience to the order of the sovereign and the father, and it teaches one to make light of his or her own life, because compliance to Deus' will takes precedence over everything else. The intention is implied to subvert and take over the country and to destroy the Law of Buddha and the (Confucian) precept of the sovereign."

In *Myotei Mondo*, he attempts to defend the Christians against a similar charge by invoking the third commandment. He insists that the Christian oaths are reliable and demand allegiance to the sovereign, parents, and friends, because the oaths are predicated upon the name of the true and immutable God.

Here in *Ha-Daiusu*, however, Fabian abandons the transcendent basis for one's loyalty and quotes the words of Chu-hsi: "One needs not look for precepts for attaining the ultimate good outside the reality of morals which are maintained in people's daily life." (This, incidentally, does not indicate that Confucian morality is lacking a transcendent basis; Tao or Heaven does possess a transcendent quality as the supporting principle for morality. But the transcendent nature of the Christian God is by far more eminent because of the heavy emphasis Christianity places on the separateness between God and the world.)

The transcendent foundation of morality which he once used to defend the Christians' loyalty and reliability as members of the feudal society now serves as a major weapon for attack. In order to support his new logic against Christianity, Fabian cites as evidence the Christians' willingness to submit themselves to any kind of persecution including physical torture and violent death. This, in his opinion, illustrates their grave offense against the order of the sovereign and the kind love of their parents.

Fabian's ideological somersault concludes with a familiar tune: Japan as the *shinkoku* (the country of gods). This man who was able to demonstrate a critical intelligence remarkable for his time soul-searched many different religions and philosphical views and yet ended with the shinkoku ideology without himself subscribing ultimately to any one of these religions.

Following the seven areas of polemic against Christianity, Fabian adds several more points on which he also criticizes Christianity. These points contain mostly his own emotional reaction to some aspects of Christian teachings and practices. First, he attacks the doctrine of the eucharist which, as confirmed not long before Fabian's time at the Council of Trent, teaches that during the liturgy the bread and wine are transformed into the very body and blood of Christ (i.e. a change in the substance but not in the appearance). This rational critic brushes aside this teaching, calling it totally incredible.

The next target at which Fabian takes aim is the padres, whom he accuses as being so "arrogant that even the devil could not surpass them." "Because of arrogance, they engage in brawls and quarrels with the padres of other factions, competing for influence, and outdoing secular people in their conflicts. It is so ugly, you can't even imagine." He even exaggerates the disagreements between the Jesuit missionaries and those of other orders by blaming them for involving themselves in physical combat. (There is no evidence that the padres indeed did so.)

Fabian's verbal assault on the padres' alleged arrogance continues on to his deep resentment toward their way of treating the Japanese. He charges: "Being arrogant, they do not even regard the Japanese as persons. The Japanese, in their turn, deem it inexcusable. There is, therefore, no intimate communication between them." They made it a policy, according to Fabian, not to ordain the Japanese. As mentioned earlier, these effusive statements have prompted some modern scholars to suspect that this alleged "policy" was the real reason for his departure from the Jesuit order. It may well have been, but this cannot be ascertained.

With the same acerbity, Fabian accuses the padres for their discriminating attitude toward the poor in favor of the rich, and their sexual immorality (for evidence he cites some unspecified incidents in the Philippines, Mexico, and Europe, but none from Japan). He also discredits the padres regarding their claim of authority to forgive their penitents' sins. The Christian belief of divine miracles for martyrs is also questionable to him; he says that he has neither seen nor heard them happen even once. And anyway, miracle stories are found in Buddhism as well, he contends.

Fabian closes this whole series of bitter innuendo against the padres with an expression of fear of possible retaliation by the Christians. That is the reason, he insists, why he has not written this book for many years after apostatizing.

The foregoing discussion of Fabian's writings has revealed the author as an extremely intriguing figure—an intelligent man who demonstrated a critical mind extraordinary for his day and who took a drastic ideological somersault to become a bitter foe of Christianity after some twenty years of a very active life as a Jesuit brother. At each stage of his career, he left impressive traces of his work.

After all this long journey of soul-searching, however, what in effect did Fabian discover? Despite his great abundance of knowledge about many religions and a considerable amount of valuable information with regard to European culture, he settled with none of them. His understanding of Christianity was basically of an intellectual nature; the Christian faith never really became indigenous to his soul. So what then was truly indigenous to him?

Toward the end of *Ha-Daiusu*, Fabian mentions the shinkoku ideology, which seems to indicate the basic direction of his thought, though he did not elaborate on it. Many rulers and their supporters of those days used it for political advantage, as we have observed previously. Fabian, however, was not a politician and was intelligent enough to discern the shallowness of the political exploitation of this ideological assertion.

What then is his version of the shinkoku thought? Shichihei Yamamoto, a modern Japanese critic, has called it "Japanism," i.e. a quasi-religion which "religionizes" Japan itself. According to Yamamoto, not only Fabian but also most Japanese throughout history belong to this "religion." Japanism, neither Buddhism nor Confucianism nor Shintoism, is the real foe of the Christian missions, as it tenaciously refused and violently persecuted the Christians because of the "foreignness" of their doctrines and practices. Japanism is by nature syncretic, combining these three religions. It rejected Christianity because the Christian faith could not be blended into this syncretism.

Even today when there is no official rejection of Christianity in Japan in Yamamoto's opinion, the same mental and emotional tradition is operative in the people's minds, which prevents them from truly accepting the Christian message. This question will be discussed more in detail in the epilogue. This chapter continues by considering several more cases of the Japanese polemic against Christianity during the pre-modern era.

SESSO

We have referred to Masashige Inoue, who exerted an uncommon shrewdness as the inquisitor general against the Christians. One of the various tactics he employed in order to force the Christians to apostatize was the vigorous "counter-missionary" efforts of using Buddhist priests. Several monks of Zen Buddhism, in particular, were actively involved in this venture. One of them was Sesso, the abbot of the cathedral temple in Bungo which belonged to the Rinzai sect, a major branch of Zen Buddhism. In the Bungo domain which was the former fief of the Otomo clan (a prominent protectorate of Christianity), there were still a considerable number of Christians secretly practicing their faith. The abbot's mission was to win them over to his brand of Buddhism.

The details of his activities are not known, but his writing called *Taiji-jashumon* (On Subduing the Evil Religion) has been preserved. It was written in 1648 on the basis of sermons he delivered at the Kofuku temple in Nagasaki during May 6–26, 1647. It was not published, however, until 1861 when a revival of Christian persecutions took place.

The tract opens with remarks on how Christianity was introduced to Japan, containing many instances of historical inaccuracies. The abbot then attempts to explain why this western religion succeeded in attracting the gullible masses. The reason lies, according to him, in a deceptive tactic of the Christian missions: the Christian missionaries have shown kindness to the people by first offering them charity without openly revealing their teachings or criticizing other religions. But they, when the occasion arose, then extolled their faith and tacitly put down other faiths. As soon as they discovered those who exhibited some interest in Christianity, they shut them in a church for a week in order to indoctrinate them in their teachings and in malicious invectives of other religions.

Sesso contends that Buddhism, in particular, has been a major target of their vicious attacks since it teaches the hereafter as Christianity does. "Those fools," as the Zen monk calls these "gullible masses," thinking of Christianity as a wonderful religion which guarantees pleasures in this as well as in the next life, have been thus taken in.

In his writing, Sesso distorts many facts. For instance, the missionaries were from the beginning quite outspoken in denouncing the Japanese religions, instead of being shrewdly diplomatic. That was, in fact, a major reason for inviting the horrible persecutions. Sesso, however, rightly concedes that the personal kindness and social charity offered by the Christians helped their cause. He is correct also when he says that the Christian preaching, particularly about a hereafter, appealed to the masses. Sesso adds to his original sermon some explanatory comments on Christian teachings, most of which he apparently borrowed from Fabian and Ferreira without much alteration.

Sesso proceeds to talk about the Christians' attitude toward the Buddhists and Shintoists. We see here again basically what we have read in Fabian's books. What then is Sesso's major contention? The answer is quite simple: Christian doctrine is a superficial imitation of Buddhist notions. He insists the following: Jesus learned Buddhism but failed to comprehend its real essence, and thus came up with a quasi-Buddhistic set of teachings simply by changing names such as Bonten-O (a creator deity of ancient India) to Deus, the enlightened ones to angels, the heavenly firmament to paradise, the human world to purgatory, the Buddhist hell to inferno, kanjo (a water purification ceremony of Buddhism) to baptism, the Buddhist five commandments to the Christian ten commandments, and so forth.

This kind of polemic against Christianity by the Buddhists is not new to us; it had been often presented since the time of Xavier's mission. There is nothing new in his defense of Buddhism either. He stresses the transcendent Buddha as representing the absolute truth against the Christian contention that the Buddha was merely a human being. He questions the compatibility between the Christian belief in hell and that of the almighty and all-loving Deus. Such a question and other accusations against Christianity are again familiar to us.

As one who worked for the bakufu's anti-Christian policy, he too alleged the subversive intention of the Christian missions and harbored a strong negative reaction toward its European character. Though he tried to reproduce rather accurately the basic Christian teachings as a basis for his criticism of them, he had no deep understanding of them at all. Like all other critics, he never mentioned such an important Christian doctrine as the Trinity. He brushed aside as deceptive notions the teachings of Christ's incarnation and redemption from sin. It is indeed unfortunate that he, with such a brilliant mind, failed to examine more closely the subject he was criticizing.

### SHOSAN SUZUKI

Like Sesso, Shosan Suzuki (1579–1655) was also a Zen monk who engaged actively in anti-Christian propaganda. He belonged to the Soto sect which constituted one of the two major sects of Zen Buddhism along with the Rinzai sect. Despite their different sectarian affiliations, Shosan and Sesso were close acquaintances since their training days under the same master, Genshun-Risshi. Likewise, their anti-Christian activities were commonly sponsored by the bakufu at the hand of Inoue and also by the local feudal lords in Kyushu.

Like Sesso, Shosan also wrote a tract denouncing Christianity. It is entitled *Ha-Kirishitan* (The Contra Christians). (It was translated by G. Elison in his *Deus Destroyed*, pp. 375–389.) In order to clarify the reasons for his opposition to Christianity, a consideration of his background is necessary.

Shosan Suzuki was a unique Zen monk because of his background and thought. Until forty years of age when he became a monk, he had been a warrior (samurai) from Mikawa, a territory where the first shogun Ieyasu Tokugawa originated. His fealty toward Ieyasu was impeccable as he proved by his bravery during the warfare with the

Toyotomi forces. His experiences of constant exposure to the threat of death on the battlefields led him to a profound reflection on the meaning of life and death.

The answer Shosan found after serious soul-searching lay in Zen Buddhism. He in fact called his religion "Buddhism for cowards." This is an ironical way of suggesting the idea that Zen would set one free from the fear of the extinction of one's self. The fear would be eliminated by truly realizing that there was no such solid and permanent entity as a "self."

The way Shosan adopted to reach this inner enlightenment was what he called Nio Zen, Zen meditation in the style of the guardian king of ancient Indian mythology, Nio. Unlike usual Zen meditation which taught absolute serenity, Shosan's Nio Zen was done with strenuous concentration—a strained back, clenched fists, gritted teeth, and fiercely focused eyes—the appearance of Nio. Such an approach certainly stemmed from Shosan's samurai background.

One other unique feature of his religious discipline was the use of *nembutsu* (recitation of the name of Amida Buddha which was a practice vital to the Pure Land sect, but not to the Zen sects). Shosan repeated it in a vigorous manner during the meditation in order to induce the total concentration of his mind. Such a mental discipline, he taught, should be done with intense feeling as if every moment were the last moment of one's life, a self-awareness in the midst of battle.

The rigorously samurai-style Buddhism of Shosan accompanied one more samurai characteristic—loyalty to the sovereign. As mentioned above, Shosan was a warrior ardently devoted to Shogun Ieyasu, and his dedication to the master never changed even after he became a monk. He served the Tokugawa family faithfully and bravely with the sword, and he continued to do so as a Zen monk by promoting Buddhism. It was his firm conviction that Buddhism, not any other religion, should be the spiritual foundation for the long-lasting prosperity of the Tokugawa bakufu.

Shosan believed that the government officials, including the shogun, should exercise the spirit of Buddhism when ruling the country, and that every member of the society should do the same in his or her daily occupation. For example, farming was a way for farmers to practice Buddhism, and to serve the sovereign with selfless loyalty was a way for samurai to do likewise. It followed that Shosan's Buddhist version of the "Protestant work ethic" was, in effect, a strong endorsement of the contemporary social order under the rule of the bakufu. The organic unity of church and state was his ideal.

Such a religio-political ideology prompted Shosan to participate vigorously in the bakufu's anti-Christian campaign. During 1641–1644, he was particularly active in working for this cause in Amakusa, Kyushu, in support of his brother, Shigenari Suzuki. Shigenari was appointed by the bakufu to govern that province after the Christian-peasant revolt had taken place there.

Shosan's main task was to inculcate in the people of that whole region his Buddhist ideology, thereby eradicating what he called the "pernicious teachings of Christianity." His doctrine of the "practice of Buddhism through farming" was systematically promulgated among the peasants there through thirty-two local temples of the Pure Land sect and the Zen sect which he used as bases for his activities. (The former sect was the one to which the Tokugawa family belonged, and the latter was his own.) This effort was coordinated with his brother's policy of keeping rigid control over the peasants of Amakusa among whom Christan roots were still deeply embedded.

As a part of his anti-Christian propaganda, he wrote a tract entitled *Ha-Kirishitan*, copies of which were distributed and kept at each of these thirty-two temples. This booklet was published posthumously in 1662. As for its contents, there is nothing new in his argument against Christianity. Since both Sesso and Shosan firmly believed in the universal truth of Buddhism, both regarded Christianity as a superficial imitation or a fraudulent version of Buddhism and not as a totally independent religion. Shosan calls Deus a false Buddha and likewise Jesus Christ the same false Buddha who appeared in the land of the "southern barbarians."

Deus is fraudulent, Shosan insists, because he, though allegedly the creator of the universe, had been known only among the "southern barbarians," and only now is he known to the rest of the world including Japan. He is either cruel or impotent because he left his son on the cross, crucified by the "unenlightened mass." The Christians are fools, because they venerate this false Buddha instead of the many truly enlightened Buddhas. It is indeed audacious for the padres to come to

Japan, the country of gods and Buddha, to oppose the true law of Buddha—an action which can be likened to a firefly's attempt to debate his brightness with the moon!

Compared with Fabian, Shosan seems to have been the inferior in rational and critical intellect, though some modern historians evaluate his thinking as highly enlightened. His understanding of Christianity is very superficial and his revilement of it shows no independent thinking. His mind is dominated by an insular and feudalistic mentality. His defense of Buddhism is far from persuasive. Against the Christian attack on the Japanese "worship" of the sun and the moon, for example, Shosan tries to legitimate the Japanese practice by regarding the sun *Yo* and the moon *In* as being basic principles of nature and deserving veneration by people. They are, he argues, as important as one's two eyes.

Nonetheless, Shosan is right when he complains that the padres have failed to comprehend the meaning of *mushin* (no-mind), the state of consciousness where the realization of the *mu* occurs. This is a crucial point of Zen Buddhism which the European Christians did not fathom, as we have discussed previously. A truly unfortunate fact is that most of the missionaries did not even try to understand it and the Buddhists did not attempt to make them realize its significance. Shosan, too, simply laments over Christian ignorance without elaborating on this vital Buddhist contention. This lack of attempt on both sides to communicate with each other humbly and seriously was the major cause for such a tragic outcome of this early encounter between Christianity and Japan. This was also the case in the encounter between a great Confucian mind and an excellent Christian soul, which will be discussed next.

### GIOVANNI BATTISTA SIDOTI

Because of the bakufu's systematic and devastating persecution, the Christians appear to have become virtually extinct, and yet there were, though certainly limited in number, those who continued to maintain their faith secretly at dire risk. During the second half of the seventeenth century the memory of the whole affair concerning the Christians faded almost completely from the minds of the general public as well as of the government officials. Then in 1708 they were taken by surprise by a sudden arrival of a padre. This Jesuit who dared a solitary mission to the closed Japan was Giovanni Battista Sidoti.

Padre Sidoti was born in Palermo, Sicily in 1668, and trained in Rome as a member of the Society of Jesus. While studying he developed a keen interest in the history of the missions in Japan. An opportunity came for him to get involved directly in the church's work in Asia, when the church decided in 1703 to send him to Japan in order to sound out the possibility of reopening the missions. The measure was taken because the long-awaited news had reached Rome that the official policy prohibiting Christian missions was repealed in China. It was the church's hope that the same might happen in Japan as well. In fact, in a letter from the Vatican addressed to the Augustinians in Manila, dated September 25, 1714, ardent expectation was expressed that in Japan Sidoti would produce results as great as those of Xavier.

Sidoti arrived in the Philippines in 1704, and worked in the missions there for four years, while preparing for a journey to Japan. In August 1708 he finally set sail to his destination on a ship furnished by the Spanish governor of the Philippines. After a hazardous trip over the sea, the ship reached an island called Yaku, located off the southern tip of Kyushu.

Sidoti's lone venture began after the ship dropped him there. The helpless padre, hungry and fatigued, approached a villager who, despite the fear caused by the sudden encounter with a stranger, carried him home with the help of his fellow villager, took him in, and gave him food and water. According to what Sidoti later told the interrogator in Nagasaki, even though he offered some pieces of gold and a sword (he assumed the appearance of a samurai), the villagers declined to accept them.

The news of the landing of an European was conveyed immediately to the commissioner in Nagasaki, who ordered that he be brought to his custody for interrogation. The case was evidently not so easy for the official to handle, for first of all he could not find an interpreter. The bakufu's expulsion of the Iberians had nullified the necessity of translators, and nobody dared to learn the languages of the forbidden countries.

But there was one at the Dutch farm who was able to manage some Latin. It was reported that Sidoti showed quite openly his ill feelings toward the Dutch, which puzzled the Japanese because they were unaware of the continued intense hostility between the Catholics and the Protestants in Europe at that time.

Sidoti's identification of his origins was also unfamiliar to the interrogators, as their memory was that the padres were connected with either Portugal or Spain and not with Italy. The Italian identity of Valignano and Organtino had faded into oblivion as well. Such was the situation in Japan when Sidoti arrived.

The officials at Nagasaki eventually found out the fact that Sidoti came from Rome with the intention of spreading Christianity in Japan by the order of the pope. According to the formal report from Nagasaki to Edo, the padre insisted that though he was quite aware of the national policy against the propagation of Christianity, he nevertheless would like to go to Edo in order to appeal directly to the government to repeal the prohibition. He also stated that he was willing to submit himself to any punishment the authority should choose to inflict on him, such as an immediate deportation back to the Philippines, imprisonment, or even execution. The interrogators were seemingly quite impressed by his sincere and serious attitude.

Sidoti was then sent to Edo for further interrogations. This measure taken by the bakufu indicates again a change of the situation in Japan; if it had been forty years before, any padre who made a secret entry to the country would have been executed immediately. This time, however, the bakufu decided to investigate this daring missionary in a civil manner. The person who was appointed to carry out this task was a widely respected Confucian scholar by the name of Hakuseki Arai. He was also a trusted aide of Shogun Ienobu Tokugawa.

The trial was held at the former estate of Inoue where many Christians had been interrogated, imprisoned, and tortured when the persecution was at its height. Because of Sidoti's hostility toward the Dutch, the Dutch interpreter was placed behind a paper partition in order to avoid any direct confrontation. The sequence of the conversation exchanged between Hakuseki and Sidoti affords an interesting illustration of an encounter between eastern and western intellectuals. A brief description of Hakuseki's profile is in order.

### HAKUSEKI ARAI

Hakuseki Arai was born in a samurai family in Edo in 1657. The early education he received from his disciplinarian father nurtured him into a bright and studious young man. As often the case with such intelligent youngsters in those days in Japan, he too studied Confucian thought quite intensely. Impressed by his brilliance, his teacher, Juan Kinoshita, a well-known Confucian scholar, recommended him to Tsunatoyo Tokugawa, the lord of Kofu, as his personal tutor on Confucianism.

Tsunatoyo, an ardent student of the Chinese classics, listened to Hakuseki's lectures with great enthusiasm. The tutorials continued with the same intensity even after the lord became the shogun in 1709. Serving the new shogun Ienobu (he had changed his name from Tsunatoyo to Ienobu when he assumed the office of shogun), Hakuseki contributed greatly to the government not only as the shogun's academic tutor but also as one of his most trusted aides.

When Sidoti was brought to the capital city, Hakuseki was quite eager to meet this foreigner, because he had been keenly interested in western culture since his young days. When he was a child, for example, he once suffered from a severe case of smallpox, which was cured by medicine supplied by a Dutch trader. This experience apparently provided him with a positive reinforcement to his intellectual curiosity about what Europe could offer. Later when one of his sons became ill, he asked a Dutch physician, Willem Wagemans, to treat him.

Consequently, when he faced Sidoti, he did not behave like a fearful prosecutor but more like a curious inquisitor. He kept a rather objective and rational stance throughout their conversation. It is well manifested in his booklet *Seiyo-kibun* (News of the West), which he began to write shortly after Sidoti's death in 1714 and completed a year before his own death in 1725. This treatise was produced on the basis of his own memoir and a copy of the report of the interrogation which he submitted to the shogun. It contained an intriguing record of the exchange between the Jesuit missionary and the Confucian government official.

### SEIYO-KIBUN

*Seiyo-kibun* consists of three parts: the first section traces events including the four sessions of the interrogation of Sidoti, the conversion of an elderly couple (caretakers of the padre's prison), and the death of the prisoner in a solitary cell where he was thrown because he influenced the couple to receive baptism. The report of the commissioner of Nagasaki is appendixed; it describes the arrest and investigation of Sidoti in that town. In the second section, Hakuseki narrates the political geography of the world which he had learned from Sidoti with some verification he obtained from the Dutch traders. The third section deals with matters concerning Christian doctrines.

### *(1) Interrogation of Sidoti*

According to the first section, Hakuseki, prior to the first interrogation, prepared himself by carefully reading books written by an apostate padre, Giuseppe Chiara, which explained Christianity. (He also studied works by Razan Hayashi, Fabian, Sesso, and Shosan Suzuki which we have discussed above.) The first examination of Sidoti took place on November 22, 1709.

Describing Sidoti, Hakuseki wrote: "He is tall, more than six *shaku* (one *shaku* is slightly longer than one foot). Ordinary people would not be even as high as his shoulder. His hair is black and set in a child's style (i.e. it hangs in front of the face), his eyes are deep set, and his nose is prominent. He wears a cotton-lined garment with narrow sleeves over a pongee garment which were, I heard, given to him by the lord of Satsuma. He was also wearing a white cotton undergarment."

Sidoti told the interrogator emphatically that his intention in coming to Japan was solely to introduce Christianity to the Japanese and added words of his sincere regret that his arrival had caused such trouble on the part of many people, especially the guards who had to watch him day and night in the cold weather. His statements impressed many officials who were present, but Hakuseki decided to counter him by calling his words hypocritical because he did not show enough respect to the authorities when he declined an offer of warmer clothes.

To this criticism, the prisoner meekly apologized and expressed

his genuine appreciation for the kind offer. He then modestly requested a simple cotton garment rather than the better one of silk. This
exchange evidently set the tone for the rest of the conversation—
Hakuseki became fond of the foreigner's sincerity and humbleness.
This positive impression was reinforced further in the chief investigator's mind when he inspected the house of detention during his second
visit. He saw the detainee seated in front of a cross cut out of a sheet of
red paper pasted on the western wall of the room, quietly reciting
prayers "like a Buddhist monk chanting a sutra."

Hakuseki's third investigation was devoted totally to the topics
concerning the political and cultural conditions in Europe. Information acquired from this questioning became the major source for the
second part of *Seiyo-kibun*. Hakuseki was overwhelmed by Sidoti's
"wide range of academic knowledge and his excellent memory." "No
one can compete with him as regards astronomy and geography."
Sidoti astonished the interrogators by telling the date and time precisely
without checking a clock but only by measuring his own shadow on the
ground. The padre was also able to locate specific spots on an old map
obtained from the Dutch.

Sidoti's manner throughout the interrogations was always extremely "contrite and sincere." "He tried to be accurate on even very
trivial matters." He seemed to the interrogator to be even unnecessarily
careful at times. When asked about the location of Australia, for example, he kept silence for fear that Japan might try to invade the land
militarily.

To the great delight of the padre, the fourth and last interview was
focused on Christianity. Hakuseki's former amazement and admiration
turned utterly negative this time. He reported: "What he explained
agrees with the three books (by Chiara) which the commissioner's
office has furnished for me." "There is nothing reasonable in what he
says about Christian doctrines. The brilliance he has demonstrated
disappeared. This is nothing but utter absurdity. It is as if one is listening to a totally different person."

## (2) Hakuseki on Christianity

Hakuseki consequently wrote his negative views about Christian teachings, which constitutes a major portion of the third section of *Seiyo-kibun*. He first recorded Sidoti's explanation of the following subjects: the necessary existence of the creator, the fall of Adam and Eve, Noah and the ark, the story of Moses, the birth of Jesus, his death on the cross, the establishment of the Roman Church and its papacy, and a brief conclusion referring to the three major religions of the world (Christianity, the "polytheisms" such as Buddhism, and "Mohammedanism").

Hakuseki's criticism and questions concerning these items are basically the same as those of many other Japanese detractors—e.g. what is the provenance of Deus? Was the universe not able to come to exist by its own mechanism, if Deus be autogenic? If Deus wanted to forgive the first parents' sin, he could have done it immediately rather than postponing it for three thousand years until he became a man and received a penalty by human beings, etc. etc. . . .

Just as Sesso and Shosan had done before, Hakuseki also thought that there were many parallels between the Christian teachings and those of Buddhism. These two Buddhists regarded Christianity essentially as a pseudo-Buddhist sect mainly because they wanted to insist that Buddhism was the fountainhead of all truth and that other faiths were either offshoots or imitations of Buddhism.

Being a convinced Confucian, Hakuseki harbored a negative view toward Buddhism, and thus Christianity was placed even lower than Buddhism in his mind, because it was, in his opinion, nothing but a forgery of Buddhism. In order to give historical support to this judgment, he quoted Sidoti's statement that before the birth of Jesus, the teaching of Deus had been known only in Judea and Buddhism was believed in other lands. He then distorted this information and drew the conclusion that Buddhism must have been practiced in these entire regions (including Judea) long before Christianity came to exist, and that Jesus forged his teachings out of this old religion. That is the reason, he tried to explain, why there are so many similarities between those two religions.

### (3) Hakuseki's estimate of Sidoti

Hakuseki's estimate of Sidoti comprised two totally opposite observations: he held a very high evaluation of his brilliance, knowledge, and personality, but had, on the other hand, a radically negative opinion of his religious faith. This Confucian scholar was open-minded enough to truly appreciate the various kinds of information the European visitor provided him, so much so that he even returned to talk with him several times after the official inquiry was over.

Hakuseki did not use pejorative terms such as the "southern barbarian." He instead called Sidoti a westerner or a Roman, and the Dutch, Dutch. An example which illustrates his objective attitude is found in the fact that he neither purged nor altered Sidoti's statement that Confucianism was a "small religion," which infuriated some of his fellow Confucian scholars when it became known later. They even ridiculed Hakuseki, saying that he must have been bewitched by the foreign magician because of the open and even humble stance he took toward Sidoti.

Hakuseki was quite realistic when he frankly admitted the fact that Europe was superior to Japan in such diverse fields of knowledge as astronomy, geography, botany, navigation, military arms and strategy, medical science, and linguistics. He was clearly ahead of his contemporaries in his interest and ability to digest this flood of new information.

Sidoti recognized Hakuseki's brilliance and complimented him by saying that a person like him would be born only once every five hundred years! (Such a warm mutual appraisal reminds us of a similar encounter between Xavier and Ninshitsu, the abbot of the Zen Buddhist monastery in Kagoshima in 1549.) It is indeed a pity that his compatriots, including the political leaders in Edo, in particular, did not possess an enlightened mind of his caliber. If they had, modernization would have taken place in Japan several centuries earlier. Nonetheless, Hakuseki certainly opened the path for his country's future; his influence was long-lasting among the intelligentsia in Japan, particularly in respect to the study of European culture.

As regards the religious aspect, however, Hakuseki's thinking did not go beyond the framework of the Confucian tradition. He was, moreover, a practical thinker, and was not greatly fond of philosophical speculation. In addition to his negative reactions to the Christian doctrines, Sidoti's accounts of the bloody power struggles in Christian Europe reinforced in his mind the importance of Confucian morality—filial piety, humaneness, loyalty, etc.

As mentioned earlier, it was Hakuseki's firm conclusion that the west could offer nothing to Japan as far as "spiritual matters" were concerned. This view gave rise to what later became prevalent among the Japanese intellectuals —*wakon yosai* (the Japanese mind and western knowledge).

Why did Sidoti fail to influence Hakuseki religiously? It is far from easy to answer this question. If we may venture to say, Hakuseki might have listened to the padre somewhat differently if the westerner had possessed a good amount of knowledge of Confucian ideas and had been able to utilize the knowledge skillfully during their conversation about Christianity. It seems that some basic channels of communication should have been established first in terms of vocabulary, concepts, logic, and, above all, a willingness to seek the truth together.

Sidoti, however, could not have used this approach, even if he had been well versed with Confucianism, because Matteo Ricci's utilization of Confucian notions during his missionary activities in China was condemned officially by Pope Clement XI in 1704. In fact, when Hakuseki asked Sidoti about Ricci, Sidoti first ignored the question. When pressed further, he finally said that he did not know "that person" well. Hakuseki discounted the answer, however. The padre did the best he believed he could—he told the investigator basic Christian doctrines straightforwardly and forcefully yet humbly.

## (4) Verdict on Sidoti

The failure to appreciate Christian teachings led Hakuseki as a loyal government official to confirm the official policy to suppress Christianity. The closing statement he made in *Seiyo-kibun* was an endorsement of the bakufu's method of quelling Christianity through the Buddhist parish system. But his anti-Christian parlance lacks ferocity; though he still suspected that Christian missions might possibly cause social unrest, he did recognize its intention as being "not a plot of aggression." This acknowledgement was quite unique and bold coming from an important bakufu official during an age of severe prohibition toward Christianity. It is indicative of his own perceptive and independent mind.

As for the fate of Sidoti, Hakuseki recommended to the shogun three alternatives: the first and preferable measure, he said, would be to deport him back to where he came from; the second intermediate measure would be to give him life imprisonment; the third and worst step would be to execute him.

In the memorandum he submitted, he stated that Sidoti had risked his life to come to Japan as an envoy of the ruler of his country and the "master" (pope) of his religion "without knowing the fallacy of its teaching," and thus deserved pity. He, moreover, emphasized that it would be desirable to demonstrate the bakufu's humane policy following the Confucian moral ideal. Sidoti himself asserted that he was a legitimate messenger and not a vagrant of some sort. (This self-claim, however, did not quite convince the Japanese, because he was not carrying with him any official letter—neither from the pope nor from the king.)

The bakufu's decision was to choose the second alternative which Hakuseki had suggested. Sidoti was to be kept a prisoner without strict security under the care of an elderly couple by the names of Chosuke and Haru.

In the autumn of 1714 the caretakers confessed voluntarily to the authorities that they were baptized by Sidoti. They had already received instructions in Christian teachings some sixteen years or so previously by a missionary for whom they had worked as servants. They did not receive baptism at that time, but now decided to do so because of Sidoti's influence. They were immediately taken to jail, and Sidoti was thrown into underground confinement. Describing Sidoti, Hakuseki wrote in *Seiyo-kibun:* "At this point his true feelings were manifested. He called out the names of Chosuke and Haru day and night, urging them loudly to stay firm in their faith and not to change their hearts even to death."

Sidoti died in the cell on October 21, 1714 at the age of forty-six. Chosuke also died in the same month. (The final fate of Haru is not known.) News of Sidoti's death moved Hakuseki emotionally so much that he took up a pen to write *Seiyo-kibun* in the following year. (It was not published until 1882, however, because it contained an account of Christianity.)

Sidoti was not able to accomplish his initial plans—the bakufu did not open the country to Christianity and only two people were baptized. But by way of Hakuseki, he left a unique impact on the intellectual history of Japan—an expansion of the country's mental horizon toward the rest of the world and the development of the study of western culture.

## THE UNDERGROUND CHRISTIANS

The bakufu's anti-Christian campaign was thorough; every citizen was indoctrinated from childhood and told that Christianity was an evil religion which would destroy the country. Many stories were written in order to inculcate how pernicious the Christians were. Some of these stories appear to have been produced by utilizing certain Christian sources (most likely obtained from former Christians), while others were obviously contrived out of sheer fantasy for the sake of popular entertainment. The revolt at Shimabara was a favorite subject for fictitious exaggeration, and Urugan Bateren (Padre Organtino) appeared as the most popular exotic character for those imaginative dramas.

The basic thrust common to all of these writings was that the padres came to Japan as a part of a grand plan of the southern barbarians to conquer the whole world. Many Japanese, including Nobunaga Oda, were inveigled into trusting the padres' wicked schemes. These western "defrauders" performed various magical demonstrations and taught the "occult" to their Japanese followers. But their fallacies were always disclosed by wise men of Buddhism and Confucianism.

Though all the Christians appear to have been totally eradicated from the country, there were some of them who secretly maintained their faith. They were located mostly in secluded villages in northern Kyushu and in the area of Nagasaki and on the small isles off its coast. In order to survive under such conditions for an indefinite period of time without priests and any support from outside, they formed an extremely tightly knit unit hamlet by hamlet. Each member's loyalty to the community was so strong that the secrets were hardly revealed to outsiders. Through a span of time as long as two centuries, nonethe-

less, some of them were occasionally discovered and, unless they recanted, suffered horrible consequences.

Another means for them to sustain their identity secretly was to
pretend to be Buddhists. Assuming a posture docile enough to follow
the government's requirement for every person to register as a member
at a local Buddhist temple, they outwardly lived like ordinary Buddhists, but undercover they actually practiced Christianity. For instance, engravings of the madonna with the baby Jesus were modified
to look like a representation of Kannon (the embodiment of Buddha's
mercy) holding a child. The sign of the cross was often concealed at
the back of a Buddha's statue.

The Christian rites and education were also done undercover with
chosen personnel in charge of particular functions (which we have
already referred to before). It was an absolutely indispensable practice
for these "undercover" Christians to offer prayers of contrition in order
to express their profound remorse after attending Buddhist temples for
some special occasions such as funerals. It was also hoped that these
prayers would "cancel out" the pagan rituals which they, though nominally, did participate in. Because all funerals were supposed to be
conducted in the Buddhist way, the Christians were obliged to follow
the rule, but they held their own secret funeral ceremonies afterward.

Basic Christian doctrines, prayers, and rituals were taught and
passed on orally from one generation to another. A very few of them
were preserved in written form. During the course of a long span of
time, memory sometimes failed and heterogeneous practices crept in.
For example, when the French priests arrived in Japan, as it finally
opened its doors to western countries in the nineteenth century, they
were appalled at what they deemed the atrocious contents of a small
book of supposedly Christian doctrines which was given to them by
some local people who had been practicing their underground Christianity. It is of interest to consider just how Christian teachings were
distorted in this booklet.

### TENCHI NO HAJIME NO KOTO

Despite the title *Tenchi no hajime no koto* (Concerning the beginning of heaven and earth), Deus' creation of heaven and earth is stated

rather briefly at the opening of this writing, but an account of the fall of Adam and Eve is described in detail. This is followed by an elaborate tale of the birth of Jesus and his discussion with the wise men who are Buddhist monks. The story then moves on to a narrative of Christ's passion and crucifixion.

As will be discussed shortly, these versions contain numerous distortions and modifications of the biblical account. What follows the topics mentioned above is also quite fanciful. It says in a language reminiscent of the Apostles' Creed that Christ descended to "the bottom of the earth," after which he ascended on the third day to heaven to sit on the right hand of Deus. Then it states that he descended to the earth again to stay at the "temple of *Santa-ekerenjia*" (holy ecclesia) to save the living and the dead.

The Trinity, according to this story, consists of Deus the father ("pater"), Mary the mother (the intercessor), and Christ the son (the savior). Mary is not the wife of Deus, however, because Mary's marriage with Joseph is said to have been consummated in heaven with Deus' approval. The story has a human touch as it mentions that the infants killed by King Herod (who is called *Yorotetsu* in the story) were raised to paradise, and that Veronica received the "rank" of *Aneisu-teu* (Agnus Dei, with no explanation as to what kind of rank this is). The last subject in this book concerns eschatology. Each person is said to be judged upon his or her death, and then the final catastrophe of the whole world is predicted.

It is understandable that without proper instructions the original meaning of the Latin words were lost and a lapse of memory regarding the biblical stories occurred during the process of more than two hundred years of oral transmission. For example, the "biruzen" (virgin) is understood in the story as something of a spiritual exercise, such as that in which Buddhist monks engaged. Maruya (Mary) is said to have been able to perform miracles (e.g. causing a snowfall in June), give birth to Hiriyo (filius, son in Latin; here it is used like the name of Deus' son), and ascend to heaven, all because of the merit of her "biruzen." She is elevated to be even the third person of the Trinity! Mary, representing eternally compassionate love and care, must have been especially important to those underground Christians undergoing severe persecutions.

Mary is said to have been a humble maiden who lived in the

country of Ruson (Luzon, the Philippines). Deus "jumped into her body" through her mouth in the form of a butterfly and thus she conceived Hiriyo, the son of Deus. The young Hiriyo received baptism by San Joan (St. John) and became a monk (here again a Buddhist term is used). He was then educated by the angel called "Sacrament" at the monastery in Zezemaruya (Gethsemane). His debate with the Buddhist monks at Baran-do (Vatican? basilica?) made them his disciples, and he became the abbot of the magnificent temple of Santa Ekerenjia in the country of Rome.

The story clearly reflects the extremely precarious condition of those underground Christians who were desperately and covertly fighting back (yet also being greatly influenced by) the Buddhist pressure which was imposed on them constantly. Nonetheless, they do not seem to have lost their hope by virtue of clinging to the belief that paradise would be opened to them someday.

The biblical world was, in a way, made into their own world. For instance, the place where Adam and Eve were placed is not the garden of Eden, but nowhere else than the area of Nagasaki, the locale of this story's provenance. Mary's birthplace is claimed to have been located in the Philippines, where the padres came from, and the story also says that Jesus lived in the monastery in Rome, the place of "pappa" (pope).

Despite numerous distortions and diversions, the story retains some important aspects of the genuine Christian teachings which the padres taught the local people. First of all, Deus, though called the king of heaven many times and even Buddha a few times, is described as a monotheistic God, the supreme creator. This fact is significant since the circumstances faced by the underground Christians must have tempted them to transform their monotheistic faith into some form of pantheism. In some of their groups, in fact, such a transformation did take place. But as far as this story is concerned, there is no trace of it.

Secondly, the importance of the paradise to come is underscored again and again throughout the story. This must have been the crucial item of belief which sustained them through the years of horrendous persecution. Their faith was decidedly otherworldly.

The third genuine aspect concerns the story's emphasis on sexual morality and a prohibition of suicide. The story tells us that the son and daughter of Adam and Eve lost their blood-relationship by Deus' will—a statement, though not found in the Bible, which is intended to clarify that incest did not take place at that time. The looseness of sexual conduct was one of the social conditions the padres found in Japan and criticized in strong terms. The underground Christians did not forget that admonition.

Suicide was committed quite often in Japan in those days. An honorable suicide was, in fact, praised highly by the samurais in particular. The Christian prohibition of suicide was said to be cowardice and a dishonor. In this story we read Jesus' words of sorrow after he was informed of Judas' suicide—that even a traitor like him could have been saved if he had not committed suicide.

One other observation is that this story fails to mention the redemptive significance of Christ's death. The author of the story apparently did not know the reason why Christ had to die on the cross. He therefore artificially connected the story of the massacre of the infants by King Herod (Matthew 2:16) with the arrest and execution of Christ. This should be deemed as a vital defect of this story as literature narrating Christianity. No wonder the French missionaries who came to Japan in the nineteenth century were so vexed by the contents that they eventually discarded the book.

A dearth of the proper understanding of this crucial point of the Christian faith does not seem to be a problem of this writing alone. We have noted previously the fact that even such a well-educated person as Fabian does not appear to have had a profound existential realization of the meaning of Christ's death. This seems to have been a serious weakness in the content of the faith of the Christians (at least for some of them) in pre-modern Japan.

### THE END OF THE PRE-MODERN ERA

There was a persistent conviction which never ceased to exist among the underground Christians in pre-modern Japan: that the prohibition of Christianity would be repealed someday. It did become a reality when the country finally opened its door to westerners again in the nineteenth century. That marked the end of the pre-modern era of Japan's history. By the beginning of the nineteenth century the Tokugawa bakufu in Edo had considerably weakened politically. It had lost its tight control over the feudal lords, so that some of them became strong enough to assert themselves against the bakufu authority.

There were also economic problems. Famines struck the land several times, which caused social unrest. Peasants, in particular, who constituted the basis of this agricultural society, had to bear the heaviest burden of these economic and social ills. They, joined by dissatisfied and masterless samurais, started rebellions and attacked wealthy landowners and merchants as well as the local magisterial offices. These incidents occurred in many places in the nation.

Perhaps the biggest problem the bakufu government had to face was how to deal with the foreigners who began to knock on the country's hitherto tightly closed door. First the Russians came to Hokkaido (the northernmost island called Ezo in those days) in 1792 and demanded trade. They were soon followed by the English in 1797 and by the Americans in 1837.

The resourceless bakufu officials tried simply to keep the closed-door policy which they had inherited. But the news of China's miserable defeat during the Opium War (1839–1842) greatly disturbed them. In 1844 the Dutch, who had been the sole western trading partner, advised them strongly to open their country. Around that time the French reached the Ryukyu islands, which were under the political influence of both China and Japan (according to Japan's understanding, it was under the jurisdiction of the Satsuma fief).

Faced with a forceful demand made by the American Commodore Perry, who anchored his squadron of four warships in Uraga (located at the mouth of the Tokyo bay), the Japanese government reluctantly signed a treaty with the Americans in 1854, which was followed by similar treaties with the English and the Russians. Within a few years, the French joined as well.

The bakufu's new political move, however, infuriated many nationalists. Here again the ideology they relied on was the fanatic belief in Japan as the divine country (shinkoku). It had been used, as we have referred to more than once, to persecute the Christians since the sixteenth century. This time as well it furnished a nationalistic fuel against what those nationalists called "foreign invaders."

Inspired by Shintoism, educated in the Japanese classics, and trained with Confucian morality, these zealots launched vigorous movements aiming at a restoration of direct rule by the emperor and a total expulsion of all foreign powers. They considered the Tokugawa bakufu too incompetent to handle foreign affairs in addition to domestic problems. Being fiercely anti-foreign, they were passionate foes not only of Christianity but of Buddhism. The latter too was branded as a foreign religion. Many temples and monasteries were demolished in those days because of this trend.

Some influential feudal lords, while competing with one another, took the lead in the anti-bakufu movements. The relatively young samurais of middle rank from these fiefs were particularly active, and they, in fact, played a major role in pushing ahead the pro-emperor forces.

The last shogun, Yoshinobu Tokugawa, surrendered the hegemony of the country to a new government based on the imperial authority in 1867. Thus the feudal era ended. In the following year the imperial residence was moved to Edo, now renamed Tokyo, which became the new capital of the nation. The new era was called Meiji.

The passionate nationalists who succeeded in establishing the Meiji government by toppling the Tokugawa regime could hardly afford to remain naive about the mounting pressures exerted by the westerners. Faced with the overwhelming superior military power of these nations, there was no choice but to open the country.

Though giving up their desire to expel the foreigners, they continued to assert vigorously the Shintoistic tradition as the spiritual foundation of Japan because it was organically connected with the imperial system. As a result, the anti-Christian policy enforced by the bakufu was kept intact by the Meiji government. However, it was finally abandoned in 1873 because of repetitive strong demands by the western diplomats.

### THE ARRIVAL OF MISSIONARIES

Just as many of the underground Christians in Japan never gave up hope for regaining their freedom to exercise their faith openly, the church in Europe did not lose its vision of resuming its mission in

Japan. In 1653 the Society for Foreign Missions in Paris (*Société des Missions Etrangérs de Paris*) was established, and it began to send its member priests to Asia. Several of them reached Ryukyu by the middle of the nineteenth century, looking for an opportunity to commence their missions in Japan.

The long-awaited chance finally came when the bakufu government signed treaties with the five western nations. In 1859 Grudence Seraphim Girard, the superior of the missions, landed at Yokohama (near Tokyo), and a few years afterward Fr. Bernard Thadée Petitjean (1829–1884) and several other French priests arrived and opened their residences at three port cities: Yokohama, Hakodate (located at the southern tip of the island of Hokkaido), and Nagasaki.

Nevertheless, any missionary activities aimed at the local Japanese were still strictly forbidden by the law. These priests were allowed to stay within certain confined areas of these cities solely for the sake of taking spiritual care of the westerners there. They seldom had any chance to have contact with the local people. A church was built in Yokohama in 1862, and another one in Nagasaki in 1864. The exotic sight of the church buildings with gold crosses (a sign forbidden for two hundred and fifty years!) on the top of the steeples startled many Japanese, who flocked to see them.

From the moment they stepped on Japan's soil, the priests were quite anxious to find out if there were any Christians still in existence in Japan. But much to their dismay, any chance of inquiry seemed impossible under the constantly watchful eyes of local officials. However, it was about noontime on March 17, 1865 when an old woman, who had been with some other sightseers standing outside the church, approached and whispered to Fr. Petitjean, "The hearts of all of us here are the same as yours."

The woman's words sounded like joyous music to him. She was one of the underground Christians by the name of Yuri Isabelina Sugimoto, who lived in the village of Uragami near Nagasaki. (Uragami is now a part of the city of Nagasaki.) She told Petitjean that all of her fellow villagers were also Christians. At her request, he guided her to a statue of the madonna and Christ, where she and others (who turned out to be her family members) prayed. They asked him whether or not he was observing the *kanashimi no setsu* (season of sorrow) as they were.

"Yes!" answered the priest. It was indeed the season of Lent. (This dramatic scene of Petitjean's first encounter with these Christians is recorded in Francisque Marnes, La "religion de Jésus" ressuscitée au Japan, Paris, 1896, vol. 1, p. 488.)

It was thus that the resurrection of the Catholic missions began in Japan. Petitjean and the Christians in Uragami kept in contact with each other despite the awful risk they were taking. He learned that Uragami had not been without Christians since the sixteenth century. Baptisms, daily family worship, and the holy weeks according to the Catholic calendar had been faithfully observed throughout that long period of time. According to Petitjean, most of these peasants knew by heart the Lord's Prayer, the Angelic Salutation, the Apostles' Creed, the Salve Regina, and the Act of Contrition. This was also the occasion when the priest received the book Tenchi no hajime no koto (Concerning the beginning of heaven and earth), which we discussed earlier.

The priest's excitement increased further as he continued to discover many more Christians in other villages and even in the islands of Goto off the coast of Nagasaki. Within a few months he learned that in total several thousand of them were living in the isolated hamlets and isles in the whole region. Fr. Girard's letter to the mission board in Paris mentioned fifty thousand as an estimated number of Christians and urged a reinforcement of missionaries. The priests, despite the official prohibition, commenced their pastoral ministry to these Christians.

(There were, however, some of those Christians who refused to believe that the French missionaries brought back the religion they had been following. Their "Christian" teachings and practices had changed greatly through the many years. In an attempt to convince them, some priests even visited them in seventeenth century Portuguese costumes, but to no avail; their suspicion was so deep that they did not open their minds. Even now the descendants of these "separatists"—hanare in Japanese—live in Kyushu.)

### LAST FLARE OF PERSECUTION

Greatly encouraged by the arrival of the priests, these Christians became bolder. Not only did they begin to invite the priests to their homes, though still cautiously during the dark of night, but some of them buried their dead according to the Christian way without asking local Buddhist priests to conduct the funerals as prescribed by the authorities. Such open violations, needless to say, provoked local officials to launch investigations, which resulted in massive arrests, and they were thrown into jail.

Hearing of this development, the western diplomats immediately strongly protested to the Japanese government, which flatly refused their pleas, insisting that the practice of Christianity was unlawful in the country, but pledged that the prisoners would be treated in a humane way. Contrary to the official words of assurance, the prisoners were treated horribly; severe torture was inflicted on them. The investigators succeeded in forcing some of them to apostatize, but many others showed not even a sign of surrender. The hunt and seizure of the Christians continued, and so did the excruciating torture.

In 1869 the new Meiji government, which was as violently anti-Christian as the old Tokugawa bakufu, decided to imprison 3,400 Christians in twenty-two different places in the country. Their families were split and their properties were lost. The prison conditions in the places of exile were unbearable, yet many of them managed to survive through hunger, thirst, illness, winter's cold, summer's heat, and physical and mental abuse.

Meanwhile, the pressures were mounting from the western governments to terminate such barbaric treatment of the Christians. Some of the forward-looking Japanese politicians and intellectuals, including those who visited the western countries, began to speak up for the freedom to believe as one may choose. In 1873 the Meiji government finally set free the exiled Christians and allowed them to go home. The constitution promulgated in 1889 formally included the guarantee of freedom of belief.

These legal provisions by no means heralded the arrival of a golden age for Christianity. Since then, largely by virtue of the endeavor of foreign missionaries, the number of Christians (including both Catholics and Protestants) has increased, and Christian contributions to Japanese society have been considerable particularly in the areas of education and social charity. (Protestant Christianity was introduced by missionaries from the United States and England. The first

Protestant church was built in Nagasaki in 1861.) Nonetheless, Christianity has remained a foreign religion.

Even today the number of Christians (Catholics, Protestants, Orthodox, all combined) constitutes less than two percent of the entire population. Why so? Is it because there is some formidable factor deep-seated in the Japanese mentality itself which prevents most of the people from accepting Christianity? If so, this "factor" may have been a major reason why Catholic Christianity, despite its initial success, had to suffer horrendous persecutions for as long as almost three centuries. It is our task next to reflect on this Christian history in the pre-modern era in a summary fashion and then to discuss what that "factor" may be in the chapter which follows.

# EPILOGUE

## REASONS FOR THE INITIAL SUCCESS

Reflecting upon the Catholic mission in pre-modern Japan, one would certainly wonder why, despite impressive initial success, it had to suffer from persecution of such great magnitude. Let us begin by recapitulating the reasons why so many Japanese accepted Christianity to the extent that they did prior to the Tokugawa bakufu's wholesale oppression.

### (1) Historical reasons

We should consider first of all the historical context in which Catholic Christianity was first introduced to Japan at the hands of the Portuguese Jesuits. It was an age of civil war—the old regime had collapsed and numerous warlords were anxiously attempting to expand their power. This unstable social condition, though involving possible physical danger, also provided an opportunity for the missionaries to exercise their influence on the local people.

Such a situation also enabled the missionaries to have relatively free access to all parts of the country (which was not the case in India and was much less so in China). Despite the political turmoil, the nation was quite homogeneous, which made mission activity much easier. (Again this was not the case in the other two areas of the Jesuit mission.) One common language, for example, facilitated the mission work (in contrast to the multi-lingual situation in the rest of the mission lands in Asia).

The absence of rigid control by the central government also

prompted many warlords to exercise their own will. Not only were they militarily daring but they also became adventurous intellectually; many of them looked eagerly for new things, new ideas, and new resources. The social climate was thus more receptive than it would have been earlier to a new value system such as that of European Christianity. Nobunaga Oda perhaps represented such a dynamic trend; he took a keen interest in European culture and willingly supported the padres, the bringers of a new civilization. This dynamism, propelled by avidity and curiosity, was, however, curtailed severely when an unmalleable social structure was established by the Tokugawa bakufu. With that as well, the Christian missions had to suffer doom.

## (2) Economic reasons

As a second reason for the initial success of the Christian missions, we may cite an economic factor. The power vacuum in the nation's capital quickened the competing warlords' desperate search for economic resources themselves. There was also a newly rising merchant class which, by taking advantage of the confused situation of the society, succeeded in accumulating a considerable amount of wealth.

Both groups discovered a tremendous opportunity for financial growth in foreign trade. Here lay the diplomatic usefulness of the European missionaries; their intermediary role was vital in various commercial and diplomatic transactions. Even those who opposed Christianity inwardly found it necessary to resort to the contribution the padres were able to offer. Benefits from the trade furnished a sizable income for the missions as well. However, when the trade with the Iberians was terminated under the Tokugawa bakufu's policy of closing the country, the diplomatic value of the padres also diminished.

## (3) Sociological reasons

We should also note a sociological factor which attracted many Japanese to Christianity. Despite the Jesuit mission policy of placing priority on work among the higher echelon of society, the padres failed to gain converts from the wealthy and intellectual class for many years.

Unlike Matteo Ricci in China, the Jesuits in Japan did not struggle to create intellectual rapport with the literati.

However, as soon as the missionaries succeeded in winning friendship from the political leaders (shogun and warlords), they were able to expand the mission fields. In this sense, their mission strategy did succeed by taking advantage of the feudalistic social structure and mores. This approach, nonetheless, entailed also the consequence that the fate of the mission was controlled by their political patrons. As we have observed, much evidence corroborated this fact. The adoption of an anti-Christian policy by Ieyasu Tokugawa was a case in point: Christianity thrived when it was tolerated by Ieyasu, but as soon as he turned against it, it faced disaster.

Though they were violated from time to time during the era of civil wars, the feudalistic mores demanded absolute loyalty of a subordinate to the suzerain. When a lord decided to convert to Christianity, consequently, many of his retainers were obliged to follow suit in order to express their fealty. Thus mass conversion took place in the domains of the Christian lords such as Otomo, Arima, Omura, and Takayama.

As for the peasants, a strong sense of loyalty toward their own community generated mass conversion. A village was an extended family; there was an inseparable identity between the group and the individual. Once a community as a whole chose to become Christian under the leadership of elders, every member was bound to join the church. This village solidarity was incredibly firm, as was evinced by the fact that a considerable number of the "underground Christians" survived with the support of this community spirit throughout two hundred and fifty years of severe persecution.

The sense of loyalty in these cases was not totally a product of feudalism and traditional collectivism; the Christian faith certainly provided an ultimate object of dedication—one absolute God. The belief in the supreme master in heaven, in fact, led some Christian warriors even to defy their lords when faced with the demand of apostasy. The "underground Christian" peasants did likewise against the bakufu's order of the eradication of Christianity. The Christians' faithfulness to God was considered by Hideyoshi and the Tokugawa shoguns as a sign of rebellion against their authority. This accusation constituted one of the major reasons for the Christian persecution.

## (4) Cultural reasons

There was also a cultural reason why the Christian mission made such successful inroads into the Japanese society. We have already noted the dynamic nature of this period—the old social mores were challenged and new culture was explored. The European culture the padres introduced fascinated much of the population from the top to the lower echelons. For the local people the appearance of the Europeans itself was an object of tremendous curiosity.

The churches and the liturgy observed therein were exotic and enchanting. Padre Organtino capitalized on this foreign charm in the most effective way for his missionary cause. Visitor Valignano played an important role in introducing European literature, music, and painting to Japan. The colegios and seminarios functioned as the main loci for these cultural activities as well. The Jesuit emphasis on education was admired by many of the Japanese.

The missionaries made an invaluable contribution to Japanese society with respect to medical care as well. Luis de Almeida, in particular, played a vital role in introducing European medicine and surgical techniques. He established clinics, which offered immeasurable help especially for impoverished patients, including lepers who until that time had been totally deserted by society. The friars also demonstrated a selfless dedication to this cause. Such a charitable work certainly earned great respect from the Japanese. Western medical science brought by the Jesuits was taken over and further developed by their Japanese disciples after the missionaries were expelled by the bakufu.

Other branches of European science and technology were also taught by the padres; astronomy based on the Copernican theory, for example, presented a radical challenge to the Confucian world-view espoused by Japanese intellectuals. It also supplied the Japanese with new information about the calendarial system, geography, and navigation. Along with firearms, European armed ships were eagerly coveted by the warlords.

Suffice it to say that the padres opened the eyes of the Japanese to a whole new and vast world. All this undoubtedly won the missionaries tremendous awe and admiration from the Japanese. Many converts from the intellectual class at least in the initial stage of the mission were apparently persuaded by the padres' preaching of natural theology (God's revelation through the created world) armed with the recent European scientific information.

### (5) Psychological reasons

Faced with such a flood of fresh cultural products and knowledge, the Japanese were by no means passive recipients; they were quite anxious to pursue them by themselves. (This desire continued clandestinely even after the country was officially closed by the Tokugawa bakufu.) The first missionary, Francis Xavier, soon noticed the Japanese penchant for novelties. Hoping to take advantage of this national characteristic for his missionary purpose, he urged the General of the Jesuit Society in Rome that padres equipped with good scientific learning as well as spiritual excellence be sent to Japan. Valignano, the chief architect of the Christian mission in Japan, made the identical request repeatedly to Rome. Not only these two leading Jesuits but Japan experts, such as Frois and Organtino, reported to Europe such a nature of the Japanese as well.

This national psychological feature seems to have been nurtured by the country's experiences of being influenced by the outside world. The cultural roots of Japan were mostly in China. Examples of the Chinese influence on Japan lie in profusion: Buddhism, Confucianism, the writing system, the structure of the government, moral codes, art, and literature. All of these cultural products were brought to Japan usually by way of Korea from the early period down to the Tokugawa era in Japan's history. The Japanese, therefore, had been quite used to accepting foreign influence long before the arrival of the Europeans in the sixteenth century.

The heavy influence of the Chinese culture, however, did not result in the simple "sinization" of Japanese culture. The Japanese, in other words, did not adopt foreign imports automatically; instead they altered them to a great extent so that they suited the taste and convenience of the Japanese. The Chinese ideograms, for example, were not only appropriated in order to represent the Japanese phonetic system but were also simplified in such a way that the Japanese alphabet was created out of them. Buddhism, which taught the salvation of every sentient being, was accepted by Japanese from a national point of view rather than in its original universal nature. (For this question, see Hajime Nakamura, *Ways of Thinking of Eastern Peoples*, tr. by Philip Wiener, Honolulu, 1971, p. 529. In this erudite study, Nakamura also explains that in contrast to the Japanese openness and attraction to foreign influence, the Chinese have generally tended to despise and ignore it.)

Such an insular process of the "Japanization" of the foreign products intimates the Japanese people's clever skill of imitation as well as an often superficial comprehension of foreign cultures. A well-known scholar of the history of Japanese thought, Sokichi Tsuda (1873–1961), for instance, has indicated that Japanese intellectuals had been exposed to Chinese thought throughout history but their understanding had tended to be arbitrary because they had learned it mostly through books. The superficial adaptation of Chinese philosophies, according to Tsuda, has caused numerous instances of distortion and fraudulent appropriations; nonetheless, this adoptive process, in effect, enriched Japan's culture.

An identical response was shown by the Japanese when the Portuguese arrived in the sixteenth century. The newcomers were welcomed and their cultural products were cherished by many of the Japanese. The people realized with great fascination the fact that China and Korea were not the only foreign countries which could offer useful things. Like Neo-Confucianism which was a new philosophy from China at that time, Christianity presented itself as a brand new religion which attracted the attention of a number of people. The missionaries, therefore, were objects of curiosity as well as affection as long as they did not offend the local religions. Even Kiyomasa Kato, a notorious foe of the Christians, liked to wear Portuguese clothing.

For an example of a cunning use of Christian ideas, we may refer to Atsutane Hirata (1776–1843), a fanatic Shintoist. His xenophobic zeal prompted him to direct vehement attacks on Buddhism and Confucianism as foreign and corrupted religions. In order to construct a Shinto cosmology and theology centered around a monotheistic supreme creator (identified with the Japanese national deity), he covertly utilized the Christian notions of God's creation and the hereafter which he had borrowed from some Christian literature published in China.

The Japanese psychological characteristics of having a love for novelty and arbitrarily adopting foreign products became even more manifest after the fall of the Tokugawa bakufu. From the Meiji restoration to the present (except during World War II), western culture has been insatiably absorbed and "conveniently" Japanized.

## (6) Religious reasons

Lastly we consider a specifically religious aspect of the initial success of the Christian missions. We should note first the fact that Buddhism was then at a low ebb, which provided an opportunity for Christianity to penetrate the Japanese society. Though some fanatic Buddhists succeeded in attracting the poor and discontented peasants and disenfranchised warriors and thereby expanded their influence, Buddhism in general had lost the spiritual vitality it previously possessed and had been quite secularized. The fanatic Buddhists grew into a formidable political power, but finally succumbed to the merciless forces of Nobunaga Oda. This despot favored the Christians because of his intense dislike of those Buddhists. But in a later reversal the Tokugawa regime used Buddhism as a tool to eradicate the Christians.

Christianity, in a way, provided the people with a religious alternative to Buddhism. It was a fresh teaching, radically different from any of the hitherto known religions in Japan. The Christian promise of a hereafter was appealing particularly to those who were utterly weary and hopeless in the war-torn condition of the time. Fortified with scholastic theology, the padres never ceased to tell their audience of the existence of the immortal soul and its final destiny. The necessary presence of the almighty creator God was also their favorite subject against the Buddhist and Confucian opponents, in particular.

The doctrine of Christ's redemption of sinners does not seem to have sounded cacophonous to many of the Japanese. George Sansom, a celebrated Japanologist, has said that "it seems very clearly to mark off the Japanese as different from other Asiatic peoples in their attitude towards the crucifixion." "To most people in other parts of eastern Asia . . . the doctrine of atonement was repugnant. They were shocked by the idea of a divine person undergoing torture and death and disliked a symbolism that had to do with blood."

Sansom explains this religious psychological feature of the Japanese by pointing out a "masochistic strain in Japan, where the religious ascetic usually mortified the flesh only by living frugally in a mountain hut or by practicing such minor austerities as bathing in very cold water." Such a mental trait, he also maintains, disposed the Christians of the pre-modern Japan toward the suffering they would face under the persecution. (Cf. his *The Western World and Japan: A Study in the Interaction of Europe and Asiatic Cultures*, N.Y., 1973, p. 130.)

Sansom seems to be accurate in recognizing this Japanese emotional trait which made them as a people susceptible to the Christian message of the vicarious death of Christ. It had a dramatic effect on the sentiments of many of the listeners: "The Son of God died for everyone, even a wretch like me!" And the opponents of Christianity criticized this teaching not because of the repugnant idea of the suffering and death of the Son of God but because of the apparent cold indifference on the part of God the Father toward his own Son who submitted himself to such a horrendous fate. Christ's death, they felt, betrayed Deus' incompetence as well as his cruelty.

Sansom seems to be right also when he calls this emotional trait of the Japanese a "masochistic strain," even though the examples he presents are not quite convincing because they are not unique to Japan. This "masochistic strain" may be exemplified better by the emotional tendency of the Japanese called *hangan-biiki*. "Hangan" refers to Yoshitsune Minamoto, a tragic war hero of the twelfth century, and "biiki" means favor. Using Yoshitsune as an example, the "hangan-biiki" indicates a sentiment which is favorable and sympathetic toward tragic heroes, unfortunate losers, and victims of circumstances. Many highly emotional stories and dramas depicting such unlucky historical characters have been enormously popular in Japan for centuries. The audiences appear to love to empathize with the sad fate these individuals had to undergo.

The Christian story of the suffering and death of the innocent Son of Deus was, therefore, quite agreeable to such an emotional strain common among the Japanese. From the point of view of the Christian mission, needless to say, it was advantageous that there was no emotional stumbling block on the part of the Japanese to an acceptance of the most important message concerning Christ's redemption of sinners.

It is difficult to assess exactly the degree of Japanese comprehension of the Christian doctrines, because most of the documents written by the Japanese Christians were systematically destroyed under the Tokugawa bakufu's anti-Christian policy. The padres were seemingly quite impressed by the intellectual curiosity and ability of the Japanese to understand Christian theology, as reported by Xavier, Frois, Valignano, Organtino and others (except for people like Cabral) in their letters.

Japanese preachers such as Lourenço, Yohoken and Fabian (before his apostasy) evidently were able to digest Christian teachings remarkably well. Many of the novices and dojukus, according to Valignano, proved to be excellent students and useful mission workers. Compared to the converts in India (most of whom he called "rice-Christians"), the Visitor testified that the Japanese converts "all have this in common, that after they become Christians they pay no regard whatsoever to their idols" (Eng. tr. by Boxer, op. cit., p. 94). As for the mission's opponents, some Buddhist monks were known to have asked highly sophisticated questions of the padres. Padre Torres honestly admitted that even St. Thomas and Duns Scotus perhaps could not answer some of those questions.

The obstacles to a comprehension of Christianity stemmed from the basic difference of philosophical and religious concepts and logic in addition to that of language. Despite the high intensity and intelligent quality of debate between the two religious groups, a truly fructuous dialogue seemingly never took place, and instead the encounters often ended in mutual obloquy (as typically exemplified by the argument between Razan Hayashi and Fabian). It was indeed unfortunate that an intellectual exchange like the one which Matteo Ricci fostered in China did not take place in Japan.

Nonetheless, it is unfair simply to blame the missionaries for the failure. Indeed they made Herculean efforts against incredible odds. Not only did they suffer the deadly danger and hardship of the long journey by sea all the way from the other side of the earth, but many of them did their best to overcome the difficulties arising from such a totally different climate, life-style, diet, language, and culture.

As far as the European missionaries who came to Japan (and

China) were concerned, they, for the most part, did not actively work for the political and economic interests of the colonial policy of their mother countries which supported them. In this respect, they were quite different from those in other mission lands such as in the South and Central Americas, South Asia, and Africa.

Visitor Valignano clearly spelled out an adaptational mission policy and strongly opposed any aggressive or confrontational approaches. The friars who arrived later, despite conflicting with the Jesuits in various ways, followed a non-aggressive course as well. (This, however, does not mean that they were total pacifists; many of them on at least one occasion considered the possibility of resorting to the use of military force.)

Many of the padres were, as a matter of fact, greatly loved and respected by the Japanese. We can name some of them without hesitation: Xavier, Torres, Frois, Organtino, Valignano, and many friars who bore witness to the spiritual virtues of poverty, humility, and devotion. Their genuine affection for the local people and selfless dedication to their religious cause were major reasons why many of the Japanese listened to them and became Christians. Their personal inspiration was more effective than their missionary rhetoric. Their moral aptitude also elicited the people's admiration as it was contrasted to the moral decadence of the Buddhist monks by Nobunaga Oda, for example. We should add that many of the Japanese Christians also led an upright and exemplary life, which won the respect of the general populace.

We have thus far recapitulated systematically the positive reasons for the remarkable success the Christian missions had until the Tokugawa bakufu launched the nationwide persecution of the Christians during the 1600s. Our next task is to consider in a summary fashion the reasons why Christianity was rejected to the extent it was.

### REASONS FOR THE REJECTION OF CHRISTIANITY

### (1) Political reasons

One direct reason why the suppression of Christianity began was basically political. The first official persecution took place in 1587 when Toyotomi Hideyoshi suddenly ordered the edict expelling the padres and demanded the apostasy of Ukon Takayama, a capable Christian lord as an expression of fealty toward him. Though the real reason for this abrupt move against the Christians is unclear, it is beyond a doubt that Hideyoshi feared that the rapid growth of Christian population and influence would be disadvantageous to the hegemony he had recently established. This drastic decision was made immediately following the conclusion of his successful campaign in Kyushu, where he had personally observed the enormous popularity of Christianity. Even without the instigation by Seyakuin, his anti-Christian companion, the despot probably would have taken some course of action inimical to Christianity.

Nonetheless, Hideyoshi apparently did not intend to eradicate the Christians totally from the country, at least at that time. He was keenly interested in trade with the Europeans for which the padres were still useful, and he greatly enjoyed procuring new information and products from Europe. His thinking seems to have been that for financial and cultural benefits, Christianity was to be tolerated.

Hideyoshi, for his own part, showed no serious interest in Christianity; he never attempted to learn or understand its teachings. He was satisfied with the syncretic religious tradition of Japan, an amalgam of Confucianism, Buddhism, and Shintoism, which he used as a political ideology in support of his reign over the nation. Christianity was first of all excluded because of its highly foreign nature, second for its demand of ultimate fidelity toward Deus, and third for its strict moral injunctions.

Hideyoshi's adventurous personality perhaps would have allowed him personally to accommodate the exotic or foreign nature of Christianity, but as the national ruler he must have been concerned about possible negative repercussions it might cause among loyal Buddhists, Shintoists, Confucians and nationalists in general. No domestic turmoil was tolerated under his control particularly when engaging in the aggressive invasion of Korea.

The second negative reason mentioned above was crucial in Hideyoshi's mind. As a despot, he did not want any higher authority over him. (The emperor had no practical power over him, and he simply made use of the imperial court for his personal advantage.) The Christians' loyalty to him was questionable as long as they held to their belief in a supreme God. Ukon Takayama's refusal to submit to his order because of Christian beliefs confirmed this suspicion.

This suspicion of the troublesome potential of Christianity was indeed a decisive problem which invited persecution. The repeated and desperate attempts by the Christians to overcome the problem failed. Not only at the time of Hideyoshi but also throughout the Tokugawa era and even the period from the Meiji government until the end of World War II, Christians were often suspected and accused of a questionable loyalty to their country. This suspicion was uncalled for, however (the Christian participation in the revolt at Shimabara was a rare exception). Most Japanese Christians always anxiously tried to present themselves as patriotic throughout those periods (unfortunately, including the time when militarism dominated the nation).

The source of this unwarranted suspicion of the loyalty of Christians was an insular nationalism which rendered Japan ignorant about world affairs, thereby causing the country to dwell simultaneously in complacency and insecurity. Hideyoshi called this nationalism *shinkoku* (Japan as a divine country), and used this slogan often in his public statements in order to legitimate policies which included his infamous anti-Christian edict.

This "shinkoku ideology" was not at all a well-defined system of thought. Rather it resembled a religious sentiment of national identity, which may be called "Japanism." The archenemy that the Christian mission encountered in Japan was this crypto-religion (i.e. it did not claim to be an independent religion but it, in reality, had a highly religious nature). (This subject will be discussed further later.)

As far as the Tokugawa bakufu's policy regarding Christianity was concerned, the first shogun, Ieyasu, adopted a course identical to that of Hideyoshi, i.e. he overlooked the religious practice of Christianity because of the diplomatic utility of the padres. For this reason, he was even eager to keep in contact with the friars from the Philippines. But when trade with the Spaniards failed to develop to the extent that he had hoped and the Dutch arrived with a new prospect of trade, he turned completely against Christianity. He and the cabinet of his close aides decided that Christianity was potentially inimical to the stability of their regime. The slogan used to legitimate this policy was the old and by now familiar shinkoku ideology.

Ieyasu was not a xenophobe, but his successors were. His grandson, Iemitsu, in particular, evidently harbored a deep-seated phobia of the aggressive expansion of European colonialism and regarded the Christians as a potential "fifth column." The revolt at Shimabara in 1637 seemed to him to corroborate this judgment. Hence the bakufu's persecution of the Christians reached its height under his reign. The anti-Christian hysteria became nationwide as well as endemic.

Reflecting on the whole political background of the Christian persecution from a Christian point of view, it was most unfortunate that the religious cause was misunderstood to be a part of the European colonial scheme. But this misunderstanding on the part of the Japanese political leaders was not entirely without reason. They were informed of the close collaboration between military aggression and missionary endeavors during the European expansion in the Central and South Americas and South Asia. Colonial expansionism, in this sense, constituted one of the root causes for the failure of the Christian mission in pre-modern Japan.

## (2) *Religious reasons*

The political reasons for the suppression of Christianity in Japan was, needless to say, closely connected with religious reasons. The exotic appearance of Christianity worked both for and against missionary activities in this Asian country. It offered utterly fresh religious ideas and practices, which on the one hand attracted a number of people but on the other hand alienated many conservative nationalists. Many Buddhists, in particular, felt threatened and consequently engaged in a rabid anti-Christian campaign. Buddhist intellectuals like Sesso and Shosan Suzuki considered Christianity a sort of corrupted offshoot of Buddhism without appropriating an accurate understanding thereof. Not only those Buddhists but noted Confucian scholars such as Razan Hayashi and Hakuseki Arai also tried to explain Christian teachings as inferior parallels of Buddhist doctrines.

Japanese opponents of Christianity did not have a monopoly on the lack of a proper understanding of the other party's beliefs. The padres failed to comprehend the Buddhist notions as well. They, for example, thought *mu* (no-thingness) meant simply non-existence.

Their scholastic intellectual training led them to try to explain away the totally heterogeous eastern ideas. Padre Frois, for instance, determined (inaccurately) that *Dainichi* ("Great Sun") was equivalent to the scholastic concept of "prime matter." Both the Japanese Buddhists and the European Christians tried to force artificially the others' ideas into their own frame of thinking rather than shift their mental gear in order to adjust their thinking and grasp what the other party was really saying.

It is of course quite understandable that both the Japanese and the Europeans had grave difficulty in accurately communicating, since, after all, it was historically their very first encounter. Not only the language barrier but the differences in terms of ways of thinking, living patterns, and cultural background were enormously profound. (Padre Frois mentioned more than six hundred instances of sharp contrast between the European people and their customs and those of the Japanese. See his *Kulturgengensätze Europa-Japan*, tr. by Josef Franz Schütte, Tokyo, 1955.)

To discourse about highly personal and spiritual matters despite all these divergences was not an easy task at all. Xavier, for example, experienced embarrassing frustration when he had to change suddenly the message of his street-corner preaching from "Believe in Dainichi!" to "Don't believe in Dainichi!" It must have undermined the credibility of his sermon! The padres simply could not find an equivalent Japanese word for the God of Christianity.

Besides these anti-Christian Buddhists, the imperial court and the Shinto protagonists (save a few) were also consistently antagonistic toward Christianity. They, like the Buddhists, felt threatened by this foreign religion which taught the supreme authority of God over any other sovereignties including that of the imperial tradition. It was Xavier's original aim to approach and hopefully convert the emperor and his entourage. And even after this initial failure, several other attempts were made by the padres and their Japanese associates, but to no avail.

The failure of entering into good terms with all the dignitaries in Japan (except Nobunaga Oda) stands in clear contrast to Ricci's success with the Chinese imperial court. Ricci was able to create a friendly relationship with the Chinese intellectuals and he enjoyed the respect of the dignitaries. He concentrated his efforts on searching for points of contact between Christian and Confucian doctrines because he had realized that Confucianism provided the Chinese society with religious as well as political authority. Exploiting the Confucians' dislike for the Buddhists, he censured Buddhism from the Christian point of view. But in Japan such a shrewd course of action was not taken by the Jesuits, who instead directed unceremonious denunciation toward any and all groups of the Japanese religions.

Ricci's approach, however, involved the possible risk of syncretizing Christianity with Confucianism. This was in fact the reason why the Catholic Church later decided to condemn it officially, bringing to an end the Catholic mission in that country.

As Confucianism was vital to China, so was what we have already called "Japanism" to Japan. Shintoism, being connected with the imperial heritage, constituted a significant part of this national tradition. Buddhism and Confucianism, though of foreign origin, came to be assimilated into "Japanism." Razan Hayashi, for example, succeeded in making the Chu-hsi school of Confucianism (then a new import from China) a part of the ideological power structure of the Tokugawa bakufu by relating it to Shintoism (e.g. his identification of the Confucian notion of *taikyoku*, the Great Ultimate, with the Shinto deity). A younger contemporary Confucian scholar by the name of Ansai Yamazaki (1619–1682) furthered Razan's idea and organized a Confucian-Shinto cult. The amalgamation of Buddhism and Shintoism occurred throughout Japan's history as well. In an attempt to claim their Japanese identity, Japanese Confucians often reproved Buddhism as a foreign religion.

So strongly convinced were they of the absolute superiority of Christianity and the European culture, the missionaries in Japan, unlike Ricci, never tried to find "contact points" with the local traditions. Several of the missionaries such as Frois, Vilela, and Valignano studied Buddhism seriously, but they did so with the sole intention of refuting it. To their western eyes, Shintoism looked to be nothing other than a devil worship of magic and superstition. As for Confucianism, there is no evidence that any of the padres paid it serious attention.

It is extremely unfortunate that a humble and sincere dialogue never took place between the Christians and those who followed the eastern religions. As indicated previously more than once, the religious debate which did occur usually failed to produce any constructive

results. If an attempt had been made to create positive mutual understanding instead of mutual denunciation, it might have had the effect
of changing the course of history: not only Hideyoshi but also the
Tokugawa bakufu might not have treated the Christians in the vicious
way they did.

It was a vital mistake that the Christian lords such as Yoshishige
Otomo, Ukon Takayama, and others, with the padres' encouragement,
ordered the systematic demolition of Buddhist temples and monasteries
and Shinto shrines in their fiefs, exiled the clergy associated with those
religious institutions, and confiscated their properties for use as Christian facilities.

Such an overzealotry eventuated in inner turmoil and sometimes
serious civil war within the domains of some of these Christian lords.
These unwarranted confrontational incidents were used persuasively as
the excuse for the persecution of all Christians by the anti-Christian
instigators (such as, for example, Seyakuin). By pointing to these actions as signs of arrogant subversion, the Tokugawa bakufu effectively
indoctrinated the general populace to cooperate in its attempt to eradicate Christians from the country.

In addition to the serious conflict with religious opponents, the
Christian mission had another formidable problem which considerably damaged its cause, that is, the disunity among the missionaries.
This problem began with opposing views as to mission policy. Padre
Cabral represented what we have termed the confrontational approach, against which Visitor Valignano and Organtino advocated an
adaptational policy.

The collision of these adverse opinions created embarrassing ten-
sions in the mission fields. While Organtino succeeded remarkably in
his mission assignment in central Japan, Cabral antagonized many
Japanese Christians. Communication between the padres and the Japanese mission workers turned scabrous at times. Fabian, for example,
expressed his anger over what he called the padres' "inhuman treatment" of the Japanese brothers. Valignano worked hard to solve this
problem.

Another case of disturbing disunity erupted between the Jesuits
and the friars of three different orders (the Franciscans, the Dominicans, and the Augustinians). The former order was represented mostly

by the Portuguese, the latter by the Spanish. Their national rivalry continued in the mission land. Being first-comers, the Jesuits insisted on having a monopoly of the religious activities in Japan, but the friars condemned the Jesuit policy of adaptation while they maintained a more "purist" approach.

These Catholic missionaries not only engaged in an inner feud but they also had to confront attacks from the Protestant Europeans. The conflict between the Catholics and the Protestants in post-reformation Europe was enacted in the mission lands as well. Vicious hostilities were openly exchanged between them.

Padre Orphanel, for example, was convinced that the vilification of the Catholics by William Adams (the English pilot of a Dutch trade ship who became the shogun's interpreter) was the direct cause of Ieyasu turning against the Catholics. Padre Sidoti, who impressed the inquisitor Hakuseki Arai tremendously with his admirable personality and brilliance, flatly refused even to meet the Dutch merchant who was asked by the bakufu to serve as the interpreter during his interrogation. The antagonism demonstrated by this gentle and pious man puzzled the Japanese officials considerably. All of these cases of strife among the Europeans happily provided the Japanese opponents of Christianity with just one more reason for the persecution of the Christians.

### (3) Financial reasons

In addition to all these problems with which the Christian missions had to struggle, the perpetual lack of financial security posed a vexing dilemma to them from the beginning. It required an enormous amount of funds not only to sustain the daily living of the padres and the Japanese mission workers but also to develop and run the mission bases which included the churches, colegios, and seminarios. Promised support from the royal treasuries in Europe often failed to reach the mission land. Individual donations by the traders were erratic. Participation in the silk trade provided the bulk of financial resources, but this was terminated by order of the Vatican. A remedial plan which was seriously discussed was that the mission purchase land to raise food. This plan was also abandoned because it would violate mission policy.

The lack of material wherewithal thus considerably undermined the stability of the Christian work in Japan. Though the mission was successful in attracting many local people, it was still too young and insecure to establish a self-supporting parish system. This stood in contrast to Buddhism, which was, despite being at a low ebb, deeply rooted in the populace through the parish structure.

The Christian mission was hence forced to look for financial favor from the feudal lords. Fate, therefore, often required that the mission be at the mercy of those patrons (who themselves were not always secure during times of civil war and were accountable to higher powers under the feudalistic social scheme). When the Tokugawa bakufu established firm control over the feudal lords, they no longer could help the Christians even if they had wanted to do so. Padre Sotelo, for instance, kept on vainly hoping for Lord Date's assistance until his death.

We have thus far reflected on the major reasons for the suppression of the Christian missions in pre-modern Japan. There is no doubt that the persecution originated with the central political power (Hideyoshi and the Tokugawa bakufu). Does this fact lead us to the conclusion, reached by some modern historians, that though the populace welcomed Christianity, only the government rejected it? The answer does not seem to be in the affirmative, because despite the great success of the Christian mission up until the commencement of massive oppression by the bakufu, a deep-rooted opposition to Christianity persisted generally in Japanese society. In fact, even after the suppression was officially terminated in the Meiji era, the majority of the people still did not accept Christianity. There seems to be some factor in the Japanese mentality itself which hinders them generally from becoming Christians. What is it? We shall discuss this question next.

### JAPANISM

"A muddy swamp"—this is how the Japanese Catholic novelist Shusaku Endo (1923–   ) describes the "factor" inherent to the Japanese mentality which stubbornly rejects Christianity. In the novel *Silence*, which deals with the persecution of Christians in pre-modern

Japan, the author has the apostatized Padre Ferreira say to the recently captured Padre Chiara (in the story, Rodriguez):

> This country is a swamp. In time you will come to see that for yourself. This country is a more terrible swamp than you can imagine. Whenever you plant a sapling in this swamp the roots begin to rot; the leaves grow yellow and wither. And we have planted the sapling of Christianity in this swamp.

The swamp Japan, in Endo's opinion, welcomed the padres, who were then able to plant the sapling of Christianity with relative ease since the mud was soft (i.e the Japanese pantheistic mentality is quite tolerant and it shows no stiff and outright opposition). But the swamp consumed the young plant quietly and steadily, i.e. Christianity is transformed into one of the religious components of the Japanese culture. (For Endo's thought and literary works, see the present writer's "Shusaku Endo: Japanese Catholic Novelist," in *Religion and Intellectual Life*, vol. 3, no. 3, 1986, pp. 101–113.)

What is this "swamp-like" mentality of the Japanese? A modern Japanese social critic, Shichihei Yamamoto, presents an interesting suggestion in this regard. He says that the Japanese have been neither irreligious nor anti-deity. On the contrary, they have always been religious; nonetheless, most of them have not really committed themselves to any particular organized religion.

In their mind, Yamamoto maintains, there is a characteristic religious mentality which allows different religions to co-exist "peacefully." It refuses to accommodate any religion or philosophy which rejects this "peaceful co-existence" with other religions. Therefore, both intolerant Christianity and an exclusivist Buddhist sect like the Fuju-fuse sect were violently denounced. Since this religious mentality is essentially tied to the nation itself, Yamamoto calls it "Japanism." (He has published many books dealing with this theme in Japanese, but only his first book which became a best-seller in Japan, *The Japanese and the Jews* [tr. by Richard L. Gage, N.Y. & Tokyo, 1972], has been translated into English.)

Yamamoto marshals numerous examples from Japan's history to illustrate the nature of "Japanism." Among others, he refers to the

"shinkoku" ideology and the apostate Brother Fabian. The former, as
we have discussed previously, certainly affords an instance which
places the three religions together in such a "convenient" way as to
serve as an ideological identity for the nation.

In the case of Fabian as well, Yamamoto seems correct; Fabian,
after all, remained as a member of "Japanism" all through his life. He,
with his brilliant rational mind, understood Christian doctrines well,
but existentially he failed to come to grips with the heart of Christianity. And after apostatizing, he did not return to any of the old religions,
though he approvingly used their ideas in his refutation of Christianity.
His final choice was the shinkoku ideology, an amalgamation of
Shintoism, Buddhism, and Confucianism in a peculiarly Japanese
way—Japanism.

Yamamoto's "Japanism" is, of course, a metaphor. No Japanese
has ever consciously identified himself or herself as a member of this
"religion." It has no doctrine, no scripture, no liturgy, no institution. It
is "nationalistic" in the sense that it ascribes a supreme value to the
deeply felt sentiment which arises out of the shared human relation-
ships one holds as a Japanese.

Shintoism as the national cult of Japan has been an integral part
of "Japanism." Buddhism and Confucianism were considerably modified in order to conform with this national sentiment. The former,
Buddhism, was incorporated into "Japanism" as early as the opening
year of the seventh century by the hand of the political reformer,
Prince Shotoku (574–622). The latter, Confucianism, has been with
the Japanese as long as Buddhism, and in a revitalized form (Neo-
Confucianism) it was adopted to bolster the feudalistic social system
ideologically during the Tokugawa period. After the Meiji Restoration,
"Japanism" was used by the imperialistic government to promote its
expansionist policy.

Such an insular nationalistic mentality was, needless to say, essentially at odds with the universalism of Christianity. Japanism, furthermore, stands in sharp contrast to Christianity, because of its immanent
nature as against the transcendent God of Christianity. (For an explanation of the incompatibility between Christianity and the Japanese spiritual tradition, see *Mount Fuji and Mount Sinai: A Critique of Idols*,
Orbis Press, 1984, by Kosuke Koyama.)

Explaining the Japanese mentality, Nakamura states: "the Japanese are willing to accept the phenomenal world as absolute because of their disposition to lay a greater emphasis upon intuitive sensible concrete events, rather than upon universals" (*op. cit.*, p. 350). In this sense, it can be regarded as possessing a "pantheistic" nature. The gods of Japanism are objects which cause a feeling of awe, be it of the astral bodies, the mountains, the sea, animals, spirits, or anything which truly fascinates people. This notion of gods is akin to what the German theologian Rudolph Otto called "numinous" (cf. his *The Idea of Holy*, tr. by J.W. Harvey, 1923).

The gods of Japanism can include also human beings, who are typically exemplified by ancestors and emperors. The so-called Japanese "ancestor worship" should not be taken in the same way as Christian worship of God. Inspired by the Confucian virtue of filial piety, the "worship" of ancestors is more of a religious expression affirming one's indebtedness to his/her ancestors. In contrast to the individualism which characterizes the west, the Japanese tend to regard themselves as a part of the same national entity including the living and the dead.

As for the so-called "emperor worship," it is actually a reverence of nationhood as represented symbolically by the emperor. No individual emperor or empress has claimed himself or herself to be, or has been claimed to be, divine in the western sense of the word. In fact, the emperors have acted quite human throughout Japan's history, except during the modern era running from the Meiji period to the end of World War II when militaristic nationalism fanatically glorified imperial authority. Individual emperors were challenged and even deposed sometimes, but the emperor-system itself has never once been defied.

"Worship" in both cases, ancestor and emperor, is a "liturgical act" of Japanism, so to speak. The purpose of this "liturgical act" is to appreciate the essential unity with the national numinous.

Because of its emphasis on the phenomenal world as absolute, as Nakamura says, Japanism has a distinctively this-worldly orientation. This was the reason why the padres' message stressing a belief in the hereafter presented a formidable challenge to the Japanese.

The this-worldly orientation of Japanism is closely related to the Japanese love of nature. This deep sense of unity with nature provides a salvific effect for the Japanese mind. A love of nature is, needless to say, universal, but there seems to be a uniquely Japanese way of having a spiritual experience through nature. The following sketch by Lafcadio Hearn of a shrine in Kyoto seems to capture this religious mentality very well:

> Perhaps the ascent begins with a sloping paved avenue, half a mile long, lined with giant trees. Stone monsters guard the way at regular intervals. Then you come to some great flight of steps ascending through green gloom to a terrace umbraged by older and vaster trees; and other steps from thence lead to other terraces, all in the shadow. And you climb and climb and climb, till at last, beyond a gray torii, the goal appears: a small, void, colorless wooden shrine—a Shinto miya. The shock of emptiness thus received, in the high silence and the shadows, after all the sublimity of the long approach, is very ghostliness itself. (L. Hearn, *Kokoro: Hints and Echoes of Japanese Inner Life*, N.Y., 1896, p. 51. Hearn was born in England, went to Japan in 1890, became a naturalized citizen, and taught English literature there for many years. He wrote a number of quite perceptive essays about Japan.)

The contrast is unmistakably clear between the religiosity as described here and the padres' scholastic theology. Japanese spirituality is decidedly intuitive, aesthetic, emotional, and naturalistic, while the padres' religion is essentially logical, rational, propositional, and transcendental.

The naturalistic character of Japanism is not only related to its love for the natural world but also with the naturalness of human affairs. Nakamura states: "Just as the Japanese are apt to accept external and objective nature as it is, so they are inclined to accept man's natural desires and sentiments as they are, and not to strive to repress or fight against them" (*op. cit.*, p. 372). To illustrate this, we may well recall the extreme sorrow of the Japanese converts when told by Xavier that the souls of their ancestors had been eternally lost and there would be no means to rescue them. Another example is afforded by the accusation of the opponents of Christianity concerning the impassivity of Deus who left Adam and Eve to fall into sin and also let his Son Jesus suffer on the cross. In both cases, the Japanese felt strongly that the Christian teachings violated a natural humanness.

The importance which the Japanese attribute to this naturalness is crucial to Japanism. "Let nature take its course" is its basic doctrine, which is to be applied to every human activity including religious beliefs, ethical conduct, cultural activities, and daily life itself. Desirable human actions are to follow and promote the natural course rather than to alter it from some external vantage point such as the demands of a certain theological or ideological persuasion.

To such a naturalistic mind, the Christian spirit of martyrdom was incomprehensible and unacceptable; it seemed unnatural to the Japanese mind. The natural course is supposed to continue from eternity to eternity owing to its own mechanism. The doctrines of the creation of a world out of nothing by the transcendent God, and of the end of history which is to be brought about by the same God, are too disturbing to Japanism. Nonetheless, as mentioned before, Japanism would react violently to what it considers to be threatening. It is not at all a consistently harmless, peace-loving tradition.

We have thus far discussed the basic nature of Japanism, and we have noted the profound incompatibility between Japanism and Christianity, which constitutes the very root of the Japanese rejection of Christianity. Japanism is the source of what Endo calls "a swamp" which rotted the padres' Christianity in the pre-modern era. It seems also to be the reason why Christianity remains still a religion of a small minority in Japanese society even today.

According to a recent survey, less than two percent of the entire population of Japan profess to be Christian. About seventy percent say that they are not serious about any religion but yet not adverse to religion. Almost all, nonetheless, do participate in various religious ceremonies and religion-related practices. When they do, many of them get involved in several different religions; for example, a Japanese may go to a local Shinto shrine in order to pray for his/her children's healthy growth, then visit the ancestral grave at the Buddhist temple, and then have a marriage ceremony at a Christian church. He or she enjoys Christmas as much as the Buddhist and Shinto festivals. In other words, the Japanese engage themselves in such multi-religious activities without really being bothered by the obvious confusion. This strange practice, as Yamamoto says, stems not from their religious tolerance but from the very nature of Japanism. (An English report of this survey is provided by Jan Swyngedouw in *Nanzan Bulletin*, no. 9, 1985.)

Is Japan then a hopeless country as far as the Christian faith is concerned? The padres' attempts ended in a horrible tragedy in the pre-modern era. Nonetheless, we should remember the fact that even in this "God-forsaken" land there were a number of people (mostly nameless peasants) who indeed genuinely believed in Christianity to their death. As far as these Christians were concerned, Japan was not a barren swamp. If so, there must be hope. What then is the way to establish a meaningful understanding between Christianity and the traditional religions in Japan?

### DIALOGICAL RELATIONSHIP

We have observed three different approaches taken by the European missionaries who engaged in the propagation of Christianity in pre-modern Japan: confrontational, purist, and adaptational. Notwithstanding the clear differences among them, they shared the same basic stance toward the Japanese religions: an outright rejection of them as "doctrines of devils."

It was the missionaries' firm conviction that Christianity had absolutely nothing in common with these pseudo-religions which would lead people to eternal damnation. The Catholic Church was the only vehicle which the true God would use to teach the absolute truth to the world. This exclusivistic position has been upheld by the Catholic Christians from the medieval era down to Vatican Council II (1962–1965). (This church council brought about an open and positive stance in the missions of the contemporary Catholic Church; it reversed the traditional assertion that there is no salvation outside the church.)

Ironically, however, not every Japanese convert seems to have affirmed this assertion of their missionary teachers. One distinctive example is Lourenço, the Japanese preacher who contributed to the mission perhaps more than many of the missionaries. He evidently embraced the idea that the Japanese religions constituted a preparatory stage leading to the final religious truth, i.e. Christianity.

This view represents an inclusivist position as it is willing to accept the non-Christian religions as having some positive value. It believes that the God of Christianity has guided various peoples of the world in different ways such as the Jewish, Muslim, Hindu, Buddhist, Confucian, and Shinto. All of these religions possess partial truth; they see the light only dimly. But Christianity reveals the whole truth, nothing but the truth, and the light, nothing but the light.

This inclusivist position has been quite popular among modern Christians. Many noted contemporary theologians provide us with examples. Hans Küng maintains "an inclusive Christian universalism claiming for Christianity not exclusiveness but certainly uniqueness" (cf. his *On Being a Christian*, Doubleday, 1976, p. 112). Karl Rahner calls a devout Muslim or Hindu or Jew, etc. an anonymous Christian (cf. his *Theological Investigations*, vol. 14, Seabury, 1976, chap. 17).

Both the exclusivist and inclusivist positions hold to the claim of the absolute superiority of Christianity. More recent theologians (e.g. John Hick, Paul F. Knitter, Raimundo Panikkar, etc.), however, intend to go beyond this basic premise and advocate a position which may be termed the dialogical approach. This viewpoint does not uncritically presuppose one particular religious persuasion to be superior to other religious traditions; it intends to create an open dialogue among different religions without preconceived aims and results. A sincere dialogue between authentic religions would be a living encounter with mutual respect; thus it would involve not simply an intellectual comparison of various religious ideas.

The dearth of such a creative openness was the fatal cause of the tragedy which occurred when the Christians attempted to stretch their roots into the soil of Japan during the pre-modern era. Many Japanese, particularly those in the higher political echelons, considered Christianity as an utterly foreign religion which would undermine the security of the nation and its heritage and made no attempt to understand what it really was. And on their part the missionaries imposed Christian teachings on the people out of their sense of religious and cultural superiority. Some of them did try to learn the local religions, but did so always with the intention of refuting them.

The openness which the dialogical approach advocates entails in no sense a watering down of one's religious tradition for the sake of seeking friendship from others at any price or of creating a new religious coalition. It instead enriches one's own faith by means of critical examination. Through this process, one may eliminate misunderstandings and prejudices about one's own and the other's religious beliefs. A meaningful encounter with different religions and cultures also serves as a catalyst for one to gain new insight into one's own tradition; it enables one to discover and rediscover the relevance of one's cultural and religious heritage.

One of the most important lessons we may learn from the tragic encounter between Christianity and Japan in the pre-modern era is that differences should be taken as the occasion for mutual growth rather than as a threat. If the people of that time, both Japanese and European, realized this simple point, the subsequent history of Japan might have been quite different: the horrendous persecution would have been avoided, and Christianity might have found a home there; the understanding of Christianity would have been enlarged; the colonialistic notion concerning the Christian mission could have been altered; the modernization of Japan might have taken place much earlier than it actually occurred, and with the insular mentality lessened, this could have even led the Japanese to a path somehow different from military expansionism. But, alas, all this did not happen.

Today ignorance, narrow-mindedness, and complacency are no longer acceptable. The modern pluralistic world presents a serious demand: we should all be joint-seekers of truth. An understanding of the historical encounter between Japan and Christianity can, if we are willing to learn from it, contribute to a fructuous dialogue today.

# SELECTED BIBLIOGRAPHY

There are numerous books and articles written in Japanese about the Christian mission work in pre-modern Japan, but unfortunately most of them have not been translated into English. Nor have the books, reports, and letters of the Europeans of that time, save those of Francis Xavier, been made available in English. Since the present book anticipates a general audience, precise citations from non-English sources have not been included in the text. Unless indicated, any translations of these works were done by the present author. In the following bibliographical list Japanese books and articles, with the exception of a few notable ones, are excluded.

Agency for Cultural Affairs, *Japanese Religion: A Survey*, Kodansha, 1972.

Anesaki, Masaharu, *A Concordance to the History of Kirishitan Mission*, Tokyo, 1930.

———, *History of Japanese Religion*, Tuttle, 1963.

———, *Kirishitan Dendo no Kohai*, Tokyo, 1930.

———, *Kirishitan Kinsei no Shumatsu*, Tokyo, 1926.

———, *Kirishitanshumon no Hakugai to Sempuku*, Tokyo, 1925.

Bangert, W.V., *A History of the Society of Jesus*, Institute of Jesuit Sources, 1986.

Bellah, R., *Tokugawa Religion*, Beacon, 1957.

Ben-Dasan, I. (Shichihei Yamamoto), *The Japanese and the Jews*, tr. R.L. Gage, Weatherhill, 1972.

Boxer, C.R., *The Christian Century in Japan 1549–1650*, University of California Press, 1967.

————, *The Church Militant and Iberian Expansion 1440–1770*, Johns Hopkins University Press, 1978.

Burkham, T.W., "The Uragami Incidents and the Struggle for Religious Toleration in Early Japan," *Japanese Journal of Religious Studies* 1 (1974) 143–216.

Caron, Francis & Joost Schouten, A *True Description of the Mighty Kingdom of Japan and Siam*, tr. C.R. Boxer, London, 1935.

*Cartas que os Padres e Irmãos da Companhia de Iesus secreverão dos Reynos de Iapão e China aos da mesma Companhia da India, e Europa, desde ano de 1549 ate o de 1580*, Evora, 1598.

Cary, O., A *History of Christianity in Japan: Roman Catholic, Greek Orthodox, and Protestant Missions* (two vols. in one) Tuttle, 1976 (first published in 1909).

Ching, J. & Hans Küng, *Christianity and Chinese Religions*, Doubleday, 1989.

Cieslik, H., "The Case of Christovão Ferreira," *Monumenta Nipponica* 29/1 (1974) 1–54.

Cobb, J.B. Jr., *Beyond Dialogue: Toward a Mutual Transformation of Christianity and Buddhism*, Fortress, 1982.

Coleridge, H.J., *The Life and Letters of St. Francis Xavier*, 2 vols., London, 1902.

Cooper, M., *Rodrigues the Interpreter: An Early Jesuit in Japan and China*, Weatherhill, 1974.

————, *The Southern Barbarians: The First Europeans in Japan*, Kodansha, 1971.

————, *They Came to Japan: An Anthology of European Reports on Japan 1543–1640*, University of California Press, 1965.

Crasset, Jean, *The History of the Church in Japan*, 2 vols., London, 1905–1907.

Dawe, D.G. & J.B. Carman (eds.), *Christian Faith in a Religiously Plural World*, Orbis, 1978.

Deplace, Louis, *Le Catholicisme au Japon 1540–1593*, Malines, vol. 1, 1909, vol. 2, 1910.

Doi, T., *The Anatomy of Dependence*, tr. J. Bester, Kodansha, 1971.

————, *The Anatomy of Self: The Individual versus Society*, tr. M.A. Herbison, 1986.

Elison, G., *Deus Destroyed*, Harvard University Press, 1973.

—— & B.L. Smith, *Warlords, Artists and Commoners: Japan in the 16th Century*, University of Hawaii Press, 1981.

Endo, S., *Silence*, tr. W. Johnston, Taplinger, 1969.

Frois, Luis, *Historia de Japan*, ed. Josef Wicki, Lisbon, 5 vols., 1976–1984 (German tr. by G. Schurhammer, Leipitz, 1926).

——, *Kulturgegensätze Europa-Japan*, tr. J.F. Schütte, Tokyo, 1955 (originally written in 1585).

Fujita, N.S., "Shusaku Endo: Japanese Catholic Novelist," *Religion & Intellectual Life* 3/3 (1986) 101–113.

Gernet, Jacques, *China and the Christian Impact*, tr. J. Lloyd, Cambridge University Press, 1985.

Giron, Avila, *Relaçion de Reino de Nippon*, ed. D. Schilling & Fidel de Lejarza, *Archivo Ibero-Americano*, vol. 36, 1933, vol. 38, 1935.

Goodman, G.K., *The Dutch Impact on Japan, 1640–1853*, Leiden, 1967.

de Guibert, J., *The Jesuits: Their Spiritual Doctrine and Practice*, tr. W.J. Young, The Institute of Jesuit Sources, 1972.

Guzman, Luis, *Historia de la Missiones de la Compañia de Jesús en la India Oriental, en la China y Japón desde 1540 hasta 1600*, Bilboa, 1891.

Hall, J.W., et al. (eds.), *Japan Before Tokugawa: Political and Economic Growth, 1520–1650*, Princeton University Press, 1981.

—— & M.B. Jansen, *Studies in the Institutional History of Early Modern Japan*, Princeton University Press, 1968.

Hartmann, A., *The Augustinians in Seventeenth Century Japan*, Ontario, 1965.

Hearn, Lafcadio, *Kokoro: Hints and Echoes of Japanese Inner Life*, N.Y., 1896.

——, *Japan: An Attempt at Interpretation*, Boston & New York, 1904.

Hick, J., *God Has Many Names*, Westminster, 1980.

—— & P.F. Knitter (eds.), *The Myth of Christian Uniqueness: Toward a Pluralistic Theology of Religions*, Orbis, 1987.

Jadot, J.L., "The Growth of Roman Catholic Commitment to Inter-religious Dialogue since Vatican II," *Journal of Ecumenical Studies* 20/3 (1983) 365–378.

Jannes, Joseph, A *History of the Catholic Church in Japan*, Tokyo, 1973.

Kitagawa, J.M., *On Understanding Japanese Religion*, Princeton University Press, 1987.

Knitter, P., *No Other Name? A Critical Survey of Christian Attitudes Toward the World Religions*, Orbis, 1985.

Koyama, K., *Mount Fuji and Mount Sinai: A Critique of Idols*, Orbis, 1984.

Küng, H., *On Being a Christian*, Doubleday, 1976.

———— & Jurgen Moltmann (eds.), *Christianity Among World Religions*, Edinburgh, 1986.

Loures, J., *Kirishitan Bunko: A Manual of Books and Languages in the Early Christian Missions in Japan*, Tokyo, 1957.

————, *The Catholic Church in Japan*, Tuttle, 1954.

Lucena, Afonso, *Erinnerungen aus der Christenheit von Omura*, tr. J.F. Schütte, Tokyo, 1972.

Marnas, Francisque, *La "Religion de Jésus" (Iaso Ja-kyo) ressuscitée au Japan*, 2 vols., Paris, 1896.

Minamiki, G., *The Chinese Rites Controversy*, Loyola University Press, 1985.

Morejón, Pedro, *A Brief Relation of the Persecution Lately Made Against the Catholike Christians in the Kingdom of Iaponia*, Pt. I, tr. W. W. Gent, The English Jesuit College of Saint Omer, 1619.

Murdoch, J. & I. Yamagata, *A History of Japan during the Century of Early Foreign Intercourse, 1542–1651*, Kobe, 1903.

Nagayama, T., *Collection of Historical Materials Connected with the Roman Catholic Religion in Japan*, Nagasaki, 1924.

Nagazumi, Y., "Japan's Isolationist Policy as Seen through Dutch Source Materials," *Acta Asiatica* 22 (1972) 18–35.

Najita, T. & I. Scheiner (eds.), *Japanese Thought in the Tokugawa Period 1600–1868*, University of Chicago Press, 1978.

Nakamura, H., *A History of the Development of Japanese Thought from 592 to 1868*, Tokyo, 1967.

————, *Ways of Thinking of Eastern Peoples: India, China, Tibet, Japan*, tr. P.P. Wiener, University Press of Hawaii, 1964.

Nosco, P. (ed.), *Confucianism and Tokugawa Culture*, Princeton University Press, 1984.

Ooms, H., *Tokugawa Ideology: Early Constructs, 1570–1680*, Princeton University Press, 1985.

Orfanel, Iacino, *Historia Eclesiastica de los Sucessos de la Christiandad de Japon*, Madrid, 1633.

Pagés, Leon, *Histoire de la religion chrétienne au Japan 1598–1651*, 2 vols., Paris, 1868.

Panikkar, R., *The Intra-Religious Dialogue*, Paulist, 1978.

————, *Myth, Faith and Hermeneutics*, Paulist, 1979.

Pollack, D., *The Structure of Meaning: Japan's Synthesis of China from the Eighth through the Eighteenth Centuries*, Princeton University Press, 1986.

Rahner, K., *Theological Investigations*, vol. 14, Seabury, 1976.

Reischauer, E.O., *Japan: The History of a Nation*, Knopf, 1981 (3rd ed.).

Ricci, Matteo, *The True Meaning of the Lord of Heaven*, tr. D. Lancashire & P. Hu Kuo-chen, Taipei-Paris-Hongkong, 1985.

Rodrigues, João, *Historia da Igreja do Japão*, ed. João do Amaral Abranches Pinto, 2 vols., Macao, 1954–1955.

————, *This Island Japan: João Rodrigues' Account of 16th Century Japan*, tr. M. Cooper, Kodansha, 1973.

de Sande, Eduardus, *De Missione Legatorum Iaponensium*, Macao, 1590 (Jap. tr. 1942).

Sansom, G., *A History of Japan*, 3 vols., Stanford University Press, 1963.

————, *The Western World and Japan*, Knopf, 1973.

Schütte, J.F., *Valignanos Japangeschichte* (*Analecta Gregoriana* XXXII), Rome, 1954.

————, *Valignano's Mission Principles for Japan*, tr. J.J. Coyne, Institute of Jesuit Sources, Pt. I, 1980, Pt. II, 1985.

Schurhammer, G., *Die Disputationen des P. Cosme de Torres S.J. mit den Buddhisten in Yamaguchi im Jahre 1551*, Tokyo, 1929.

————, *Francis Xavier: His Life, His Time*, tr. M.J. Costelloe, 4 vols. Loyola University Press, 1973–1982.

Steichen, M., *Les Daimyos chrétiens, ou un siècle de l'histoire et politique du Japan, 1549–1650*, Hongkong, 1904.

Swidler, L. (ed.), *Toward a Universal Theology of Religions*, Orbis, 1987.

Swyngedouw, J., "The Quiet Reversal: A Few Notes on the NHK Survey of Japanese Religiosity," *Nanzan Bulletin* 9 (1985) 24–35.

Takase, K., "Royal Patronage and the Propagation of Christianity in Japan," *Acta Asiatica* 22 (1972) 1–17.

Thelle, N.E., *Buddhism and Christianity in Japan: From Conflict to Dialogue 1854–1899*, University Press of Hawaii, 1987.

Tillich, P., *Christianity and the Encounter of the World Religions*, Columbia University Press, 1963.

Toby, R.P., *State and Diplomacy in Early Modern Japan*, Princeton University Press, 1984.

Tong, P.K.K., "A Study of Thematic Differences Between Eastern and Western Religious Thought," *Journal of Ecumenical Studies* 10 (1973) 337–358.

Totman, C., *Politics in Tokugawa Bakufu 1600–1843*, University Press of Hawaii, 1988.

Toynbee, A., *Christianity among the Religions of the World*, Scribner, 1957.

Tsunoda, R., W.T. de Bary, & D. Keene, *Sources of Japanese Tradition*, 2 vols., Columbia University Press, 1958.

Tyler, R., *Selected Writings of Suzuki Shosan*, Cornell University Press, 1977.

Uyttenbroeck, T., *Early Franciscans in Japan*, Himeji, 1958.

Valignano, Alessandro, *Catechismus* (Jap. tr. 1963).

———, *Historia del Principio y Progresso de la Compañia de Jesús en las Indias* Orientales (1542–1564) ed. Josef Wicki, Rome, 1944.

———, *Sumario de las Cosas de Japon*, ed. José Luis Alvarez-Taladriz, Tokyo, 1954 (Jap. tr. 1965).

Wray, H. & H. Conroy, *Japan Examined: Perspectives on Modern Japanese History*, University Press of Hawaii, 1983.

# INDEX

Adam and Eve, 239
Adami, Joseppe Mateo, 197
Adams, William, 156–157
Adaptation, policy of, 88–91,
 105
Alcaçova, Pedro de, 54
Alexander VI (Pope), 128
Almeida, Luis de
 arrival of, in Japan, 52
 confraria and, 169
 in Kyoto, 60–61
 missions of, 53
 Sumitada Omura and, 51
 surgical skill of, 53–54
 Torres and, 52–53
 Yoshisada Arima and, 51
Alvares, Jorge, 13
Amakusa, Shiro, 185
Americans, 242
Amida Buddha, 6, 225
*The Analects*, 106
Anjiro, 15, 21–22, 30
Ansei. *See* Anjiro
Arima, 79
Arima family, 51, 158–159. *See
 also* specific names of
Arroyo, Alonzo, 201, 202

Ashikaga bakufu, 3, 5
Asia, 14–15. *See also* specific
 countries in
Azuchi, 80

Bakufu, 3. *See also* specific
 names of
Baptism
 Fabian on, 218–222
 in *Ha-Daiusu*, 218–222
 in Japanese religions, 16
 under Xavier's mission, 17
Bautista, Pedro, 134, 139–140,
 142–143
Belchior Nuñez, 20, 55–56
Bernal, Anri, 127
Bernal, Diego, 127
Bobadilla (Brother), 15
Buddha, 30
Buddhism. *See also* specific sects
 of
 Anjiro and, 15
 Christian censure of, 31
 Christianity and, alternative
 to, 254
 debate of, versus Christianity

Kirishito-Ki (Record of the Christians) 200